DEATH AND JUSTICE

DEATH
AND
JUSTICE

AN EXPOSÉ OF OKLAHOMA'S DEATH ROW MACHINE

MARK FUHRMAN

wm WILLIAM MORROW *AN IMPRINT OF* HARPERCOLLINS*PUBLISHERS*

HarperCollins books may be purchased for educational, business,
or sales promotional use. For information please write:
Special Markets Department, HarperCollins Publishers Inc.,
10 East 53rd Street, New York, NY 10022.

FIRST EDITION

Designed by Gretchen Achilles

Printed on acid-free paper

Library of Congress Cataloging-in-Publication Data
Fuhrman, Mark.
Death and justice/Mark Fuhrman.— 1st ed.
p.   cm.
Includes index.
ISBN 0-06-000917-9
1. Criminal justice, Administration of—Oklahoma.
2. Capital punishment—Oklahoma.   3. Prosecution—Oklahoma.
4. Evidence, Criminal—Oklahoma.   I. Title.
HV9955.O5 F85   2003
364.9766'38—dc21
2002040992

03   04   05   06   07   WBC/RRD   10   9   8   7   6   5   4   3   2   1

FOR MY SON AND DAUGHTER

CONTENTS

ACKNOWLEDGMENTS

The author would like to thank the following people:

STEPHEN WEEKS Steve worked really hard on this one. Aside from his writing and research, Steve counseled me when times were tough, which was quite often. I can always count on his honesty, loyalty, and judgment. One day, I might actually start listening to him.

JACK DEMPSEY POINTER For introducing me to Oklahoma City, particularly the gang at the Oyster Bar: Dave, Eddie, and everybody else.

ROBERT A. MANCHESTER He offered first his support and then his friendship.

LEE ANN PETERS She provided assistance and entrée at Oklahoma Indigent Defense System.

BOB RAVITZ He opened his office and gave generously of his time and energy.

CLARK BREWSTER AND GUY FORTNEY Their investigation into

Oklahoma County law enforcement in many ways paralleled my own and hopefully will surpass it.

ERIC SKINNER AND THE GANG AT SANDPOINT.COM For their help and toner and jokes.

PETER MICO AND MIKE "RUG" RUSKEY For asking the question: "What About Us?"

THE BIG BOY BALLET COMPANY For giving me a chance to dance.

ROB AND DAWN AND BARBARA For all those Sunday evenings.

STEVE'S PARENTS For sending him to college instead of jail.

DIANE REVERAND Who had the courage and the vision.

MEAGHAN DOWLING Who saw Diane's vision to completion.

JENNIFER SUITOR Who makes the media gauntlet easier to bear.

AL LOWMAN AND THE STAFF AT AUTHORS AND ARTISTS Who make these books possible.

REBECCA MACK Who gets me on the air every day.

LYNDA BENSKY Who helps in many ways, some she realizes and some she doesn't. Lynda's another one I'm going to start listening to.

WELCOME TO DEATH ROW

THEY CALL OKLAHOMA STATE PENITENTIARY AT MCALESTER "THE WALL," and once you see it, you know why. At the entrance to the prison grounds, there's a high, wide wall with guard towers at each corner. The Wall is made of brick that has been painted white so many times the paint itself has become part of its structural integrity. Some of the arches are beginning to sag or lean, but The Wall isn't coming down.

I had come to McAlester to visit death row. I was researching the death penalty. There had been a series of high-profile releases of inmates from death row, several of them in Oklahoma, and I wanted to find out exactly what happened and why. The media has a way of simplifying crime stories so that they stray further and further from the truth the more attention is paid to them.

At first I suspected that most of the inmates released from death row might actually have been guilty of the crimes for which they were convicted. I'd seen it before. All convicts claim they are innocent, and sometimes their defense attorneys get their cases reversed on a technicality. Yet in several recent death row releases, there had been evidence like DNA that could not be dismissed as a technicality. Since 1977, more than one hundred inmates have been released from death row in the United States. Many of them had arguable claims of innocence. Some had clearly been railroaded, perhaps even intentionally framed.

Was there something wrong with the death penalty? I decided to look into it myself. As I looked at individual cases in isolation, I saw some terrible miscarriages of justice. Police had fabricated confessions. Criminalists had lied or enhanced evidence. Prosecutors had cut corners. I wanted to understand how this happened and why. So I decided to focus on one jurisdiction and examine several cases together, looking not just at innocent people who had been convicted but also at guilty suspects. I felt that the answer would lie not in the isolated cases but in the entire process itself. From arrest to execution over a period of several years and many different cases, I wanted see how the death penalty worked.

Oklahoma executed twenty-one convicts in 2001—more than any other state. Thirteen of those executed had been tried and convicted in one county by one district attorney. Oklahoma City, a relatively small jurisdiction, was producing an extraordinary number of death penalty convictions (and two innocent men had been released from death row). Oklahoma County, which encompasses Oklahoma City, seemed like a good place to conduct my investigation. I hoped to reach some conclusions about the death penalty.

I arrived at McAlester on Good Friday morning in 2002. It was the first day that felt like spring, and dozens of inmates on low-security work detail were out mowing the lawns and raking up the clippings. The smell of freshly cut grass and clover filled the air. All the lawns are well maintained. Everything is painted white. Even the inmates wear white pants and T-shirts that are white, except for the word *inmate* printed on the back. It was only nine o'clock and already warm. Their T-shirts were soaked with sweat.

You have to remind yourself that these people are convicted criminals. Don't make eye contact. Don't get too close to them physically. Watch your back, just in case. Because there's another wall, the one that prison makes you put up between yourself and others—don't show any emotion, any weakness, any sympathy, or any fear. If you do, someone will take advantage.

The people who work at McAlester never let themselves forget why the inmates are there. Outside The Wall is a collection of houses for prison administrators and employees, a neighborhood of sorts. The administrators drive from their nearby houses to their assigned parking spaces and stay, as much as they can, in their offices. When I arrived, no one was outside except the inmates and an occasional corrections officer. I didn't see anybody who looked like a civilian resident. A nearby playground was empty.

Construction on McAlester began soon after Oklahoma achieved statehood in 1907, and the main building was finished in 1909 by inmates who lived in what are now the stables for the prison rodeo. The prison is well maintained: everything that can be polished or trimmed or painted has been. Across from the main entrance is the warden's residence, a sprawling house, a mansion in fact.

In front of the main entrance is a chain-link fence and a guard tower of white-painted brick. A guard stood in the tower, surveying the outside grounds from behind the tinted glass. I could feel him watching me as I walked up the stairs with my partner, Stephen Weeks.

I was on the guard's side. We were both members of the law enforcement community. Still, I felt a chill on my back as he watched me.

Climbing the steps, we passed a young girl walking down from visitor processing. She was around eleven years old, the age at which girls first start looking like the women they will become. (I have a daughter the same age.) This girl was pretty, with dark features. Her brown hair was tied back neatly into a bun. She wore a brand-new Easter dress but on her feet were dirty sneakers with no socks. The girl must have been visiting her father, and maybe her mother sent her back to the car to wait. Her eyes were wet and reddened, but when she saw me looking at her, she set her face—stubborn, almost proud—stared straight ahead, and walked deliberately down the concrete steps toward the guard tower. She was not going to let anyone see her cry.

Our contact at the prison was Lee Mann. Her official title is spokesperson, but she handles a variety of functions, including fielding media questions and requests, dealing with family members of inmates, and presenting the public face of McAlester to the world outside. Ms. Mann is an attractive woman, tall and slim, with short white hair. Her manner is candid and direct, even warm. She could be the tour guide at a dead president's home instead of a maximum-security prison. Inside her office the decor was civil-service functional, aside from a collection of baseball caps from local homicide divisions, and any posters or pictures were generic. This was a room where inmates' families, maybe sometimes inmates themselves, would come. Nothing personal, nothing human.

Lee Mann led us back outside, and we waited beneath the front tower while the guard lowered down a set of keys in a gray plastic bucket at the end of a long, knotted piece of rope. These were the keys to the deputy warden's minivan, which would take us to H-Unit, the maximum-security block of McAlester, where the death row inmates are housed.

H-Unit—lock-down, supermax, whatever you want to call it—was built in 1990, following a violent prison riot in 1985, during which guards were taken hostage and several of them seriously injured. I talked to several prison employees who were there in 1985. They showed me pictures of the riot—inmates swarming the yard, guards bloody and bound. The prison museum has a collection of shivs and other weapons taken from the rioters. Having survived one nightmare, the Oklahoma Department of Corrections decided not to risk another. So they built H-Unit.

Designed by a prison committee to create a supermaximum facility in which physical contact between inmates and staff was kept to a minimum by a series of elaborate electronic security features, H-Unit is almost entirely constructed of steel and concrete, an "earth-sheltered facility" rising up out of the ground like some kind of huge root cellar.

Once we entered H-Unit's Plexiglas and metal doors, the guards made us empty our pockets and take off our shoes. They patted us down but let us keep everything except for cell phones. A guard inside the control room gave Mann a set of archaic-looking keys, then opened the first of two steel-barred doors. We stepped inside— it was the size of an elevator—and the first door shut behind us with a resounding metallic thud. Then the second door opened and we walked out onto H-Unit. The floors were concrete, sealed and polished as smooth as glass. The walls and ceilings were also concrete. We walked down the hall—no windows or doors or people, just a long, narrow concrete maze. The bars ahead of us had been freshly painted.

"The inmates on death row take pride in their unit," Mann said, after I remarked on how clean everything was. "And we don't have a shortage of labor."

Still, beneath the polished concrete and painted bars, there was a thick, heavy funk—the smell of men together, as in a barracks or a locker room, only worse. There was a feeling of suppressed violence, the tension one feels just before a fight. At the same time, you knew nothing was going to happen.

We passed a barred door that said LIBRARY. Inside were several individual metal cages, where the inmates could study the law or work on their cases without coming into contact with each other.

At the end of the hallway, H-Unit splits into four rows of double-tiered corridors or "pods," each containing fifty double-occupancy cells. This is death row itself. We entered another set of double metal doors and stood in a cage that looked over two of the pods. Each of the pods is two stories high, with cells along the far wall (in addition to the double cells there are eight "punishment cells" for solitary confinement). Outside the doors is a narrow hallway and then a cage of metal bars enclosing the large open space between the pods, which run parallel to each other. Three times a day, a dumbwaiter carries meals from the ground floor up to the second level, where a trustee delivers the food to his fellow inmates.

Each cell is marked with a pair of letters—AA, BB, and so on. Behind the small, barred windows flicker the lights of small televisions. There is a man in each one of these cells, but you can't hear them. The pod itself is eerily quiet, with only a muffled echo of what might be voices somewhere off in the distance. Each double cell measures seven feet seven inches by fifteen feet five inches, with two poured concrete bunks on either side of an uncovered toilet and sink. The only furniture consists of four shelves, also of poured concrete, that the inmates use as tables and TV stands. The walls are unpainted concrete, and the inmates are not allowed to decorate them in any way. The doors are solid metal, with a Plexiglas window covered by thick metal bars. There are no windows. Other than the glow of the TVs, the only light comes from two bare lightbulbs. Each cell is linked to the central command tower by intercom, which the guards control. The guards turn on the intercom when they need to communicate with the inmates; otherwise, it is kept off.

At one end of each pod is an exercise yard, nothing more than a dozen square feet of cement with a thick Plexiglas ceiling, so a little sunlight bleeds through. In one of the yards, five men were playing handball. In the other, a basketball game was going on. Death row prisoners are under twenty-three-hour lockdown—they get one hour outside their cells every day during the week and are confined to their cells during the weekend. They can spend their five hours a week with visitors, studying in the library, taking one of their three fifteen-minute showers allotted per week, or exercising in the yard.

Although they are not allowed to work out with weights, the inmates are in good shape from doing push-ups, sit-ups, and other isometrics. They run around inside the small concrete yard, sometimes laughing or joking, but always with a guarded manner, never letting down the wall.

Televisions and radios are a privilege that prisoners have to earn the right to have and pay for with their own funds. If they break prison rules, their televisions and radios, along with other privileges like visitors, can be taken away.

"We don't coddle our prisoners," Mann said.

Lee Mann pointed to a cell on the second floor. This was LL, where a prisoner awaiting execution was held. He was put there approximately a month before his execution.

"No one has ever come into this cell and left," Mann said.

Death row houses the worst of the worst. The bottom of the gene pool. The men and women who have made the worst choices in life. It's pretty hard to feel sorry for them.

We were still inside the cage overlooking the pods when we heard a cell door open behind us. A black guy with long dreadlocks walked out of the shower room. The prisoner greeted Mann and asked how she was doing. She stiffened a little. Dropping the friendly manner with which she had been addressing us, she answered him with a few clipped words.

She took us back out into the hallway and upstairs, past the visiting windows, where inmates' families and friends can speak to them over telephone receivers and touch the thick Plexiglas, barred and embedded with chicken wire. Inmates are allowed four hours of visiting a week. Once they enter death row, inmates have no physical contact with friends or family. When inmates meet with their attorneys, officers view them through a one-way mirror. In addition to talking with their lawyers, inmates are allowed one fifteen-minute personal call a week on a mobile phone brought into their cells. When a prisoner is brought into LL, his phone and visiting privileges are expanded.

Down the hall from the visitors' window is a door painted bright yellow. Behind that door is the death chamber.

Lee Mann opened the yellow door and led us into a narrow room with a split-level floor filled with two rows of cheap metal folding chairs. This is where the execution is witnessed by family and friends of the inmate, as well as Department of Corrections VIPs and any members of the media.

In 1966, James Donald French was the last person to be electrocuted in "Old Sparky." The electric chair is now displayed in McAlester's museum, where visitors can sit and pose for pictures. Lethal injection as a method of execution was developed in Oklahoma by a state senator and a medical examiner. In 1977, Oklahoma passed the first bill authorizing the use of lethal injection—Texas passed a similar bill the next day. After the Oklahoma law was passed, then warden of McAlester Norman Hess resigned, saying he did not want to participate in executions using lethal injection. In 1990, Charles Coleman became the first Oklahoma inmate to be killed by lethal injection. In case lethal injection is ever declared unconstitutional, the state has electrocution and firing squad provisions already established.

The Supreme Court struck down all existing death penalty statutes in 1972. In *Furman* v. *Georgia,* the Court ruled that the death penalty, as administered, was cruel and unusual punishment.

Four years later, several states, including Oklahoma, rewrote their death penalty statutes to remedy the Supreme Court's concerns. The Court upheld these new statutes, and executions were legal once again, although because of the appeals process guaranteed by these new laws, it took several years for executions to recommence.

The first person executed under the new guidelines was Gary Gilmore in 1977. When Gilmore was shot by a firing squad in Utah, I wrote a letter that was published in the *Los Angeles Times:* "One small step for Gary Gilmore. One giant step for mankind." I believed that everyone on death row was guilty and deserving of death.

Oklahoma had its first execution by lethal injection in 1990. At that time the media requests were so numerous that the Department of Corrections (DOC) had to establish rather elaborate criteria to decide who got to see one (the largest and smallest newspapers, the largest and smallest television stations, a local radio station). Today there are very few media witnesses—usually just the Associated Press and one or two reporters from local newspapers. The district court judge who presided over the inmate's trial is allowed to witness, as are the detectives involved in the original investigation, if they are still alive. Before executions became commonplace, there were two chairs for citizens at large, selected by lottery. At that time, many people wanted to see executions. Now interest has waned among the general public.

I asked Ms. Mann if she had ever witnessed an execution.

"I don't think it's something that would make my job any better," she said. "I'd rather not have any tugs that way."

The death chamber is separated from the witness seating area by a wall, most of which consists of a large, clear plate-glass window with a set of dark blinds that were raised for now.

Behind the witness observation room with its two rows of chairs is an even smaller room, with a single row of chairs behind a one-way tinted window. This is where the family and friends of the victims watch the inmate die. Family members of the victims are escorted into their seats well before the inmate's witnesses enter.

Lee Mann opened another door and we walked into the death chamber.

The room measures some ten by fifteen feet. A small podium stands against the wall. This is where the warden will log, with minute precision, every action associated with the execution, what happened and when.

The execution gurney takes up most of the room. Without a human being strapped down on top of it, the gurney looks pretty harmless, a cross between a dentist's chair and a massage table. The gurney is a converted American Sterilizer operating table taken from a hospital emergency room. The table has been customized, with crudely welded metal armrests and wool and leather wrist restraints and black nylon and Velcro body straps. White sheets and sterile paper cover the worn black vinyl cushions. A small pillow lies where the inmate's head will rest.

A microphone is positioned on the wall above the head of the gurney. When the inmate is ready to give his final statement, the microphone will be lowered into place. Against the wall by the plate-glass window is a shelf holding a video monitor. The execution will not be recorded, but sometimes it is necessary to televise the execution on closed circuit so that additional witnesses, usually family members of victims, can watch in another room. Lee Mann told me that they would never record an actual execution because they are afraid of the tape getting "into the wrong hands."

Across from the gurney is a white door that opens into LL cell.

On the day of execution, the inmate is woken around 6:00 or 7:00 A.M. The warden meets with him and tells him exactly what will happen that day. They take care of legal matters like the inmate's will, if he needs one, and the disposition of his body.

Two corrections officers stand outside LL cell all day. The inmate is allowed visitors most of the day, but they are not permitted to touch; instead, he speaks with family and friends through the visitors' windows.

Some inmates have been able to convince visitors to smuggle in drugs so they can tranquilize themselves or even commit suicide. In August 1995, Robert Brecheen overdosed on drugs hours before his scheduled execution. Prison officials rushed him to a local hospital and had his stomach pumped. Once Brecheen was conscious and stable, he was brought back to H-Unit and taken to the death chamber, where he was given a lethal injection. The state-contracted doctor who was to witness the execution followed Brecheen to the hospital and insisted that he perform the medical procedures in the emergency room. Then, after saving Brecheen's life, the doctor accompanied the inmate to the execution chamber, where he made a formal pronouncement of death.

In addition to family, friends, and lawyers, the inmate may get visits from law enforcement officials who hope that he will be able to help them solve some of their open cases.

After spending the morning with his visitors, the inmate eats his last meal at noon. He is allowed to have anything available in the local community that costs up to fifteen dollars. Inmates are not allowed to use their own funds. Many of them order something they haven't had for a long time, often junk food. Some of them want just Coke and potato chips or doughnuts. Others ask for food that has some sentimental value to them, like a breakfast cereal they ate as a child. Most order from one of the several Italian restaurants or fast-food joints in town. Most have had at least ten years to think about this meal. Many are disappointed.

"They've been watching television for fifteen years," Lee Mann said. "When they finally get to eat a Wendy's hamburger, it's not what they saw in the commercial."

After his last meal, the inmate is allowed to have his visitors back for a couple more hours. If the execution is scheduled for later at night, the inmate can eat a regular prison dinner off the line, if he's still hungry. Recently, McAlester has been scheduling executions in the early evening; therefore, the noon meal is the last thing an inmate will eat.

An hour before the execution, the visitors are escorted out of LL. The prison chaplain comes into the cell to speak with the inmate, and to hear his confession and give him last rites if he is a Catholic.

The inmate is dressed in a light blue outfit that resembles surgical scrubs. About twenty minutes before the execution, the warden comes into LL and asks, "Are you ready to walk with me?"

The inmate follows the warden through the door and into the death chamber. Aside from Robert Brecheen, there has never been a problem.

"By now they know, this is it," Lee Mann said. "They accept the fact that they are going to die."

Minutes before the execution, H-Unit erupts into noise. Inmates bang on their cell doors and rattle the bars. They shout and wail. This continues until they know that the time of execution has passed and the inmate is dead.

At every execution, a group of family members of murder victims and death penalty supporters gathers outside the prison wall. Many of them arrive together in a large motor home. They have a somber tailgate party near a large signboard covered with photographs of their family members and other murder victims. Nearby, opponents of the death penalty hold a candlelight vigil. Again, often the same people show up for each execution. Depending on whether the crime was high-profile or not, the media presence can range from hundreds of journalists to merely a handful.

On the day of an execution, H-Unit basically shuts down. No inmate other than the one to be executed leaves his cell. There are no visitors other than those visiting the condemned.

While the inmate's visitors are secured elsewhere, three men enter the prison. They arrive separately and do not know each other's names. Their identities are kept secret from nearly every other prison employee.

They are the executioners.

Each man walks alone past the control room, through the double doors, down the empty hall, upstairs, and past the visitors' windows. He opens the yellow door and walks into the death room. Behind a white door within the chamber itself, the three men gather in the executioners' room, where they wait for the order to proceed. Each one of them wears a black hood.

The hoods were made by one of the secretaries at the prison from material that Lee Mann herself bought at Wal-Mart. While Mann was at the store, she saw an acquaintance, who asked her if she was shopping for Halloween costumes. I asked her why the executioners wore masks.

"The masks make it a little more palatable," Mann said.

The executioners' room is tiny, not much bigger than a large supply closet; there is one cinder-block wall—the other three are concrete—and shelving filled with sterile sheets, rubber gloves, and other medical necessities. A small biohazard trash bin sits on the floor by the door. The only light comes from a weak green bulb, which gives it the appearance of a photographer's dark room.

The executioners set up three different chemical doses and saline solutions that are run through two holes in the wall and into the IV units in the inmate's arms. A local hospital had provided the drugs, until the doctors there decided that participating in executions was contrary to their Hippocratic oath. For the same reason, the executioners are not doctors themselves, and the doctor in the death chamber is not there to participate in the actual execution, only to monitor the inmate and pronounce death, or in case of an emergency.

There is a phone in the witness seating area that a prison official uses to call the governor before the execution to make sure there will be no last-minute reprieve.

A reprieve is not likely to happen. Usually on the day before the execution, the U.S. Supreme Court will inform the inmate's lawyer that all of his legal appeals have been exhausted. Governor Frank Keating has granted only one executive clemency; he reduced Phillip Dewitt Smith's death sentence to life without parole on March 1, 2001, on the recommendation of the Oklahoma Pardon and Parole Board after the prosecution's star witness recanted testimony. Once the final word from the governor has been received, the prison official places a call to the phone inside the death chamber. When the warden gets the okay, he announces that the execution will proceed.

The inmate lies down on the gurney, which has been covered with sterile blue sheets (when the inmate dies, his bowels and bladder will release). Nylon straps with Velcro fasteners secure his body. His arms are strapped down to the metal armrests. A registered phlebotomist places an IV unit in each arm. He is hooked up to a heart monitor. A white sheet covers him from the waist down.

Once the inmate is prepped for execution, the blinds on the window of the witness seating area are lifted. The gurney has been raised so that the inmate is almost in a seated position. He faces sideways to the witnesses. Through the glass he can see the first two rows of witnesses, but he cannot see past the tinted glass to where the family members of his victims sit.

The inmate is asked whether he would like to make a final statement. If he wants to say something, the microphone is lowered down from the wall behind him, and he says a few words. Usually the condemned says good-bye to his family. Sometimes he apologizes to the victims and their families.

When the inmate is finished speaking, the warden gives the command for the execution to commence. In his log, the warden records every move, noting the time and any physical reaction by the inmate.

Inside the executioners' room, each executioner pushes a button. First, sodium thiopental is injected into the inmate, which causes unconsciousness. Next is a saline flush, which clears out the IV tubes to ensure that the chemicals do not mix inside the inmate's bloodstream. Then pancuronium bromide is injected, which paralyzes respiration. Next is another saline flush, and then potassium chloride is injected, which stops the heart from beating.

As the lethal injection is administered, the chaplain reads aloud from the Bible.

The whole process usually takes from four to six minutes. The doctor leans over the inmate and looks for signs of life. He then checks the heart monitor and officially declares the inmate dead. The warden duly notes this in his log.

"Every inmate reacts differently," Lee Mann said. "But it's generally very peaceful."

Once the inmate is declared dead, the blinds are lowered and the witnesses are escorted out—first the inmate's family, friends, and attorneys, and later the victims' families. Pains are taken to keep the two groups separate in order to avoid any unpleasantness.

The medical examiner (ME) drives up to H-Unit in a station wagon. The inmate's body is loaded off the gurney and onto a stretcher, then carried out through the witness room, through the yellow door, and down the hall past the empty visitors' windows. The body is loaded into the back of the ME's station wagon and taken to McAlester's regional hospital. Although no autopsy is performed, tissue samples are saved for the ME's records. Unless his family makes other arrangements, the inmate is buried in the DOC cemetery just outside of the penitentiary grounds. Called Peckerwood Hill, the cemetery is the final resting place for more than six hundred inmates and three babies born to female inmates.

Following the execution, members of the victims' families are invited by the DOC to the media center for public comments.

According to Lee Mann, "They often have a lot to say, and we want to give them a chance to express their feelings."

The family of the executed inmate may hold a press conference outside the prison wall.

After Mann described the execution process, we stood there in the death chamber. I placed my hand on the gurney and realized that fifty men and women had died there. Yet there was no visible sign of death. It was all clinical, pristine, even immaculate. Here is a crime scene that yields no evidence. There is no blood on the floor, no brain matter stuck to the ceiling. The bodies have been taken away and disposed of humanely. In order to investigate the death penalty in Oklahoma, I would have to look elsewhere.

CHAPTER ONE

FRONTIER JUSTICE

"IT'S A MESS DOWN HERE IN OKLAHOMA!" JACK DEMPSEY POINTER SAID IN his booming good-ol'-boy voice. "We're executing people; we don't know if they're innocent or guilty. It's a regular death factory."

Pointer, president of the Oklahoma Criminal Defense Lawyers' Association, was a guest on my radio show for KXLY Spokane in October 2001. I told Pointer I was skeptical.

"Fuhrman, you're just saying that because you're a cop and I'm a defense lawyer. It's your job to put criminals in jail and it's my job to keep them out," Pointer said. "But if you don't believe me, then come down here and see for yourself."

So I did. At first glance, I liked Oklahoma. The landscape is flat and somewhat monotonous, but the people are friendly. They wear Wranglers and eat red meat and listen to country music and vote Republican. Instantly I felt I was among friends.

In many ways, Oklahoma is like a place lost in time. The cowboy past is more powerfully felt there than in most other places because that past is still so recent. Originally a territory for displaced Indian tribes, Oklahoma did not achieve statehood until 1907. The ethos of frontier justice has dominated Oklahoma since the 1890s, when "hanging judge" Isaac Parker sent eighty-seven men to the gallows.

On my first night in Oklahoma City, I met Jack Dempsey Pointer, a jovial, outspoken man who is so large that he can barely fit in the front seat of his Jaguar. Pointer took me to the Oyster Bar, a downtown watering hole where people on both sides of Oklahoma City law enforcement go to unwind, gossip, and sometimes even negotiate plea bargains.

Over the next few days I met defense lawyers, prosecutors, judges, and cops. I was taken by how friendly and open people were. Even if they didn't want to tell me anything, they would be very polite about it. After my rather chilly treatment in Greenwich, Connecticut, while investigating the murder of Martha Moxley, or Spokane, Washington, on the trail of a serial killer, Oklahoma was a pleasant surprise.

Hanging around with the folks in Oklahoma made me feel like I was back among my old LAPD colleagues. We traded stories about crime and punishment. They had a good sense of humor and weren't easily offended. Even those few who didn't want to talk to me were very gracious about it.

The attitude among most Oklahomans—not just law enforcement professionals but also waitresses, cabdrivers, and businesspeople—was basically "hang 'em high." It was reassuring to hear even some defense attorneys defend the death penalty. In Oklahoma it's politically correct to support the death penalty. If you have any doubts about it, then you must be a liberal or something even worse.

Death penalty cases in Oklahoma City are prosecuted by the Oklahoma County District Attorney's Office and investigated by the Oklahoma City Police Department (OCPD). The trial defense is either private attorneys or the Oklahoma County Public Defender's Office. The Oklahoma Indigent Defense System (OIDS) is a state agency that represents defendants in jurisdictions where there is no public defender's office and handles death row appeals for those already convicted at trial. Many Oklahoma City defendants will have a public defender at their trials and OIDS lawyers during the appellate process. The OIDS office is in Norman, on the campus of the University of Oklahoma. Although many of them have worked for the Oklahoma County Public Defender's Office, OIDS lawyers are a bit removed from the Oklahoma City law enforcement scene (they don't hang out at the Oyster Bar) and are more outspoken in their criticism of the death penalty and Oklahoma's criminal justice system. They, too, were unfailingly polite, even friendly.

When I first began this project, I didn't think there was anything fundamentally wrong with the death penalty. Instead, I had the conviction that any problems with capital punishment were rare and isolated instances where mistakes, usually unintentional, had been made. I certainly didn't want to see the death penalty abolished, which I believed was the ultimate motivation for many of its critics. They didn't want the system to work, because they wanted to change it.

I knew the system wasn't perfect, but I believed that it worked. Criminals were convicted because they were guilty. And if they weren't guilty of the crime for which they had been convicted, well, they had done something else for which they should have been punished. When it came to the death penalty, I assumed that there was an even lower percentage of wrongful convictions, since capital cases were certainly held to a higher standard than other felonies, from investigation to arrest to trial to punishment.

The scandal that had brought Oklahoma to my attention, and made Jack Pointer almost burst a blood vessel on my radio show, concerned a forensic chemist named Joyce Gilchrist. In 2001, the same year that the state of Oklahoma was executing inmates at an unprecedented rate, a series of high-court rulings, official investigations, memos, and reports, as well as the usual chorus of outraged defense attorneys, had criticized Gilchrist for lying under oath, "enhancing" the value of the evidence in her testimony, and mismanaging the OCPD crime lab.

Gilchrist had been a forensic chemist for more than twenty years. She had worked on more than fifteen hundred felony cases. Cops and prosecutors loved her; defense attorneys didn't.

"Joyce Gilchrist is a kick-ass expert witness," Assistant District Attorney Richard Wintory told me. "That's why everybody is out to get her."

"Joyce Gilchrist is the most lyingest, cheatingest bitch on this earth," said one prominent Oklahoma defense attorney.

Gilchrist began working at the crime lab as an intern in 1980, while she was still an undergraduate student at Central State University in Edmond, Oklahoma, studying forensic science. Shortly after she graduated, Gilchrist was promoted to the position of forensic chemist with the OCPD.

Gilchrist rose quickly through the ranks, earning numerous commendations and awards. In 1985 she was named Civilian Police Employee of the Year. She testified in a series of high-profile felony cases during the 1980s. In 1987 she was given the task of creating a DNA lab within the OCPD facility. At the same time, she was still doing casework and testifying. In 1990, Gilchrist was promoted to supervisor of the crime lab.

On the witness stand, Gilchrist was polished, attractive, well dressed. She spoke with authority and didn't wilt under pressure. As a black woman, she couldn't be accused of racism. She made eye contact with jurors and spoke in tones that inspired confidence that Gilchrist knew what she was talking about, even if the jurors didn't quite understand her scientific terminology.

As a forensic serologist, Gilchrist worked with hair, fiber, and blood evidence. She performed visual hair and fiber comparison, presumptive blood tests, ABO blood typing, and electrophoresis, a method of using electricity to identify specific enzymes and proteins in body fluids. During the course of Gilchrist's career, these techniques were gradually eclipsed by DNA.

DNA tests performed by the OIDS and Barry Scheck's Innocence Project proved that Gilchrist and other Oklahoma police chemists had mistakenly matched evidentiary hairs to defendants in several murder and rape cases that led to wrongful convictions, including those of three death row inmates. I will examine the case of one of those inmates, Robert Lee Miller, in later chapters. The two others, Ronald Keith Williamson and Dennis Fritz, were convicted for a 1982 rape and murder largely due to microscopic hair comparisons performed by Melvin Hett of the Oklahoma State Bureau of Investigation (OSBI). Williamson and Fritz spent twelve years on death row, before DNA tests in April 1999 proved that neither one of them was the donor of semen found in the victim or the hairs that Hett had matched to theirs. When the release of Fritz and Williamson was announced, Glenn Gore escaped from a prison work detail. Gore, who had been the last person seen with the victim on the night of her murder, was eventually apprehended. DNA tests later proved he was the killer.

To a certain degree, these and other wrongful convictions were the result of forensic science methods that were more primitive and less accurate than DNA. Microscopic hair comparison involves taking known hairs from suspects, victims, or possible donors and comparing them to unknown hairs recovered from the crime scene. Finding several points of similarity, and no striking differences, a forensic scientist can determine that the evidentiary hair *could* have come from the suspect. During an investigation, hair evidence can be used to eliminate or include suspects. At trial, hair can be used as one piece of circumstantial evidence, among others, that a skillful prosecutor can use to weave together a strong case. By itself, however, hair evidence should never get a suspect charged, let alone convicted. Yet in Oklahoma, microscopic hair comparisons seem to have been considered to be powerful evidence by chemists, detectives, prosecutors, and juries.

That was about to change.

In late April 2001 a report prepared by FBI Supervisory Special Agent Douglas W. Deedrick was made public (the report had been written three weeks earlier). Deedrick had reviewed Gilchrist's laboratory notes, trial testimony, and the physical evidence in eight different cases. He found that Gilchrist had misidentified hairs in six of the cases and misidentified fibers in one other.

On April 30, two weeks after the FBI report came out, another document highly critical of Gilchrist was made public. Captain Byron Boshell, head of the laboratory services division of the OCPD, wrote in a memo dated January 16, 2001, that Gilchrist had severely mismanaged the OCPD crime lab and DNA project and was directly responsible for evidence having been lost, destroyed, contaminated, and mishandled.

The very next day, Amnesty International published a report on the death penalty in Oklahoma. Titled "Old Habits Die Hard," the Amnesty report found that Oklahoma was executing inmates at the highest rate per capita in the United States, and that Oklahoma's execution rate was higher than official executions in China or Iran. The Amnesty report cataloged various problems with the death penalty throughout Oklahoma, although it focused a great deal of attention on Oklahoma County.

Later that same day, Oklahoma County District Attorney Robert H. Macy announced that he would retire in a few weeks with eighteen months left in his term. The legendary prosecutor stated that his premature and unexpected retirement had nothing to do with the burgeoning scandal.

During his twenty-one years as Oklahoma County District

Attorney, Bob Macy sent seventy-three people to death row—more than any other prosecutor in the United States. Twenty of them have been executed, accounting for nearly half of the fifty executions in Oklahoma since the death penalty was reinstated in 1977.

Macy was the living symbol of frontier justice, or Macy justice, as they called it in Oklahoma City. He even looked the part. Wearing a black string tie, Western-cut sports coat, white ruffled shirt, and cowboy boots, Macy resembled Wyatt Earp in his Sunday go-to-meeting clothes.

Bob Macy is a real cowboy. He raises cattle on his ranch and did competitive roping in rodeos. His son Brett, now a lieutenant in the OCPD, was Oklahoma High School Rodeo Champion and won the national championship in roping three years in a row. Macy counted as his friends several pro rodeo stars and Hollywood cowboys like Wilford Brimley and Ben Johnson.

When you speak to people in Oklahoma City about Bob Macy, you often hear the words *legend, aura,* and *presence.* Over the course of several phone conversations and one face-to-face meeting, I felt Macy's presence myself. He has a quiet, engaging power. Our conversations took place after he had left office, and he was clearly a shadow of his former self. I could only imagine how formidable he was at the height of his power and ability. The force of Macy's personality—his charm and confidence, the respect and fear he inspired—are still felt in Oklahoma City today. Lawyers and policemen still call him "Mr. Macy." Some defense attorneys who fought Macy in court refuse to criticize him unless it's off the record.

Whether they agreed with him or not, most people I spoke to thought Macy was a man who believed in what he was doing.

"Macy had a good heart," said defense attorney Gary James. "He truly believed that he was stopping crime."

"I don't think he's cynical or a hypocrite," said David Autry, an

OIDS attorney who specializes in death row appeals. "He's the type of guy who, if he gets an idea in his head or has a belief, he sticks with it, no matter what."

Bob Ravitz, who tried several death penalty cases against him, remembers Macy as "extremely likable." Referring to murder cases he was able to plead out to life imprisonment, Ravitz said, "There are people still alive today because of my relationship with Bob Macy."

Part of Macy's charm is an absentmindedness, whether calculated or not, that allows him to be engaging even to his enemies.

"Macy was very friendly," Lee Ann Peters, an OIDS attorney who specializes in capital cases, told me. "When he saw me in the courthouse, he would recognize me. He wouldn't remember who I was, but he would ask what I was doing."

Jim Rowan defended five death penalty cases against Macy. When their paths crossed, Macy would tell Rowan, "I don't like you." Then he would turn to one of his aides and ask, "Why don't I like him?" The aide would whisper in his ear and Macy would say, "Oh, yeah, that's right."

Bob Macy would be the first person to tell you that he's a simple man. And he made his simplicity work for him.

"Macy sees everything in black and white. Right or wrong," Jim Rowan said. "If you're on his side, you can do no wrong. If you're against him, there's nothing good about you."

Some people I spoke to thought Macy was more than just simple. They saw a ruthless politician and an unscrupulous prosecutor.

Macy was "vicious and spiteful," in the words of one defense attorney. "He ruined a lot of people who got in his way."

"Macy was unethical," another defense attorney said. "And I think he fostered that attitude among many of the prosecutors in the office."

In his prime, Macy was a powerfully built man, with a barrel chest and large, strong hands. A shade under six feet, he seemed taller, and by all accounts cut an impressive figure in the courtroom. If Macy wasn't trying a case himself and he entered the courtroom, defense attorneys would object—that's how intimidating he was. Sometimes that intimidation threatened to escalate into physical violence.

"Macy offered to knock my block off more than once," said Jim Rowan. Rowan claims that Macy almost hit him in court, although he says it was more for show than anything else. Macy reared back like he was going to punch Rowan, then he waited for his assistants to hold him back, according to the defense attorney.

When I asked Macy about this incident, he just laughed.

"There are a few defense attorneys," he said, "that you just want to take out in the hall and kick their ass."

I've felt the same way myself at times.

Macy carried a loaded gun at all times, even in court. Once, when the state attorney general tried to bar prosecutors from carrying weapons in the courtroom, Macy successfully lobbied the legislature to pass a law specifically permitting them to carry concealed handguns. Throughout his career, Macy received death threats, some of them credible.

In 1990, Macy was dragged from the courtroom after reaching for his gun when a jury acquitted six defendants of shooting at police officers. The officers, who had been conducting a raid on a drug house, included Macy's own son, who was uninjured in the shooting.

Macy claimed later that while he did have a 9mm pistol on him, he hadn't actually reached for it. Several witnesses disputed Macy's account, saying that he was clearly reaching for his gun, whether or not he actually intended to use it.

"We were all shocked as hell," said one juror in the case. "I know that's his son, but he's the district attorney."

Another juror said that Macy was "too personally involved" to be in the courtroom. I can imagine the anger and rage that Macy must have felt when someone shot at his son. But I think Macy was grandstanding a bit, playing to the cops and the public, trying to live up to the legend he created about himself.

Macy was born to a working-class family. He grew up outside Indianapolis. His father was a truck driver, and Bob was the first person in his family to go to college. After playing fullback for the high school football team, Macy won a scholarship to Earlham College, where he also worked in the horse stables and began his romance with the cowboy life. Macy served in the air force, then became a policeman in Oklahoma City. He worked nights as a police officer and attended law school at the University of Oklahoma during the day, still wearing his patrol uniform and gun. Shortly before he graduated from law school, Macy worked as a legal aide to the state treasurer. In 1961 he got his law degree and worked briefly as an assistant district attorney in Pontotoc County. He also worked as an assistant state attorney general in Oklahoma. In Washington, D.C., he served as an assistant to the director of the Farmers Home Administration (part of the federal Department of Agriculture) and an adviser with the U.S. Justice Department's Law Enforcement Assistance Administration. For one year he served as deputy public safety administrator in St. Petersburg, Florida. And he worked with the Indiana State Police, investigating organized crime, for two years. Then he came back to Oklahoma, starting a private practice in Ada.

The way Bob Macy tells it, he never planned to be district attorney. He had been making good money practicing corporate law in Ada. Then Andy Coats, the Oklahoma County DA, decided to run for the U.S. Senate and had to step down from his position. (Coats lost the election and later became mayor of Oklahoma City.) Macy knew the governor of Oklahoma, George Nigh, and was good friends with Nigh's counsel David Hudson. A friend of Macy's had asked him for his recommendation to the DA's office. Macy called Hudson, who was handling the vetting process. After Macy's friend was taken out of consideration because of health problems, Hudson and Macy started throwing names back and forth as possible candidates.

"What about Bob Macy?" Hudson asked.

Macy said that until Hudson suggested it, he hadn't thought about being DA. He told Hudson he'd have think about it. Then Macy called a judge and asked for his advice. Macy says it was on the judge's encouragement that he agreed to take the post. And so a man with very little criminal trial experience became one of the most powerful figures in Oklahoma law enforcement.

When he took office, Macy says he only wanted to stay for the remainder of the term and then go back to private practice. But after a year or so on the job, people started urging him to run for election.

During his first term, Macy was praised for insulating himself from Oklahoma City's old guard. In fact, he was building his own power base, to a degree independent of the wealthy businessmen and influential politicians who ran the city and the state at that time.

"I had pissed off every politician in the state of Oklahoma," Macy told me. "I had put the deputy tax commissioner in jail and a whole lot of political people just hated my guts."

A review of the public record of Macy's first few years in office shows him to be a DA with a great deal of energy but no real mission. He initiated a variety of ingenious and low-risk crime-fighting measures—antifraud stings against TV- and car-repair shops, mandatory sentencing for drunk drivers, and neighborhood-watch groups. In one highly publicized case, Macy put two high school students on "DA probation" for throwing a pie in their teacher's face.

Macy cultivated a close and mutually advantageous relationship with the daily *Oklahoman,* the state's largest newspaper and the voice of the Oklahoma City establishment. The *Oklahoman* is owned by the Gaylords, one of the richest and most powerful families in the state. Macy was always good copy, providing vivid quotes and generating a great deal of controversy. The DA was often consulted before the newspaper expressed an editorial opinion on an issue that concerned him. I've read every *Oklahoman* article in which Macy was mentioned over the course of his twenty-year career, and it is difficult to find a critical word about him.

"Eddie Gaylord might slap Macy on the wrists editorially once in a while," one of Macy's former campaign managers said, "but he was always behind Macy when it counted."

Whether the office grew on him, or he had always wanted to remain DA, Macy decided to run for election in 1982. He ran a hard-fought campaign against former Olympic Gold Medal wrestler Wayne Wells. Wells accused Macy of being soft on crime. Macy countered with charges that Wells associated with corrupt individuals. Macy won 63 percent of the vote.

That campaign would be the only truly contested election in Macy's career. He would go on to be reelected four more times, always winning in a landslide. In his final campaign, he would run unopposed.

When Macy first took office, the death penalty had only recently been reestablished in Oklahoma. And while the state had quickly passed legislation in 1977 bringing the statutes up to the Supreme Court's new standards, there had been only a handful of capital convictions, and no one had been executed since 1966.

During the 1980s, Oklahoma City experienced a rise in violent crime. Many of these crimes were horrific: home invasions that resulted in rape and/or murder, the sexual homicide of children, drug and gang violence. Throughout the country, this kind of violent crime was on the rise. Bob Macy was determined to wipe it out in his town.

"I couldn't understand why we were having all these horrible murders in Oklahoma City," Macy said. "I thought, if we give them the death penalty and execute a few of them, maybe it would go down."

During his first full term as DA, Macy built a system for prosecuting death penalty cases. When a murder was committed, he would rush to the crime scene. There he would tell the media that they would find the killer and give him the death penalty. OCPD detectives would identify the suspect and the police chemists would find forensic evidence linking him to the crime. At trial, Macy would leave most of the heavy lifting to one of his assistants.

"The way Bob Macy tried cases—he kind of knew what was going on," Gary James told me. The weekend before the trial began, Macy would invite his assistant prosecutors to his ranch. They would bring their boss up to speed on the case. On Monday he'd be in the courtroom. Macy might not have been skilled at arguing complex legal issues, but he would give a powerful "fire and brimstone" closing argument. Often he would break into tears.

Gary James defended organized crime figure Benito Bowie on murder charges in a case where Macy was asking for the death penalty. In his closing argument, James told the jury, "Now Mr. Macy is going to stand in front of you and start crying." When the time came for Macy's closing argument, he couldn't summon the tears. During deliberations, the jury deadlocked on an eleven-to-one vote in favor of the death penalty. The judge imposed a life sentence.

Capital cases in Oklahoma are divided into two separate parts. The guilt phase is a regular trial that ends in the jury's verdict. If the jury decides that the defendant is guilty, then a second, much shorter, trial called the penalty phase takes place. At the end of the penalty phase, the jury decides the defendant's punishment. Macy would give closing arguments in both the guilt and the penalty phases.

Macy knew how to work a jury, particularly in a death penalty case. Juries in Oklahoma capital cases must be death qualified, which means that during jury selection, prospective jurors are asked whether they are capable of rendering a death verdict. This skews the jury toward the prosecution, because any prospective jurors who have qualms about giving the death penalty are excluded. During jury selection, the same people who had voted overwhelmingly for Bob Macy were now sitting in the jury box.

A campaign card Macy used during one of his elections showed him riding a horse in a rodeo event. The card bragged of his being the "Nation's leading death penalty prosecutor; Sent 42 murderers to death row."

Yet none of Macy's convicts were executed until 1999. Most of these delays were due to the litigation procedure of death penalty appeals (a process that was considerably shortened by changes in state and federal laws in the mid-1990s). Each death penalty conviction has a long series of appeals, some of them automatic, others generated by the appellate counsel for the condemned.

District Court judges are elected in Oklahoma County, and Macy's endorsements were crucial. Any judges who ran afoul of Macy risked having him actively campaign against them.

Judges on the Oklahoma Court of Criminal Appeals are appointed, but they run on retention ballots. Two judges on the state court of criminal appeals, Ed Parks and Charles Chapel, were singled out by Macy after having written strong opinions criticizing the prosecutor and overturning some of his death penalty convictions. According to several courthouse observers, Macy engaged in a campaign of public comments and private lobbying that pressured Parks and Chapel to start siding more with the prosecution.

Macy's influence extended beyond the courthouse. While police chiefs came and went, Macy always had an excellent relationship with the rank-and-file cops.

"We always felt like his door was open for us," one retired cop told me. "If we had a problem, or wanted him to know something, we could just walk in and talk to him. He always had time for cops."

The Police Academy included a lecture by Macy on law and procedures as part of its officer-training program. In this way, Macy left an impression on every officer before he or she even hit the street.

"In my heart," Macy said, "I've always been a police officer."

Macy was extremely loyal to the police. He took pride in never prosecuting a cop for anything but financial corruption. "I'll never prosecute a cop for doing his job," he would say. At his father's retirement dinner, Brett Macy reminded the audience that Macy had never prosecuted a cop for wrongful shooting. The crowd cheered.

"If you were a cop in Oklahoma City, you'd be crazy not to like Bob Macy," Bob Ravitz said. "He filed everything. He sought harsh sentences. And the only charges he didn't file were against police officers."

When I worked the streets, I welcomed any prosecutor or politician whose attitude reflected my own—zero tolerance of crime, strong sentencing, the death penalty. Macy's public statements would have been music to my ears and to those of most working cops. It would have been easy for detectives to clear homicides, since Macy was eager to prosecute. A lot of the cases for which Macy got the death penalty would have been kicked back by any DA in Los Angeles. Sometimes DAs refuse to prosecute with good reason; sometimes they're just afraid to file the case. I also think that if I had had Macy as a DA, I might have gotten sloppy and made some serious mistakes. That's the risk when everybody thinks the same way, and no one is willing to rock the boat.

Macy created a legacy of frontier justice that continues today. He trained a generation of district attorneys. Many of his protégés have remained in the DA's office as career prosecutors, others have been elected judges.

Throughout Macy's career as Oklahoma County DA, there was

talk of his pursuing higher office. Macy himself made no secret of his ambition to be governor. Yet he never ran for any other political office. One political insider told me that Macy had conducted polls that showed his popularity was limited to Oklahoma County. The gun incident in the courtroom had severely damaged his credibility, particularly statewide, and might have been a factor in his deciding not to run for governor.

In some ways, Macy didn't need to be governor. He was already one of the most powerful politicians in Oklahoma. As DA of the largest county in the state, Macy would investigate any corruption case where the state attorney general might have a conflict of interest, which meant that just about every state corruption case wound up on his desk.

In 1994, Macy oversaw a grand jury investigation that resulted in an indictment of Governor David Walters on campaign finance violations. After a grueling negotiation with the governor, Macy accepted a plea deal that dropped all but one of the charges and allowed Walters to remain in office. The public was outraged that Walters was not forced to resign and face charges in court. Seeing public opinion turn so quickly against him, Macy then called for the governor's resignation. It was too late. Macy had severely miscalculated the fallout from accepting Walters's plea. Although Macy would go on to be reelected twice more, he lost all chance at a higher office.

Walters was the highest-ranking state official to be investigated by Bob Macy, but he wasn't the only one. Macy investigated other law enforcement officials, other state and county agencies, other DAs. He investigated the politicians who controlled his budget, bringing down several county commissioners who had crossed him and effectively placing the DA's office outside of normal budget considerations.

Macy's political power in Oklahoma County was immense. He still commands a great deal of respect, even fear.

"Macy was J. Edgar Hoover—Oklahoma style," said one local attorney. "I always thanked God he was a friend of mine."

Macy was also a player on the national level, counseling presidents and attorneys general. He campaigned for both George Bushes and served on the transition team for Attorney General John Ashcroft. As head of the National Association of District Attorneys in the early 1990s, Macy represented prosecutors nationwide. He lobbied vigorously on every major federal crime bill. During the signing ceremony of the 1993 federal crime bill, Senator Joe Biden of Delaware pointed to Macy and said, "I wouldn't want to be in his county if I got arrested."

While Macy gained some prominence nationally, it was always, in the words of a longtime friend, "as a local character."

On two separate occasions, Macy was offered prominent and lucrative positions in the National Rifle Association (NRA), as either coordinator of a national anticrime program or the gun lobby's president. Both times, Macy told the press that the NRA was courting him. Yet he never took either job.

In the end, Macy stayed in Oklahoma County. Several people I spoke to said that Macy thought of himself as a small-town sheriff in a place that happened to be a modern city. Today, a large framed photograph of downtown Oklahoma City hangs in Macy's living room. Beneath the picture is the inscription "Macy's Town." When he was DA, a framed poster of the movie *Tombstone* hung on his office wall.

The same poster hangs in my family room. To me it depicts a place and time where I would much rather have lived—if only it were real.

Bob Macy believed in frontier justice, and that was part of his appeal. He saw himself as one of the good guys, sworn to protect the innocent and fight evil.

"I like to think I'm an honest man," Bob Macy said the first time I spoke with him. "I did my best to be one."

Yet there were those who questioned Macy's integrity.

"The dangerous thing about Bob Macy," said Pat Williams, a Tulsa defense attorney, "is that he was a guy with a lot of skills, but he just couldn't try a case straight."

I wanted to go beyond the media clichés and easy answers and get to the truth about Bob Macy, Joyce Gilchrist, and the death penalty, so I went to Oklahoma several times, including a visit to McAlester's death row. I interviewed scores of people working in or associated with Oklahoma County law enforcement. And I reviewed the press reports, trial transcripts, appellate rulings, and other documents from a score of death penalty cases.

How bad were the problems with the death penalty in Oklahoma County? Did Macy and Gilchrist knowingly convict innocent people, or were they just a couple of law enforcement professionals, imperfect like us all, who were being crucified by the media, defense attorneys, and political activists?

CHAPTER TWO

THE GUEST HOUSE MURDERS

BOB MACY WAS SWORN IN AS OKLAHOMA COUNTY DISTRICT ATTORNEY on June 16, 1980. Less than three weeks later, a triple homicide was committed at a local motel. The Guest House Murders would be Macy's first death penalty case. And one of his most controversial.

On July 6, 1980, at approximately 2:00 A.M., Ray Peters, Lawrence Evans, and Marvin Nowlin were shot and killed as they sat by the pool at the Guest House Inn Motel in Oklahoma City. The murder weapon was never found. Bullets and shell casings recovered at the scene showed the killer used a .45-caliber automatic with Winchester Western silver-tipped hollow-point bullets. Several witnesses reported seeing a man near the pool area before the shooting occurred. After the witnesses heard gunshots, they saw the man run off, get into a waiting car, and drive away.

Because of the crime's MO and the known criminal associations of the victims, authorities believed that the Guest House Murders were an organized crime execution. Bob Macy was determined to keep organized crime from infiltrating Oklahoma City.

Based on the physical descriptions provided by Mary Lee Chilton and Carrie Pitchford, two witnesses who were at the motel on the night of the murder, the police circulated a flyer with a composite sketch and the following description of the suspect: a white male, six foot one, 210 to 250 pounds, potbellied with medium-length salt-and-pepper hair, pale with a week's growth of beard, wearing a red baseball cap, long-sleeved blue shirt, faded blue jeans, and brown work boots.

When Detective Dave McBride saw the description, he immediately thought of Clifford Henry Bowen. As head of the OCPD's Organized Crime Detail, McBride (who later became police chief) had investigated Bowen in 1975. Bowen, who said he made his living playing poker, had a record for burglary and attempted bank robbery. He was reputed to have connections to the Dixie Mafia—an organized crime ring that operated in several southern states.

Another suspect was Harold Dean Behrens, a former OCPD detective who was involved in narcotics trafficking. Ray Peters, one of the victims, had been working for Behrens as a drug dealer. A month prior to the murders, Peters had been arrested in Pauls Valley, Oklahoma, on charges of drunk driving and drug possession. Behrens had gotten Peters out of jail and was reportedly concerned about Peters's excessive drinking and drug use—and how it compromised Behrens's drug business.

Before he left the OCPD to pursue his second career as a drug racketeer, Harold Behrens had been a detective on McBride's Organized Crime Detail. Behrens was the one who first brought in information concerning Bowen and his possible criminal activities. Bowen was investigated and surveilled, but he left Oklahoma City, and no charges were brought.

McBride thought Bowen perfectly fit the suspect's description in the Guest House Murders. He later testified to the details that matched, adding that Bowen always wore horn-rimmed glasses (glasses were not mentioned in any of the witness reports or the description). McBride notified homicide detectives about Bowen and gave them his picture. The detectives showed their witnesses two groups of five photographs. The first group included Bowen, without his glasses. Both witnesses identified Bowen from the photographs and then again in a live lineup.

Police got an arrest warrant for Bowen on August 27 (he was in Texas at the time). The same day murder charges were filed against Harold Dean Behrens and John Doe in the Guest House Murders. On August 29, Bowen was interrogated by OCPD detectives. He had his lawyer present and was subsequently taken into custody. Bowen's name was substituted for John Doe on the information.

Macy went down to Texas himself to arrest Bowen, eventually tricking the local authorities into releasing Bowen into his custody. The headlines in the newspaper the next day read: OKLAHOMA DA KIDNAPS PRISONER.

Behrens and Bowen were tried separately. Behrens went on trial first. He did not testify at Bowen's trial. (Behrens testified once during all of Bowen's proceedings. This was an offer of proof at the first motion for a new trial, when Behrens stated that he did not know Bowen and had never seen him before.) The prosecutors had offered Behrens a ten-year sentence for the three murder charges in return for testimony that he knew Bowen.

"I would gladly testify," Behrens replied, "but I don't know the dude."

With little more than evidence of his criminal association with Ray Peters and the theory that he had hired Bowen—who had yet to stand trial—Behrens was convicted and given a life sentence for the three murders. He entered the witness protection program, providing information about his various criminal associates in Oklahoma and several other states.

Macy had hoped that Behrens would roll on Bowen. He had no evidence against Bowen except for the two witness identifications. Before going to trial, Macy declared that he would seek the death penalty against Bowen. During the trial, Macy argued that Bowen had killed Ray Peters on Behrens's orders for money but was unable to offer any evidence to prove that Bowen had been paid.

Jack Zumwalt, Behrens's gay lover and partner in the drug business, appeared as a witness for the prosecution. Shortly before the murder, Ray Peters and his lover Herman Borden had been sitting together by the Guest House pool. Behrens came up, put his hand on Peters's shoulder, and said that he would see him tomorrow. Zumwalt testified that Behrens was not in the habit of making physical contact with people. Macy argued that this meant Behrens must have been fingering Peters for a hit man.

Bowen took the stand in his own defense, denying that he committed the murders. His attorneys also presented twelve alibi witnesses who all testified that the defendant was at a rodeo in Tyler, Texas, on the night of the murders. The shootings had occurred at 2:00 A.M. One of the state's witnesses had seen the suspect around the motel near midnight. Defense witnesses testified that Bowen had been at the rodeo as late as 1:00 A.M. Tyler is some three hundred miles from Oklahoma City. In order to have committed the murders, Bowen would have had to travel three hundred miles in one hour.

Macy waited until the final day of the trial and then offered a novel theory about how Bowen would have been able to travel from Tyler to Oklahoma City in time to commit the murders. Bowen could have chartered a Learjet, Macy told the jury, and flown from a small airport in Tyler to the downtown airpark in Oklahoma City. Macy called as a witness a pilot who testified that it could have been possible for a jet to have transported Bowen from an old airfield near the rodeo grounds to Oklahoma City within a time frame that could place him at the crime scene when the murders were committed. But Macy offered no evidence that showed Bowen had actually done this. There were no flight logs, no witnesses, no airport records corroborating Macy's theory.

Bowen was found guilty of three counts of murder and given the death penalty. He immediately filed a motion for a new trial, alleging ineffectiveness of counsel. That motion was overruled and Judge Raymond Naifeh signed the death warrant.

During subsequent hearings, Bowen's lawyers were able to present evidence that neither the Tyler airstrip nor the Oklahoma airpark was equipped to handle a jet, that no jets had landed or taken off at either facility, and that the Tyler airstrip had been long closed at the time of the murders. A judge who later ruled on the Bowen case had flown in and out of the Oklahoma airpark and had personal knowledge that a flight such as Macy had described was impossible.

"The downtown airpark had no lights for a night landing and didn't have a runway that would accommodate a Learjet," Bowen's appellate attorney, Pat Williams, said later. He called Macy's argument "totally outside the record and false."

While Bowen's appeal was pending before the Oklahoma Court of Criminal Appeals, he filed a second motion for a new trial based on newly discovered evidence and the prosecutor's failure to disclose exculpatory evidence to the defense.

The newly discovered evidence involved a corrupt South Carolina policeman named Lee Crowe, who had originally been a suspect in the murders but was eliminated once the two witnesses picked Bowen out of a photo lineup—before even seeing another photo lineup that included Crowe.

I find it difficult to believe that both of those witnesses, seeing a person at night across a courtyard, could have given the detectives an absolute 100 percent identification. And even if the witnesses did give a strong ID, the detectives should have continued their investigation, since the witness IDs were all that implicated Bowen.

Dave McBride eventually became OCPD chief, which indicates the status and respect he had among his fellow officers. When he came up with a theory of the crime, it apparently went unchallenged. And there's no doubt that McBride had an ax to grind against Behrens and Bowen.

The evidence concerning Lee Crowe was uncovered by none other than Harold Behrens, who, as part of his witness protection deal, was testifying about the drug trade in South Carolina, in which he had been involved. One day he was talking to officers from the South Carolina Law Enforcement Division (SCLED). They asked Behrens why he was in federal custody. Behrens told them how he had received a life sentence for the Guest House Murders.

"You think that's bad," Behrens told the South Carolina cops, "there's a guy named Bowen who's on death row."

Behrens said, as he had always maintained, that he didn't even know Bowen. The SCLED officers told Behrens they had received calls from Oklahoma about a dirty cop named Lee Crowe.

Crowe had been fired from the Charleston Sheriff's Department for involvement with prostitutes and felons. At the time of the Guest House Murders, Crowe was a lieutenant in Hanahan, a suburb of Charleston. Crowe matched the physical description of the suspect even better than Bowen. He was a white male, six feet two inches tall, weighing 225 pounds, with salt-and-pepper hair, a potbelly, and a pale complexion; he did not wear eyeglasses. He often wore a baseball cap and usually carried a .45-caliber automatic with silver-tipped hollow-point ammunition. And he was known to use a cross-draw holster of the same type believed to have been used in the killings.

Prior to the murders, Crowe had lived with Patsy Peters, Ray Peters's ex-wife. Patsy had once shot Ray when they were living together in Charleston. Crowe had been in Oklahoma with Patsy, visiting her family, during the first week of July 1980. The night of the murders he was 130 miles from Oklahoma City. He and Patsy left Oklahoma for South Carolina the day after the murders. Shortly after his return, Crowe resigned from the Hanahan Police Department.

A photograph taken of Crowe a few days before the murders shows him with a mustache. When he returned to South Carolina on July 8, the mustache had been shaved off. During the photo lineup, OCPD detectives had used a picture of Crowe with a mustache.

South Carolina authorities had provided the OCPD with Crowe's fingerprint card and spent casings from his .45 pistol requalification.

Neither his fingerprints nor the casings matched evidence at the crime scene. That's not surprising, as they didn't find fingerprints that matched Bowen's, either. And the shell casings from Crowe's requalification would probably have been standard-issue rounds. Even if he used the silver-tipped hollow-point rounds on the job, Crowe wasn't going to waste such expensive ammo on the range test. The police didn't take Crowe's gun and do a test fire.

Prior to the arrests of Bowen and Behrens, investigators from the SCLED had been looking into the Peters killing themselves, because they believed it might have been connected to the disappearance of Ricky Seagraves. Peters and Seagraves had allegedly ripped off Paul Mazzell, the head of organized crime in Charleston, on a 1978 drug deal involving Dilaudid, a very potent barbiturate. Behrens told the South Carolina investigators that Peters had been killed because he burned Mazzell, and that the hit man had come to Oklahoma from Charleston.

Peters's prior involvement with Mazzell and the Charleston drug trade was corroborated by South Carolina authorities. Shortly after the Dilaudid deal, Seagraves was kidnapped from a convenience store and never heard from again. Confidential informants in Oklahoma and Charleston said that Danny Hogg and Eddie Merman had killed Seagraves on Mazzell's orders. Lee Crowe had been observed at Hogg's apartment before and after the Guest House Murders. South Carolina law enforcement considered Crowe the prime suspect in Peters's murder.

South Carolina prosecutor Richard S. W. Stoney said two SCLED agents flew to Oklahoma in 1981 to interview Behrens about the Seagraves murder, "as well as to pursue SCLED agent Chad Caldwell's belief that the murderer in the Oklahoma murder of Raymond Leroy Peters was in fact one Lee Crowe."

When OCPD detectives contacted the police in Charleston, they were told that Crowe had been fired from the Sheriff's Department because of his criminal involvement. They were also told that Crowe was being investigated as a suspected hit man. On several occasions, Crowe had left the state, and upon his return it was later discovered that a homicide had been committed where he had been. They also learned that Crowe carried a .45-caliber automatic wherever he went and that he always used silver-tipped hollow-point ammo. Crowe was described as having "an extremely high temper" and was "capable of killing anyone for money." One officer told the OCPD detectives about an incident involving a former girlfriend of Crowe's who complained that a current boyfriend kept bothering her. The boyfriend was shot in the head five times with a small-caliber handgun. When Lee Crowe was asked about a similar weapon known to be in his possession, he said that he had lost it.

According to the police report, Crowe had been eliminated as a suspect because Patsy Peters's mother said that she believed Crowe had stayed in her house on the night of the murder. Patsy's mother was in Oklahoma City that night at a Jehovah's Witness convention and had no way of knowing whether or not Crowe stayed at the house. Following his interview with Mrs. Forguson, OCPD detective Bob Horn (who worked the case with his partner Bill Cook) stated that she had appeared "extremely nervous and uncomfortable." The police did not speak to Patsy's father, C. B. Forguson, until after Bowen's first trial. Forguson then told the police that Crowe had stayed at their house that night.

Lee Crowe looks like a much better suspect than Clifford Henry Bowen. He had motive, means, and opportunity. He was actually closer to the crime scene than Bowen was the night of the murders. He was known to carry a weapon similar to the one used in the killings. And he fit the physical description better than Bowen did. The suspect had been described as pale, and the defense offered evidence at the first trial that Bowen had been sun-tanned at the time of the murders. By the time of his trial and other court appearances, Bowen was more pale than usual. Of course, he had been in prison.

So why did the witnesses pick Bowen, and not Crowe, from the photo lineups?

The picture of Bowen used in the photo lineup showed him without the horn-rimmed glasses he usually wore, and which Dave McBride had remembered so well when he first thought of Bowen as a possible suspect.

None of the men in the first group of photographs, which included Bowen, had mustaches. In the second group, which included Crowe, three out of five men had mustaches. (You should never compose a photo lineup in which some subjects have different distinguishing features, like facial hair.) It was documented in the police report that Crowe had shaved his mustache around the time of the murders. Either way, the eyewitnesses reported seeing a man with a week's growth of beard but no mustache.

Although the witnesses did pick Bowen out of a live lineup, they were never given the chance to see Crowe in person. And they saw Bowen in a live lineup after they had already identified him from the photograph. Much later, Bob Macy told the *Oklahoman* that the two witnesses had been shown a photograph of Crowe before identifying Bowen. In fact, they had seen the photograph of Bowen first.

Even if Lee Crowe was not responsible for the Guest House Murders, Bob Macy should have told the defense about him. The prosecution is under a positive obligation to turn over all possibly exculpatory evidence to the defense under what is called discovery. In *Brady* v. *Maryland,* the U.S. Supreme Court ruled that "suppression by the prosecution of evidence favorable to an accused upon request violates due process where the evidence is material either to guilt or to punishment, irrespective of the good faith or bad faith of the prosecution."

While there are federal rulings that provide general guidelines concerning discovery, the specific laws and practices vary from state to state. At the time, Oklahoma had extremely limited discovery requirements (and many defense attorneys claim that Oklahoma County courts, in particular, remain very conservative, which is to say pro-prosecution, in their rulings on discovery). There was no discovery code in Oklahoma until the mid-1990s. Prior to that, defense attorneys had to file motions for discovery and exculpatory evidence. In those motions, the defense had to ask for specific items of evidence. Sometimes prosecutors would claim that evidence was work product and therefore defense attorneys were not entitled to it.

"Ray Charles could see that's *Brady* material," said Tulsa attorney Pat Williams, referring to the Lee Crowe information.

At the time of Bowen's first trial, prosecutors were obliged to turn over only what had been formally requested by the defense. In the Bowen case, Raymond Burger, the lead defense counsel for the first trial, had asked one of the prosecutors for all exculpatory materials. He was given a small folder that did not include anything about Lee Crowe. Frank Wright, another of Bowen's attorneys, asked Bob Macy if there were any other suspects in the case, and Macy had told him that there weren't. During a later hearing, Macy did not dispute

Wright's recollection of the request, saying, "I don't recall the conversation, but if they say it took place I assume it did."

Bowen's appellate lawyers argued that the prosecutors' withholding of the Lee Crowe information was a clear violation of *Brady*. Bowen's attorneys also produced a witness, Deanna Burris, who signed an affidavit stating that she had heard "Lee Crowe and Patsy Peters plan the murder of Ray Peters."

Raymond Naifeh, the judge in Bowen's trial, listened to arguments before deciding whether to hold an evidentiary hearing.

"They want you to send a man to his death without giving him a fair trial," Houston lawyer Jack Zimmerman told the judge.

Macy responded that the information about Crowe "would not have made one iota of difference" and that it would be a "travesty of justice." Macy also called Burris "a dopey prostitute."

Judge Naifeh decided to hold the evidentiary hearing.

During the hearing, Burris testified that she had shared an apartment with Crowe and Patsy Peters. "It started with Patsy wanting to have Ray knocked off and Crowe said he would do it," Burris said under oath. She also said that Crowe had asked Patsy to lure her husband to Charleston where Crowe could "take care of him," but Patsy had been unable to do so. Shortly after those conversations, Crowe and Patsy went to Oklahoma, and Ray Peters was killed. When Patsy returned to South Carolina after the murders, Burris spoke to her on the phone several times. Patsy always asked Burris whether anyone had been asking questions about Crowe.

When Burris first told her story to SCLED agent Chad Caldwell, as part of the Ricky Seagraves investigation, Caldwell was unaware of the Guest House Murders and thought that Burris's drug use cast doubt on her credibility. Drug addicts are commonly used as informants because they have knowledge of criminal behavior and a weakness that investigators can exploit. Caldwell later said that Burris had failed a polygraph examination concerning her statements.

When Caldwell found out about the convictions of Bowen and Behrens, he reinterviewed Burris and she told him the same story. This time, she was no longer on drugs. Caldwell sent both of Burris's statements along to OCPD detectives.

Burris also said that two OCPD detectives had visited her in South Carolina and told her "that I didn't know what I was getting myself into and that I shouldn't come here to testify because Lee Crowe is a dangerous man." Burris admitted that she worked as a prostitute and Crowe provided her with Quaaludes. She was afraid of Crowe, but agreed to testify because "I don't want to see anybody put to sleep for something he didn't do."

Judge Naifeh found that Burris's prostitution and drug use rendered her an unreliable witness and that the Crowe information was not credible; therefore, no *Brady* violation had occurred. He ruled that Bowen was not entitled to a new trial and set his execution date for August 12, 1985. The credibility of a person who brings forward criminal information should not be determined by his or her lifestyle but rather by the quality of the information he or she provides.

In December 1984 the Oklahoma Court of Criminal Appeals affirmed Bowen's conviction and ruled that no new trial was warranted. The court held that Frank Wright's oral request "fell short" of the *Brady* standards. Wright had not asked specifically for rejected investigative leads or other people who had been investigated and eliminated as suspects. He had only asked if there was someone else who might have committed the crime.

After the Court of Criminal Appeals issued its ruling, Macy said he was "tickled pink." Recalling the fact that he often disagreed with Criminal Appeals Judge Ed Parks, Macy said, "I'm especially happy to see that in spite of his well-publicized opposition to the death penalty, Judge Parks concurred in this case."

With Bowen's execution only three weeks away, Zimmerman

filed for a stay of execution. The stay was granted, and U.S. District Judge Thomas Brett held a hearing on possible *Brady* violation and ineffectiveness of counsel.

At the federal hearing, Raymond Burger testified that "80 to 90 percent of the prosecutors in Macy's office think Bowen is innocent." Burger also said that Macy would not have given him the information about Lee Crowe, even if he had filed a formal discovery motion.

"Prosecutors of Oklahoma, almost exclusively of Oklahoma, will hide things from defense attorneys," Burger said. "Oklahoma has a reputation for not complying with *Brady*."

Macy testified that he knew about Lee Crowe, but that Crowe had been eliminated as a suspect early in the investigation.

During the federal proceedings, Bowen's lawyers subpoenaed the homicide book, a loose-leaf binder containing all the investigative reports and intelligence information collected by the OCPD detectives working the Guest House Murders, including a lengthy report about Lee Crowe. The detectives had given the homicide book to the prosecutors in August 1980, but it was not turned over to the defense during discovery.

After the hearing, Judge Brett overturned Bowen's convictions and held that Oklahoma could retry him for the murders. Brett ruled that the oral request was enough to hold the prosecutors responsible for the Crowe material, and that even without the oral request, they were still bound by law to turn over such possibly exculpatory materials. Judge Naifeh had found that the Burris testimony was not sufficient to grant a new trial because the defense could have found her with due diligence and her testimony would not have affected the verdict, which was based on the testimony of the two witnesses who had identified Bowen. Brett disagreed with Naifeh, saying that the Burris testimony underscored the materiality of the Crowe information.

Judge Brett ordered Bowen released from death row. Macy filed a motion asking the judge to stay Bowen's release pending an appeal. Brett denied the motion, but ordered Bowen returned to prison and said he must post a $100,000 appearance bond. State officials had waited in Brett's courtroom with arrest warrants in case Bowen had been released.

Shortly after Judge Brett's decision, the foreman of the jury in Bowen's trial called it a "technicality" and said that the information about Lee Crowe wouldn't have made any difference in their decision. "We were going on the fact that two ladies said they saw him there," Jess Thomas told the *Oklahoman*. "That's the thing that makes you wonder how the judge could possibly say it wasn't fair."

"I am still convinced beyond any doubt that Bowen is guilty," Macy said. "I haven't seen anything that would change my mind about prosecuting him again."

Macy appealed Judge Brett's decision to the Tenth Circuit Court, which not only upheld Brett's ruling but also went further, saying that the Lee Crowe evidence "creates reasonable doubt" that Bowen was the killer. The court found that Macy's withholding of the Crowe evidence "raises serious questions about the manner, quality and thoroughness of the investigation that led to Bowen's arrest and trial." The homicide book, which Macy had not turned over to the defense, was characterized by the court as the "smoking gun" in the case. "With this material," the three judges wrote in a strongly worded fifty-one-page decision, "a defense lawyer of less than heroic skill could have theorized that the state found it easier to charge an admitted gambler and ne'er-do-well rather than a police officer, even an allegedly corrupt one."

"If the defense had known about Lee Crowe at trial," the Tenth Circuit concluded, "the reliability of the identification procedures could have been undermined and the witnesses impeached."

Those two witnesses were the prosecution's whole case. Bob
Macy himself admitted this in court.

Q: *If you take out the testimony of Mary Chilton, who had misidentified someone else earlier, and Carrie Pitchford, there is no case
against Henry Bowen, is there?*
A [MACY]: *There is not a total case. There is a partial case.*
Q: *Could you have gotten a conviction on the evidence you had, sub-
tracting Mary Chilton and Carrie Pitchford?*
A: *No.*

And if these witnesses had been impeached, which the Lee
Crowe information could easily have done (just a photograph of
Crowe would probably have sufficed), Macy had no case at all. He
admitted this as well.

Q: *Now, Mr. Macy, let me ask you this question. If the testimony of
Mary Chilton and Carrie Pitchford had been impeached at trial sig-
nificantly or their identification in court had been significantly
attacked or impeached, is there a reasonable probability that Mr.
Bowen would be free today?*
A: *There was a serious attempt to impeach it.*
Q: *That wasn't my question, Mr. Macy. Had they been impeached,
because their testimony was the heart of the case, isn't there a reason-
able probability that the verdict would have been not guilty?*
A: *That's true.*

Chilton's credibility could have been further undermined by the
fact that she had undergone hypnosis in order to aid her memory.
The defense was not informed of this. Instead, two police officers
denied that it had happened, despite the fact that Chilton insisted

she had been hypnotized before she identified Bowen. Chilton also misidentified one picture in the photo lineup and a police detective in the live lineup, prior to identifying Bowen.

Macy had said that when he was asked about "other suspects," he distinguished between "viable" suspects and those who had been eliminated. He stated that Bowen was the only viable suspect ever, but if the defense had asked if he had considered other suspects, he would have turned over the Crowe material. The Tenth Circuit Court didn't buy this: "According to the district attorney's analysis, if a prosecutor believes that other 'viable' suspects exist two months before a capital trial, he is obligated to dismiss the charges against the defendant. A request for all other suspects therefore must necessarily imply former or discarded suspects."

The court called Macy's jet theory "at best speculation and at worst fantasy."

Bowen's retrial was set for the summer of 1987. Before the trial began, one of the witnesses died under what Bob Macy later called "unusual circumstances." Mary Lee Chilton Brown (she had married) had been visiting her sister in rural Virginia. She became ill in a restaurant and was flown by helicopter to a hospital in Norfolk, where she died of a cerebral hemorrhage.

District Court Judge Joe Cannon ruled that Chilton's testimony from the original trial could not be used in Bowen's retrial, saying that she testified twice that she had been hypnotized by police prior to her identification of the suspect. Macy told the judge that his investigators could find no evidence that Chilton had been hypnotized, and two police officers who worked on the case, Captain Mike Heath and Detective Roy Sellers, both testified that they had no knowledge of Chilton's being hypnotized. (Why didn't they ask Detectives Horn and Cook?)

Earlier, Macy had blamed the lengthy appellate process and the higher courts for overturning Bowen's conviction.

"You can't blame that on anybody but the state of Oklahoma," Cannon said when announcing his ruling. "They failed to do what they're supposed to do in a criminal case."

Following Cannon's ruling, Macy announced that he would drop the charges against Bowen, saying his prosecutors "no longer have sufficient evidence to bring Clifford Henry Bowen to trial."

Pat Williams said that the case showed Macy's "mentality of win at all costs." Williams is a Tulsa attorney who lived and worked outside of Macy's sphere of influence. He is a former prosecutor who had been a proponent of the death penalty.

"After the Bowen case, I just thought, God Almighty, how do you unring a bell once you've killed somebody?" Williams told me.

After Bowen was finally set free Williams asked him if he wanted to file a lawsuit against Macy and the OCPD. Bowen said, "I appreciate it, but Macy will come up with some liars and I just want to get away from Oklahoma."

Despite the weak case against Bowen, Macy had been able to convince a jury that he was guilty. Williams attributes this to Macy's power. Even though he had only been DA for a few years, "a lot of people were afraid of Bob Macy. He was a powerful prosecutor and powerful politically and he ran an office that mirrored him in many respects."

I asked Bob Macy about the case, and he told me that he remained convinced that Bowen was guilty. He told me that Bowen was part of the Dixie Mafia, that he had been involved in the gang that threatened Buford Pusser in the film *Walking Tall,* and that he had been a burglar. But he offered no evidence that connected Bowen to the Guest House Murders. When I asked him about Lee Crowe, Macy said that the Oklahoma detectives had investigated Crowe "up and down, *A* to *Z.*" He also said that if Mary Lee Chilton Brown hadn't died, he would have tried Bowen again.

In the end, Bob Macy lost his first death penalty case. He was severely criticized by two federal courts (although the district and state courts found little wrong with his conduct). In the Bowen case, Oklahoma County law enforcement ignored evidence that would have exonerated their suspect. Someone should have pulled the plug on the case as soon as Bowen established a tight and unshakable alibi. If Macy didn't know about Bowen's being at the rodeo on the night of the murder, he should have. It's very troubling that Bowen went to death row without someone within the OCPD or Macy's office raising an objection about the Lee Crowe information or the lack of evidence against Bowen. And the fact that they were unable to prove a connection between Bowen and Harold Behrens calls Behrens's conviction into question as well.

Bowen was a convenient suspect. He probably made someone in the OCPD angry at some point in his criminal career, evading prosecution in other crimes, and he loosely fit the suspect description. Once Bowen was presented as the suspect, Macy never seems to have considered anyone else.

When Bowen's sentence was reversed, Macy was in the middle of his first reelection campaign. His opponent was Mike Gassaway, a criminal defense attorney who had beaten Macy in a previous murder case. (Macy had charged Royal Russell Long with abducting and killing two girls from the Oklahoma State Fair. The bodies of the two girls were never found. Long, who had been serving time in Wyoming for another murder/kidnapping of a young girl, was acquitted on the Oklahoma charges.)

Prior to the election Gassaway had been charged with felony counts of failure to file state tax returns. Gassaway said he decided to run against Macy because the charges were Macy's "retaliation" for the Long case, although he offered no proof that Macy was behind the tax charges. In August 1986, Gassaway received a suspended sentence on the state tax charges, but then he was charged with federal tax violations. Less than three weeks before the election, Gassaway was sentenced to six months in prison.

Macy won reelection with 79 percent of the vote.

Clifford Henry Bowen died in 1996 of natural causes. Bowen was a career criminal. He had the money to afford decent lawyers who eventually got him freed from death row. Was he involved in the Guest House Murders? There's no evidence that he was. Yet to be accused of a crime, even a murder in which he was not involved, came with the territory for a man like Bowen. As unjust as his trial and conviction might have been, it's hard to feel sorry for him.

CHAPTER THREE

LINGERING DOUBT

THE 1982 TRIAL OF MALCOLM RENT JOHNSON INTRODUCED A NEW MEM-
ber of Bob Macy's death penalty team—forensic scientist Joyce
Gilchrist. At the time of Johnson's trial, Gilchrist had been working
as a police chemist for a year and a half. Her testimony proved to be
instrumental.

It all started with a brutal murder. On October 27, 1981, Frank
Thompson went to his aunt's house to check on her. Ura Alma
Thompson was seventy-six years old. She lived alone, and her sister
had been unable to reach her on the phone. When she didn't answer,
Frank got the building manager to unlock the door. Frank entered
the apartment and saw his aunt's dead body on the bedroom floor.
She was naked, except for a pair of hose. An autopsy would later
determine that she had been raped and asphyxiated. Missing from
the apartment were two diamond rings, a watch, a mink coat, and
her apartment keys.

Hours before Thompson's body was discovered, Malcolm Rent
Johnson was arrested on a weapons charge at his home. Johnson, a

black man, was a parolee from Illinois who had already served three years and eight months for rape, armed robbery, and burglary. His live-in girlfriend gave police permission to search Johnson's apartment, and they found items that were later identified as belonging to Ura Alma Thompson. Johnson was arrested for parole violation and held as a suspect in four other rape cases, where the victims were all elderly women.

Shortly after his arrest on the weapons charge, Johnson was interrogated by Detectives Bill Cook and Tony Gregory, who were investigating the Thompson murder. Johnson told the detectives that his brother Rodney had given him Thompson's belongings but denied any knowledge of her apartment key. Bill Cook told Johnson that they were going to convict him because they had found his semen inside the victim.

"You couldn't have found my semen in her," Johnson replied, "because I didn't come."

The detectives took this statement as an admission of guilt, at least for the rape. But it's not so simple. Johnson's statement raised several questions. And the detectives should have answered—or at least asked—those questions instead of simply taking the statement as a confession. What did Johnson mean by his statement "I didn't come"? Was he saying he raped Thompson but didn't climax? If that was the case, then who deposited the semen in her vagina and all over the crime scene? Was Johnson saying that he didn't rape Thompson? Did that mean there was another suspect? Was this suspect responsible for the rape and/or the murder? Was Johnson saying that detectives could not have matched a semen sample to him because he surrendered only hair and blood but no semen?

"Malcolm Rent Johnson was a really dumb guy," Bob Ravitz said. Ravitz was the Oklahoma County Assistant Public Defender when he defended Johnson. When Cook told Johnson that his semen was found in the victim, Johnson had no idea that blood type could be found in the semen samples of a secretor. Ravitz believes that Johnson was saying he hadn't given a semen sample, so there was no way they could have matched the sample inside the victim to him. He thought the detectives were lying to get a confession from him.

A confession is supposed to match the evidence. Johnson's statement does not. Semen was found in the victim's vagina, in one of her stockings, and, according to Joyce Gilchrist, on her sheets and pillowcase. "I didn't come" isn't a confession to anything. It is not corroborated by the evidence, and it doesn't implicate the suspect in any crime. A simpler explanation for Johnson's statement "I didn't come" would be "I didn't do it." If anything, the statement is a denial of the crime. Detectives Cook and Gregory should have taken it as such. Instead, they called Johnson's statement a confession and charged him with the murder and rape of Ura Alma Thompson.

In addition to those crimes, Johnson was charged with four other rapes, one attempted rape, robbery with a firearm, two counts of first degree burglary, and illegal possession of a firearm.

There were two preliminary hearings, the first for the four other rapes and the burglary and robbery charges, and the second for the Thompson rape/murder. One of the victims in the first prelim, a seventy-eight-year-old woman, testified that she had just entered her apartment after a trip to the grocery store when her assailant forced his way inside and began choking her. He knocked off her glasses, ransacked her apartment, forced her to undress, and raped her on the floor.

"He broke two of my ribs. He broke my arm," the witness said, still wearing a cast on her right arm. When questioned by prosecutor Barry Albert, the woman was unable to identify Malcolm Rent Johnson as her assailant. A witness, who said he had seen the victim talking with someone in the hallway just before she was assaulted, was asked to point to the person he saw. The witness pointed to Johnson's brother, Rodney, who was sitting nearby. After being told he had selected the wrong man, the witness pointed out Malcolm, although he also stated that Johnson's appearance was somewhat different at the time of the attack. Johnson and his brother were quite similar in appearance. Malcolm's own parole officer mistook his brother for him.

When Malcolm Rent Johnson was first questioned about the items from Thompson's apartment, he said his brother had given them to him. Why didn't Cook and Gregory investigate Johnson's brother as a possible suspect? And what led the OCPD detectives to Johnson's apartment in the first place? Was there an informant involved? Was it Rodney Johnson? if so, why didn't the police investigate him as a possible material witness, accomplice, or even suspect?

In the second preliminary hearing for the Thompson case, the victim's nephew identified several belongings that he had seen in his aunt's possession, including an antique opaline box, a portable typewriter, and a gold-plated dresser set. OCPD detective Julie Smith testified that she saw these items in the apartment where Malcolm Rent Johnson lived. Smith said she had been investigating the Thompson slaying when she found them, but according to investigators' notes, Thompson's body hadn't yet been found.

The rape and murder of Ura Alma Thompson was a horrible crime. And Malcolm Rent Johnson was a dangerous criminal. Bob Macy announced he would seek the death penalty.

In order to qualify for the death penalty in Oklahoma, a murder must satisfy one or more of eight "aggravating circumstances." These conditions were part of the U.S. Supreme Court's requirements for revised death penalty statutes following their vacating of existing capital statutes in *Furman* v. *Georgia.* In Oklahoma, the eight aggravators are:

1. Murder for hire.

2. The suspect has prior felony convictions.

3. The killing of a law enforcement officer.

4. The murder is "heinous, atrocious or cruel."

5. The suspect poses a continuing threat to society.

6. The murder was committed to escape prosecution.

7. The murder was committed while the suspect was serving a felony conviction.

8. The suspect posed a great risk of death to more than one person.

Clearly, these aggravators can be satisfied by almost any murder. The "heinous, atrocious or cruel" circumstance is especially open to interpretation. Bob Macy used the "heinous, atrocious and cruel" aggravator so many times, both in the courtroom and in the media, that Oklahoma convicts began calling him "most heinous Bob."

Macy argued that the murder of Ura Alma Thompson satisfied no less than five aggravating circumstances.

"If ever released," Macy said, "Johnson would constitute a continuous threat to society. And I want to deter anyone with the propensity to commit a similar kind of crime."

Bob Ravitz was assigned to defend Johnson. At the time, the Oklahoma County Public Defender's Office had no budget for expert witnesses and very little money available for investigation. Ravitz wanted to hire an expert witness to reexamine Joyce Gilchrist's hair and fiber evidence. Judge Joe Cannon denied him the funds.

"I think I'd rather try a case anywhere else in the United States," said T. Hurley Jordan, head of the public defender's office at the time, commenting on the pro-prosecution bent of local juries. A photograph of Jordan, with his carefully curled handlebar mustache, still decorates the waiting room of the PD's office.

When Judge Cannon refused to grant Ravitz an investigative budget, the *Oklahoman* supported the decision in an editorial, saying that because the crime against Thompson was so heinous, public opinion did not support providing Johnson with even "adequate funds" for his defense. The newspaper called the ruling "reasonable and logical."

During jury selection, Macy questioned prospective jurors about whether or not they could impose the death penalty. Ravitz asked each potential juror whether he or she had the "personal courage" to stand up against the others if that one juror favored acquittal. Because jury selection took so long, and so many were excused, additional prospective jurors had to be summoned after Macy and Ravitz had gone through all forty-five on the initial list. In the end they selected a jury of eight women and four men. All of them were white. And all of them said they were capable of rendering a death verdict.

In his opening arguments, Macy described Malcolm Rent Johnson as a killer who raped Ura Alma Johnson and then neatly remade her bed after he watched her die. Macy had to say this, because the stains Joyce Gilchrist identified as semen and matched to Johnson's blood type were found on the sheets and pillowcase of a made bed.

Macy left much of the examination of witnesses and legal arguments to his assistant DA Barry Albert, who clashed several times with Bob Ravitz during the trial. The judge refused to allow the prosecution to show color photographs of the victim's nude body, ruling that their prejudicial value outweighed any probative worth. During the testimony of Fred Jordan, the medical examiner, Albert showed Jordan the color photographs, cautioning the witness not to let the jury see them. As Ravitz approached the bench to object, Albert dropped the photographs on the floor, where the jury could see them. Ravitz kicked the photos away. A fight nearly erupted. The judge called a recess and took both attorneys into chambers to admonish them.

Macy used Johnson's statement "I didn't come" as an outright admission that Johnson had raped the victim. Bob Ravitz explained what Johnson really meant to say was that he had not surrendered a semen sample, but the jury didn't seem to buy it.

Detective Cook testified that Johnson had told him that his girlfriend had found a strange set of keys in their apartment while she was vacuuming the bedroom three days before Thompson's body was found. Johnson told Cook that he did not recognize the keys, which were later determined to fit the doors at Thompson's home.

Testifying in her first capital case, Joyce Gilchrist stated that Malcolm Rent Johnson's clothing fibers, hair, and body fluids were all consistent with samples found in the bed and on the body of the victim. While she stopped short of saying that the similarities positively linked Johnson to the crime, Gilchrist testified that the hair and fiber evidence found at the crime scene was "microscopically consistent" with samples taken from the defendant and his clothing.

Johnson was a B blood type and secretor, which meant that his blood type could be detected in other bodily fluids. Semen stains found on Thompson's stockings and bed pillowcase indicated that her assailant was also a B-type secretor, Gilchrist stated. One in six blacks has type B blood and 80 percent are secretors. The victim had type O blood. Gilchrist did not perform any other tests to further narrow down the source of the semen found at the crime scene. At the time, DNA was unavailable; however, there were other forensic tests, like electrophoresis, which identifies certain enzymes and proteins in the blood, that Gilchrist was familiar with and could have performed.

Negroid hairs found on the bed were consistent with Johnson's, Gilchrist testified, stating that the only other Negroid hairs found in the apartment were her own. Gilchrist said that blue cotton fibers entwined in the Negroid hair were consistent with those of the blue shirt Johnson was wearing when arrested. While she matched the fibers to Johnson, Gilchrist also admitted that she had compared the unknown fibers to only samples from Johnson's shirt and those from police recruit uniforms. The only thing that Gilchrist can say from this evidence was that Thompson was not raped and killed by a police cadet.

Closer examination of the hair evidence, Gilchrist testified, revealed blue-tipped Negroid hairs found on the bed that matched hair taken from Johnson's arm. This was the result, Gilchrist speculated, of dye rubbing off from Johnson's shirt onto his arm hairs.

Because he had no budget, Ravitz had to act as his own expert witness. On cross-examination, Ravitz got Gilchrist to admit that while she had worked some eighty cases involving hair analysis, this was the first time she was testifying as an expert in fiber analysis. Her only training had been brief courses. Ravitz also made Gilchrist acknowledge that the blue fibers from the crime scene were compared to only one other source fiber and that she had not conducted microchemical testing to more closely analyze the fibers.

During closing arguments, Ravitz attacked Gilchrist's testimony. He stated that the blue tint Gilchrist saw in the hair evidence was, in fact, the blue lens of a comparison microscope. Ravitz argued that it was crazy to believe that Johnson would rape the victim on the bed, leave hair and semen stains on the pillowcase and sheets, and then neatly remake the bed.

Macy defended Gilchrist by saying that Ravitz had to attack her, because she was "my whole case." Macy also said that if it were up to the victim to decide punishment, "I think she'd string him from the tallest tree you could find and take a slow time doing it."

In his closing argument, Bob Macy said, "I have been in law long enough to know what the difference is between a bad case and a good case. Ladies and gentlemen, this is one of the best I have ever seen."

Macy was just getting warmed up.

"[Bob] Ravitz talked about concepts and fighting for freedom," Macy said. "I'm fighting for freedom right now. I'm fighting for Ura Thompson's discomfort in this city and this county. Not to have to live like that. Not to have to fear him any more.

"They've got a right to live without having that kind of fear and there's only one way you can stop that kind of fear and that's to march up to that jury room and convict this man because he's guilty. There's no doubt. There's only one verdict: guilty of murder in the first degree."

By the end of Macy's closing argument, several jurors were crying. So was Bob Macy. After deliberating for an hour and a half, the jury returned a verdict of murder in the first degree.

During the penalty phase, Oklahoma prosecutors are allowed to present unadjudicated acts (accusations of crimes that have yet to be proven in court) to show that the defendant is a "continuing threat to society." Macy and Albert examined a series of elderly women who testified that they had been sexually assaulted by a black man. One of the victims was able to identify Johnson, as well as several items that she claimed had been taken from her that were found in Johnson's possession. Two other victims could not identify Johnson, but they did identify their watches, which Macy said were taken from Johnson's apartment. Johnson's previous convictions of rape, armed robbery, and burglary were also introduced as evidence of continuing threat.

"Anybody who could do what he did to these old ladies doesn't deserve to live," Macy told jurors. "He's twenty-four years old and has fifteen felonies. What does it take to give the death penalty?"

At the time, Johnson had been convicted of eight felonies, including the rape and murder charges in the Thompson case.

As mitigating evidence, Ravitz presented several of Johnson's family members, who testified to various kind acts the defendant had shown them and to his difficult, often violent, upbringing.

After deliberating for three and a half hours, the jury gave Johnson the death penalty. Two of the jurors had voted against death, arguing that perhaps Johnson had not intended to kill Thompson during the attack. The two jurors stated that they favored a life term if they could be assured that Johnson would not be paroled soon. According to state law at the time, the judge could give no such guarantees, so they changed their votes to a death sentence. Even if Johnson had received life, after the Thompson conviction, there was no way he would have gotten out in less than thirty-five years. And he was still facing four additional rape and robbery charges.

Shortly after Johnson's death verdict, the *Oklahoman* editorialized: "This is one of those cases where capital punishment seems almost too kind."

At his sentencing hearing Johnson said, "I feel as though I've been railroaded, that it was racially motivated and that the sentence given to me was unjustice."

Johnson's second trial, on charges of rape, attempted rape, armed robbery, burglary, and illegal weapons possession began in January 1983. Macy said he was prosecuting Johnson on these additional charges because he wanted to have as many convictions as possible against him in case the death sentence was overturned. The initial stage of jury selection resulted in a mistrial when jurors were allowed to see Johnson in handcuffs. A new jury was chosen. After hearing less than two days of testimony, and deliberating for thirty-seven minutes, they convicted Johnson for attempted rape and robbery and gave him two seventy-five-year sentences.

The other rapes were different in several crucial respects from the Thompson case. These victims were not killed, indicating that if Johnson was the suspect, he hadn't intended to kill Thompson, and while it might still have qualified for first-degree murder, without premeditation it would have been much more difficult for Macy to get the death penalty.

Johnson was alleged to have followed these other victims home and forced his way inside while they were opening their doors. This doesn't seem to have happened at the Thompson crime scene. The apartment was neat. There were no signs of struggle. Thompson's keys were found in Johnson's apartment.

Following the second conviction, Macy stated that he would forgo prosecuting Johnson on the other rape, assault, and robbery charges (he still had three other victims) if Judge Jack Parr decided that the sentences would run consecutively, which is exactly what Parr decided to do. Even if Johnson's death sentence and conviction were both overturned, he would still be facing 150 years in prison.

During the appeals process, Bob Ravitz hired Skip Palenik, an expert witness who said that Gilchrist had testified beyond the bounds of accepted science when she matched an arm hair to the defendant. Arm hairs are generally not individual enough for such comparisons. Palenik also disputed Gilchrist's other hair and fiber testimony. However, Ravitz was unable to get an evidentiary hearing based on Palenik's findings.

In October 1987 the Supreme Court denied one of Johnson's appeals. However, Justices Marshall and Brennan, in their dissenting opinion, argued that Johnson should have been allowed an independent police scientist to examine the hair, blood, and semen evidence against him. Justices Marshall and Brennan said that because the court did not appoint a scientist for Johnson, he was prevented from raising doubts about the state's evidence and possibly finding that the evidence was, in fact, exculpatory. At the time, Marshall and Brennan were dissenting on every death penalty case, because they believed that capital punishment was unconstitutional.

With his appeals exhausted, Johnson was given an execution date of January 6, 2000. He chose not to seek a hearing before the state pardon and parole board. Johnson spent his last day visiting with eighteen members of his family. Two of Johnson's sisters, one brother, two attorneys, and a minister would stay to witness his execution. His last meal consisted of three fried chicken thighs, a dozen shrimp, Tater Tots with ketchup, two slices of pecan pie, strawberry ice cream, honey and biscuits, and a soda.

Late that afternoon, the Supreme Court rejected two last-minute appeals. Before he walked into the death chamber, Johnson met with the Reverend Charles Story, the spiritual adviser for death row inmates.

"I'm innocent," Johnson told him. "I've got peace in my heart, and I'm ready to go home."

Later, Story said that Johnson was the only convict he had ever spoken with who did not confess to the crime for which he was being executed.

When Johnson was led into the execution chamber, he made a final statement.

"I'm going to heaven on a midnight train," Johnson said, then asked God to bless his family, who sat watching in the witness chamber.

At 12:09 A.M., the executioners began administering the drugs. Johnson's right foot, clad in a blue slipper, shook nervously. He blinked three times and exhaled, his cheeks puffing. Then his foot stopped shaking. His eyes dimmed, went glassy, and slowly closed.

Malcolm Rent Johnson was pronounced dead at 12:13 A.M.

Johnson was not the first of Macy's death penalty convictions to be executed. Sean Sellers and Scotty Lee Moore had already been given the needle. Johnson's case, however, was one that would come back to haunt Bob Macy and Joyce Gilchrist.

When the Gilchrist scandal broke, Bob Ravitz and other members of the defense bar thought of Malcolm Rent Johnson. If any of

Gilchrist's death row cases who had already been executed might have been factually innocent, it was Malcolm Rent Johnson.

When defense attorneys began asking to reexamine the evidence in the Johnson case, all of the case files and much of the physical evidence turned up missing. David Prater, an assistant DA at the time, discovered this when he was reviewing the Gilchrist cases for the DA's office. The Johnson files should have been on the fourth floor of the courthouse building with all the other archived trial materials. Prater sent Wes Lane, Macy's successor as DA, an e-mail telling him about the missing evidence and saying that something needed to be done about it.

Defense attorney Doug Parr, representing the Johnson family in a possible civil rights suit, requested the serological evidence that had been used during the investigation and trial. Parr wanted that evidence sent to an independent lab for DNA testing. He was told that the evidence no longer existed. When Parr made a formal request and insisted on visiting the evidence archives himself, the evidence was right where it was supposed to be.

"I have no idea if they even looked for it, because it wasn't hard to find," Parr said.

Because the Johnson evidence was part of an adjudicated case, it was stored in the DA's office and not the OCPD crime lab, where it would have been destroyed when Gilchrist purged all the rape evidence.

David Prater sent Wes Lane a memo this time, stating that the Johnson evidence had to be sent out for DNA testing. Assistant DA Richard Wintory tried to keep the evidence from being reexamined. Wes Lane eventually decided to get the evidence retested.

Laura Schile, then an OCPD crime lab scientist, performed a microscopic examination of the evidence prior to its being sent out for DNA tests. Following her examination, Schile wrote a memo stating that "spermatozoa is not present" on six slides that Gilchrist had said contained semen matching Johnson's blood type and secretor status. Schile's conclusions were supported by three other police chemists, Kyla Marshall, Elaine Taylor, and Melissa Keith. They had all microscopically examined the smear slides prepared by Gilchrist and concluded that while there was sperm present on the slides taken from the vaginal smears, there was no sperm present in the six slides taken from the victim's bedspread and pillowcase.

During the Johnson trial, Gilchrist had testified that those six samples taken from the victim's bed showed semen consistent with Malcolm Rent Johnson's blood type. She also testified that the vaginal swab slide had contained sperm, but not enough to test. Gilchrist got it entirely wrong. She didn't see sperm where sperm was present, yet she testified to sperm being present and matching the defendant's blood type, where there wasn't any. In other words, Macy's argument that Johnson carefully remade the victim's bed after raping and killing her was unnecessary. He only said it because he thought he had to explain why Gilchrist had found semen on the sheets and pillowcase. In fact, there was no semen on the bedclothes.

The only other source of semen that Gilchrist matched to Johnson's blood type was the victim's stocking, which had not been retested. Kyla Marshall said that her examination of the slides Gilchrist had said contained sperm revealed only a few fibers from the pillowcase and bedspread. If the slides had been properly prepared, the spermatozoa, if it ever existed, would still be there: sperm does not deteriorate for decades.

In her memo, Schile recommended that a complete review of the physical evidence in the Johnson case be performed by "a trained, experienced, proficient Forensic Scientist" prior to any DNA testing. Schile quit the OCPD crime lab three days after she sent the memo.

Bob Ravitz was outraged. "It really calls into question whether Oklahoma executed an innocent person," he said.

Speaking for the DA's office, Richard Wintory said, "The evidence against Malcolm Rent Johnson is absolutely, uncontestably, overwhelming—he done it, done it, done it." Governor Frank Keating and Attorney General Drew Edmondson both stated that they were satisfied with Johnson's guilt. OCPD chief M. T. Berry said that he was willing to submit the evidence to an independent lab for further testing.

Among the physical evidence were several hairs from the crime scene. These hairs can be subjected to mitochondrial DNA testing, which was not available during Johnson's trial. Bob Ravitz offered to pay for the tests himself, but the feds seized all the evidence in the Johnson case as part of their grand jury investigation.

"The feds have no interest at all in determining whether or not Malcolm Rent Johnson was innocent or guilty," Doug Parr said. "They're ostensibly conducting a criminal investigation into Joyce Gilchrist and they're only interested in whether or not she may have lied or committed some criminal act in her involvement in the investigation and case."

The entire case against Malcolm Rent Johnson consisted of the items found in his house, the blood type evidence, the hairs, and his statement to Bill Cook. Without Gilchrist's testimony, it would have been difficult to convict Johnson.

Even David Prater admits that the "Malcolm Rent Johnson case is the one case, out of the ones who have been executed, that is questionable."

Malcolm Rent Johnson was a cheap street hood who preyed on the weak. The evidence clearly indicates that he had some involvement in the murder of Ura Alma Thompson. Still, there were so many unanswered questions about this case, that I cannot state with certainty that I believe he was the true, or the only, suspect. Certainly, his brother should have been investigated. Malcolm might have burgled Thompson's house but not raped and killed her. And considering the state of the evidence, it's unlikely that even DNA tests will conclusively prove Johnson's guilt or innocence.

In the end, Johnson was not given the due process that even a scumbag like him deserves. The first thing that should have happened was a complete investigation and a prosecution that accounted for and explained all the evidence. Once the detectives had their "confession," and Gilchrist's bodily fluid evidence, the investigation basically ended. For Bob Macy, the standard seemed to be whether or not he could get a conviction and a death sentence. Using that standard, and no others, the Johnson case was a success.

I don't know whether Johnson was guilty or innocent. And neither did Bob Macy, Joyce Gilchrist, or anyone else on the prosecution team. That's the problem. The fact that all the evidence went missing, and then miraculously reappeared, only shows that not even the prosecutors are entirely sure that Johnson was the killer.

CHAPTER FOUR

CATFIGHT IN THE
CRIME LAB

WITH THE SUCCESSFUL PROSECUTION OF MALCOLM RENT JOHNSON, Joyce Gilchrist's star began to rise in the mid-1980s. She won a certificate of achievement for her work on the Johnson case and the praise of Bob Macy. At the time, Gilchrist's immediate superior in the crime lab was Janice Davis, the senior OCPD chemist who had more extensive training and experience. Davis also had the advantage of being better liked by the detectives.

"Janice was more like one of the boys," said Bob Bemo, a former OCPD homicide detective. "She was an old country girl, kind of a cowgirl; she would chew dip with the guys, but she was an excellent chemist."

Joyce, on the other hand, had not yet been accepted by the very close-knit group of sex crimes and homicide detectives.

"She was kind of a strange lady," Bemo said. "Joyce always had a very superior attitude, like I'm smarter than you all."

Gilchrist wanted to be accepted by the detectives, to be one of the boys. She would come in and talk to them about cases and other subjects. Gilchrist not only hung around with the detectives but would also socialize with them. Soon she was being given more and more cases to work.

Bemo said that some of the results Gilchrist brought back to him and other detectives were "just unbelievable." He claims that he didn't believe Gilchrist was doing proper lab work, because her results were "too good." Bemo says that now, but it didn't stop him and his partner Bill Cook from using Gilchrist's lab results in many of their cases.

One person who did speak up was Janice Davis. Gilchrist and Davis "were always at each other's throats," according to one former cop. The crime lab was a very competitive office. Davis and Gilchrist constantly jockeyed for position.

Several people I spoke to said that the power struggle between Gilchrist and Davis came to a head when Janice Davis helped convict Dewey George Moore for the murder of a twelve-year-old cheerleader. This death penalty case was one of the highest-profile murders in the Oklahoma City area at the time, and Davis solved it almost single-handedly with hair and fiber comparisons.

Jenipher Juanell Gilbert was abducted shortly after a junior high school football game on the evening of September 27, 1984. She was last seen in the parking lot, still wearing her cheerleader outfit. The next day, Jenipher's body was found on the side of a road ten miles outside Midwest City. She was nude except for her bra and underwear. She had been strangled to death.

As a father, I cannot imagine anything worse than losing a child to murder. If someone killed my daughter in such a brutal and senseless manner, I don't know if I could handle it. Yet I have known so many families of murder victims and somehow they endure. There is no understanding why Jenipher Gilbert was killed. It was just a cruel and selfish act by an evil person.

While the crime scene was being processed, a field investigator for the medical examiner's office observed several fibers and apparently foreign hairs on the victim's body. He also noticed pieces of duct tape adhered to her hair.

Detective Bill Howard of the Midwest City Police Department was also at the crime scene, handling his first homicide. He later said that he had realized, while the crime scene was being processed, that the Gilbert murder would involve a great deal of hair and fiber evidence. Immediately, he thought of Janice Davis, who had studied hair and fiber at the FBI Academy, and had recently completed a seminar with FBI Special Agent Howard Edmond, who had helped solve the Wayne Williams child serial murder case in Atlanta.

How could any homicide detective on an outdoor scene realize, before he knew anything else about the case, that this homicide would be solved by hair and fiber evidence? There were numerous witnesses, a short period of time during which the victim could have been abducted, a variety of evidence that had not yet been found (like her cheerleading outfit), and no known suspect apprehended at that time. If Howard made this assumption at the crime scene, he was severely limiting his own case. Trace evidence is the last thing a detective should think about. And it's in the hands of the forensic technicians. Howard should have been looking for evidence that he could then follow instead of hoping that someone else would find evidence for him.

Gilbert's body was found in Harrah. She had been abducted in Midwest City, which is under the jurisdiction of the OSBI, not the OCPD. Still, Howard insisted on calling Davis in to work the evidence.

Additional fibers were recovered from the victim's body during the autopsy, which was conducted by Dr. Chaik Choy, a forensic pathologist with the ME's office. Dr. Choy determined that Gilbert had died by strangulation and/or asphyxiation. She had been bound by duct tape. Her fingernails were not broken, indicating that there had not been much of a struggle. Her hymen was intact and there was no evidence of sexual molestation.

The morning after Gilbert had been abducted, but before her body was found, Dewey George Moore was arrested for driving in a stolen car. Moore, forty-seven years old and white, had a record of sex and assault charges against children. He had been convicted of attempted rape of a five-year-old girl, assaulting two other children, kidnapping, car theft, and indecency with a child.

"This is a dangerous, violent man," Moore's ex-wife said in a letter written to the court asking for him not to be released from prison. "I find it inconceivable that a person with his violent record is able to freely walk the streets of our city while other citizens charged with less severe crimes are being sentenced to jail and/or prison."

Detectives were considering Moore a suspect as early as the afternoon of September 28, when they included his picture in photo line-ups they were showing prospective witnesses. (None of the witnesses selected Moore's or any other photograph.)

Moore told police that on the night of the murder he had gone to his brother Eddie's house, which was less than a mile from the junior high school where Gilbert had been abducted, to borrow some duct tape to seal the windows in his trailer. Dewey and Eddie watched television with Eddie's family. Dewey left the house at approximately 9:15 to 9:30, according to his brother.

The day after his arrest for car theft, Moore's trailer and his own car were searched by Midwest City detectives looking for possible evidence linking him to the Gilbert kidnapping and murder. After reviewing the evidence seized from the first search, Janice Davis requested that another search be conducted. This second search was executed on October 4. Davis participated as the primary searcher in the second warrant but had not been present for the first search. Assistant District Attorney Don Deason (now a district court judge) was present at both searches.

Between the two searches, Moore's trailer had been left unattended. Detective Jerry Garner said that he had secured the trailer with sealing tape. He also stated that prior to the second search he walked around the trailer and found the tape was still intact.

On Friday night, September 28, the detectives asked Eddie Moore to go to his brother's trailer to retrieve some heart medication. Eddie had already heard on the radio that his brother was in custody as a suspect in the Gilbert murder. Eddie Moore told the detectives that he didn't know exactly where his brother lived, but he would probably be able to find his trailer by identifying the car parked outside it.

Detectives Howard and Garner took Eddie Moore to the trailer park where Dewey lived. There Eddie identified his brother's car and trailer. Instead of letting Eddie retrieve the heart medication, the detectives began inspecting Dewey's car. Looking through the car window, Howard claimed that he saw maroon floor mats that he said were visually similar to maroon fibers that had been found on the victim's body.

This looks like a clear case of retroactive probable cause. Howard swore in both search warrants, and later testified in court, that he recognized the maroon fibers from the car floor mats as being similar to the fibers found on Jenipher Gilbert's body. There is no way he could make this comparison with the naked eye, at night, through a car window. Even if he had the fibers in front of him, Howard was not qualified to make such a match. He reportedly observed the similarity on Friday night, September 28—the day Gilbert's body was found. There is no way he had received any lab reports from either the ME or Janice Davis by then. Even if he had visually observed the maroon fibers on the victim's body, he could not have determined that they were car-floor-mat fibers. Nor could he know what the fiber colors were of the floor mats he saw in Moore's car.

Howard already had more than enough probable cause for a

search warrant. Moore had been arrested that morning, driving a stolen car. There was other circumstantial evidence indicating he planned to flee. He had prior convictions for sexual and violent assaults against children. He matched the suspect's general description and drove the same color car described by eyewitnesses. By his own admission, Moore was in the neighborhood around the time the crime was committed, and he went to his brother's house to borrow duct tape.

Even with all of this probable cause evidence, Howard apparently felt it was necessary to mention evidence that it would have been unlikely for him to have observed and impossible for him to have matched with evidence from the crime scene. I also suspect that one reason why Howard mentioned the maroon fibers is to make himself appear involved in the solution of the crime. All of the other evidence came not from his detective work but from the suspect himself.

Howard's focus on hair and fiber evidence would keep him from properly solving the case and help create reasonable doubt that persists to this day.

After the first search warrant was executed, Howard and Garner say they remembered that they hadn't retrieved Dewey's heart medicine. They called Eddie again and asked him to return to his brother's trailer to retrieve it. Eddie had to stop by the police department to get the keys. When Eddie arrived at Dewey's trailer, he later testified, he noted that it was in complete disarray. Clothes were scattered everywhere, furniture had been moved, closets had been emptied. There was no crime scene tape securing the scene. A window large enough for a man to climb through had been left open. The television was still on. Eddie gathered the medication, along with some socks and underwear, and brought them to the police station.

Taking Eddie to get the heart medication on Friday night was obviously a ruse. The detectives wanted to get a free peek at the suspect's home and trailer without having to get a search warrant. Maybe they hoped that Eddie would let them in, although he didn't have the legal right to authorize a search of his brother's home. I don't understand why they didn't just write a search warrant with the probable cause they already had, or at least admit that the heart medicine trip was a pretext to visit the suspect's house. It seems to me that Howard and Garner didn't know what they could or couldn't do during a police investigation. Even when they acted within the law— like the heart medication ruse—they felt they had to cover it up.

Later, there was some dispute as to exactly when Eddie returned to his brother's trailer. Garner claimed that he gave Eddie the keys on September 28 and that Eddie retrieved the heart medication at that time. Howard corroborated this in his trial testimony. Eddie stated that he went back a second time to his brother's trailer on September 30. The jail record shows that Dewey received his medication on September 30.

Why was there so much confusion about sending Eddie back to the trailer a second time? Once the first search warrant was executed, they must have thought that they were finished with Dewey's trailer and didn't have to worry about its being compromised as a controlled crime scene. After they gave Janice Davis the evidence they had collected on September 28, she told them to go back and conduct a second search. Apparently they had not retrieved enough evidence, or they had collected the evidence in an improper manner. Either way, Davis wanted them to search again. And she would be present at this search.

Then Howard and Garner remembered that they had sent Eddie alone back to the trailer. If Eddie got the medicine on the twenty-eighth, when the detectives said he did, then he would have done so in their presence. If he went alone on the thirtieth, then they had a real problem with contamination of the crime scene, especially since

Eddie testified that the window was open and the door was not taped secure, contrary to Garner's recollection.

During the second search, Janice Davis found clumps of red fiber in plain sight on the living room floor. These clumps of fiber were not seen during the first search. In all, Davis found hundreds of hairs and fibers that were eventually matched back to Jenipher Gilbert. Detective Howard had been right—the case against Dewey George Moore would be built almost entirely on hair and fiber evidence. The case relied on hair and fiber evidence because the detectives didn't find anything else. There were no fingerprints matched to the victim found in Moore's trailer or car. No blood or semen matching Moore was found on the victim's body. There was no confession, no strong eyewitness identification, and only a vague vehicle description.

Additional evidence was found but could not be linked to either Moore or Gilbert. On October 5, James Macon reported finding a sack on the roof of Breeden's Grocery in Midwest City. Macon lived in the same trailer park as Dewey Moore and had seen police question him shortly before his arrest. Macon had assisted in the search for the victim on the night of her murder and had complained that the police were not doing a thorough enough job. He had spent several days looking for clues in the case and remembered having seen a bag on the roof of the store a week prior. Macon had a friend, Timothy Baker, climb up onto the roof and retrieve the sack.

The items found in the sack included a knife, duct tape, eleven cigarette butts, a broken fingernail, a clothing label, a belt, a sanitary napkin, an earring, and burnt matches. The sanitary napkin was a different brand than Gilbert used and contained blood of a similar type to hers and the defendant's. The torn fingernail did not come from the victim or the defendant. The duct tape was not the same brand as the duct tape that Dewey Moore had borrowed from his brother on the night of the murder, and it did not match scraps of duct tape found beneath his trailer. Of the eleven cigarette butts, eight of them had enough saliva to determine that they had been smoked by a secretor with type O blood. Like almost half of the human species, both Moore and Gilbert had type O blood. Moore, along with 80 percent of the population, is a secretor.

Shortly after this evidence was found, Dewey George Moore was formally charged with murder, kidnapping, and unauthorized use of a vehicle. Bob Macy said that hair and fiber evidence showed Gilbert had been in Moore's car and his trailer. He also said that the sack found on top of Breeden's Grocery contained the knife Moore used to cut off her cheerleader's outfit, a belt he used to tie her up, and tape used to gag her. Based only upon the blood typing from the cigarette butts, Bob Macy introduced all the items from the sack as evidence directly connected to the murder of Jenipher Gilbert.

"There is no more cruel way to die than to have one's air passages cut off," Macy said, announcing that he would seek the death penalty.

There had been three eyewitnesses to Gilbert's abduction, but none of them could positively identify Dewey George Moore.

Paulo Gomes, a football player, saw a man struggling with a girl who might have been wearing a cheerleader's uniform. The struggle took place near a yellow car. In the courtroom, Gomes identified Dewey George Moore. But he qualified his identification by saying, "It was kind of dark. I couldn't really tell, but what I've seen looked like him." During cross-examination by Bob Ravitz, who was defending Moore, Gomes acknowledged that he had picked out another man, and not the defendant, from an earlier photo lineup and that before identifying Moore in court, he had seen him several times on television.

Bob Macy considered this a positive ID and continued to argue that Gomes had seen Moore kidnap the victim. After the trial, Gomes provided Moore's attorneys with an affidavit recanting his in-court identification. "I was a fifteen-year-old ninth grade student when I made my statement," the affidavit reads. "I was very nervous, uncertain and impressionable regarding my eyewitness recollection. . . . The 'positive' identification that I made . . . was incorrect. . . . I could not then nor can I now say with certainty that the man I saw . . . was in fact Dewey George Moore."

Cynthia Turner and her husband, Leroy, were also in the parking lot. Mrs. Turner testified that she saw a man place his arm around a cheerleader, walk her toward a car, then strike her in the face. The girl fell into the passenger side of the car and the man entered the car after her. Leroy Turner also saw the man, although he did not see him strike the cheerleader. He described the suspect as large, over two hundred pounds, with a "beer belly," a mustache, and blond hair. None of the three eyewitnesses selected Moore from photo lineups the day after the kidnapping.

With witnesses like these, and nothing else, Bob Macy's case would stand or fall on hair and fiber evidence. The defense had hired John Wilson of the Kansas City Police Crime Lab to review Davis's lab work. Wilson not only agreed with all of Davis's findings but also found two additional fiber matches that she hadn't made yet. When Wilson sent in his report, he pointed out these two matches and was surprised to see that Davis had included them in the evidence she presented in trial.

Davis also proved to be a tough witness on cross-examination.

She testified that based on the hair and fiber evidence she could conclude a positive association. "I am convinced that Jenipher Gilbert was in Moore's living room and car," Davis said under oath.

Bob Ravitz asked if it was possible that there could be another explanation.

"Anything in our society is possible, Mr. Ravitz," Davis replied. "There is a chance, it's a very remote chance, that this universe will end tonight or tomorrow. That chance exists. We don't plan on it.

But that chance exists no matter how remote it is. It is also a possibility in this case, due to fiber evidence that I will explain to the jurors, there is a remote, extremely remote, possibility that the association that these fibers and hairs represent as evidence in this case—there is a remote possibility that that could be duplicated by someone else's environment or some other human being. However, in my opinion that is extremely remote."

Here, Davis gave a prepared statement to answer a difficult question in a way that neither misstated the evidence nor followed Ravitz's tactic of wanting to get her to say that there might be another explanation for the evidence. Davis gave the jury the responsibility to decide what were the reasonable parameters of probability concerning these hair and fiber matches, without positively stating that they were definite matches and there was no other explanation for their presence than that the suspect was in contact with the victim.

The original cheerleader's uniform that Gilbert had worn the night she was abducted had never been found. A detective purchased similar uniforms to compare unknown fiber samples taken from Moore's trailer and car. At trial, Ravitz charged that detectives had bought three cheerleader uniforms, not two as they claimed, and used the third to plant the clumps of red fibers that Davis later found and which hadn't been retrieved during the first search.

After the presentation of the evidence, Bob Macy delivered a strong closing argument.

"She died in order for this baby killer to satisfy his own sadistic sexual desires," Macy said. "To satisfy him a twelve-year-old child was beat. . . . He kidnapped her. Can you imagine what that baby was going through? Took her out to his trailer, taped her up with that tape, took that knife right there and cut that uniform off her and kept her there for hours. Just to satisfy his own selfish sexual kicks."

After three hours and forty minutes of deliberation, the jury convicted Moore of murder and kidnapping.

During his closing argument in the penalty phase, Macy told the jurors, "Ladies and gentlemen, you need to recognize that you're only one piece, one little cog in the community."

This was a familiar argument to Bob Ravitz, one that had been repeatedly condemned by the Oklahoma Court of Criminal Appeals because it minimized the jurors' role and diminished their sense of responsibility in rendering a verdict. Ravitz stood up and objected. His objection was overruled. He moved for a mistrial. Also overruled. He asked that a continuing objection be entered into the record so that he would not keep interrupting Macy every time the prosecutor said something improper. The judge granted this, and Macy continued.

As he finished his closing argument, Macy asked the jury to "bring back a death verdict out of love for the Jeniphers . . . of the world and the future and past victims of Dewey George Moore."

The jury deliberated for seventy minutes before returning a sentence of death plus 999 years in prison on the kidnapping charge.

"That was the best frame Bob Macy ever put up in his life," Moore said as he was escorted from the courtroom. "My little friends out in Midwest City planted evidence all over my trailer."

District Court Judge James Gullett set the date for formal sentencing on the anniversary of Gilbert's murder. During that hearing, Gullett granted Macy's request that the 999-year sentence be run consecutively with the death sentence in order to ensure that Moore would remain in prison if the death sentence were overturned. Macy dropped the stolen car charge after the death penalty was imposed.

"The only thing wrong with this sentence," Macy said, "is that it ought to be carried out today."

"Bob Macy is a TV star," Moore responded. "He's liable to say anything."

Dewey George Moore went to McAlester's death row. He lost a series of appeals until a surprise witness surfaced, alleging that Midwest City detectives could have planted hair evidence in Moore's trailer prior to the execution of the second search warrant.

David Bruce Hawkins, a mortician who prepared Jenipher Gilbert's body for burial, swore in two affidavits that police detectives took hair samples from the victim and then went to Dewey George Moore's trailer. Hawkins states that shortly after he had finished embalming the victim's body, two Midwest City detectives came to the funeral home. They appeared nervous and, according to Hawkins, said "they had their man, and they were going to make sure he got convicted." The detectives cut several hair samples from the victim's body. Later that day, the detectives returned. This time they plucked hair samples from the victim's body. After the second visit by police detectives, Hawkins stated that John Boeing, another funeral home employee, followed the detectives from the funeral home to Moore's trailer. The detectives were carrying, among other things, "a red sweater." Hawkins said that Boeing told him that one of the police officers climbed through an open window of the trailer and unlocked the door from the inside so the other could enter. The police officers remained in Moore's trailer for some time, and later "appeared to be doing things" to his car, according to Hawkins's account of what Boeing had told him.

The second search warrant was executed after Hawkins and Boeing reportedly observed these actions by the OCPD. One or two days later, Hawkins stated, the detectives returned for a third time. By then the body had already been dressed and on display. Hawkins had to remove the body from the casket and undress it so detectives could collect more hair samples.

Hawkins said that in June 1985, prior to Moore's trial, he approached Bob Macy in the courthouse and told him what the detectives had done. Hawkins claims that shortly after this conversation, he was arrested on trumped-up charges, extradited to Texas, and imprisoned for the duration of Moore's trial. In fact, Hawkins was arrested on assault charges lodged by his ex-wife in Dallas. On September 28, 1985—the same day that Dewey George Moore was sentenced to death—Hawkins was back in Oklahoma City testifying in the preliminary hearing of Loyd Winford LaFevers and Randall Eugene Cannon, both charged with the murder and rape of eighty-four-year-old Adie Hawley. Hawkins testified that both LaFevers and Cannon had confessed to him in separate conversations at the Oklahoma County jail.

When Hawkins repeated this testimony at the LaFevers/Cannon trial, Public Defender Tim Wilson brought up Hawkins's dispute with the funeral home where he had worked. After being fired, Hawkins had picketed outside the funeral home. At a civil trial, Hawkins was ordered to stop picketing and to pay $4,300 in damages. Under cross-examination, Hawkins admitted that Bob Macy's office had agreed to recommend dismissal of three misdemeanor charges against him in return for his testimony.

All of this calls Hawkins's credibility into question.

Even if Hawkins is telling the truth, there is another possible explanation for the detectives' behavior. Janice Davis stated that she sent detectives back to the funeral home to get hair samples from the victim. (There seems to have been problems with evidence collection; Davis herself had already gone to the medical examiner's office to retrieve more blood from Gilbert's body.) The detectives could have cut the hair from Gilbert, brought the samples back to Davis, who then told them that hairs should be plucked and not cut. So the detectives could have gone back to the funeral home and this time plucked hairs from the victim. If Janice Davis was at Dewey George Moore's trailer at this time, collecting evidence during the execution of the second search warrant, the detectives might have gone directly from the funeral home to Moore's trailer to give her the known hairs. This would have compromised the chain of custody. But it doesn't mean that the detectives planted any evidence.

The fact that the detectives felt that Moore was guilty and were hoping to collect more evidence to use in court against him is not by itself suspicious. Cops say these kinds of things all the time. Hopefully, they don't say them in front of civilians who are later deposed by defense attorneys. Statements like these can be used by defense attorneys to impeach the credibility of police witnesses and present reasonable doubt hypotheses. This is exactly what happened in the Moore case. The detectives' behavior and comments appeared suspicious. And that's enough to create serious problems in the courtroom.

After hearing Hawkins's charges, the Oklahoma Court of Criminal Appeals ruled in 1995: "Although this certainly suggests that Midwest City police followed a somewhat unusual investigative procedure in this case . . . mere evidence of unusual conduct on the detectives' part, when evaluated in the context of the entire record, is not material, and does not create a reasonable probability that the trial's outcome would be changed."

In other words, the court is saying that it believes Dewey George Moore is guilty, and proof of evidence tampering and/or planting would not have changed its judicial duty or the jury's decision. Four years later, the Tenth Circuit Court of Appeals remanded the case back to federal district court so Moore's defense could pursue the possibility that evidence had been planted.

Following the Gilchrist scandal in 2001, a new evidentiary hearing was finally granted for Dewey George Moore. At the time of this writing, the hearing has not been conducted, but it will hopefully resolve the question of evidence planting in the case.

In preparation for this hearing, the federal district court hired Patricia Eddings, a consulting forensic scientist from Fort Worth, Texas, to reexamine the hair and fiber evidence in the Moore case. Even though Eddings had been appointed by a federal court, the Oklahoma County judge refused to allow her to test, or even look at, the evidence itself. All the court allowed Eddings to do was review Davis's testimony. Eddings stated that in her twenty-one years as a forensic scientist, she had rarely seen so much cross-transference of hair and fibers. She concluded that it "makes me quite curious as to the actual cause or reason for this much cross-transference." Eddings did not know about the Hawkins affidavit when she made that statement.

"Did Moore do it? I don't know," Bob Ravitz said. But he argues that it can be inferred from the missing cheerleader suit, the unsecured crime scene at Moore's trailer, Hawkins's affidavits, and the amount of hair and fiber cross-transferred that the police very well could have planted evidence against a man they believed was guilty—or could in fact be guilty.

"The evidence against Dewey George Moore was *too* good for any other explanation," Ravitz said.

Steve Pressen, a Norman, Oklahoma, attorney who now represents Dewey George Moore on appeal, argues that "we will never know for certain" if Moore is guilty, because of the questions surrounding the hair and fiber evidence. Pressen also alleged, in an appellate brief he filed for Moore, that the victim's estranged father, Howard Ben Gilbert, was investigated by the DA's office for tying his children up with duct tape. Immediately prior to her abduction, Jenipher was heard saying, "There's my dad, I've got to go." Jenipher's stepfather, Jerry Scarberry, had been looking for her in the parking lot around 9:15, but couldn't find her. Bob Macy had stated that when Jenipher mentioned her father, she was referring to Scarberry.

There is no doubt in my mind that Dewey George Moore killed Jenipher Gilbert. The issue in this case is how the detectives and prosecutors reached that conclusion and went about proving his guilt. In the first couple of days it seemed as if the detectives had sufficient evidence to win a conviction. Unfortunately, someone did not feel that they had enough hair and fiber evidence, so the detectives went out to collect more. This is what happens when the criminalist is not involved in the collection of evidence from the beginning. If Detective Howard was intent on using Janice Davis, he should have held the crime scene for her. Because the first search and the processing of the victim's body were conducted without Davis, the detectives not only had to return to Moore's home and perform a second search but also had to retrieve sample hairs from the victim when she was in the funeral home.

These actions created difficulties that persist today. Problems with the collection of evidence turn into suspicions that evidence might have been planted, which raise doubts concerning the guilt of the accused, which become claims of innocence. The police make some minor mistakes in the beginning that then escalate into a miscarriage of justice, at least according to those who want Moore to be innocent.

Of course, Moore's lawyers want to keep their client alive and possibly even taken off death row. That's their job. Some people, however, want the police and prosecutors to fail. They want the criminal justice system to be flawed. The execution of an innocent person is the worst miscarriage of justice; therefore, innocent convicts on death row are the most dramatic criminal justice stories.

You have to play by the rules. The rules may not always make sense; they might not be fair. But if you don't play by them, they will come back to bite you.

I hope that this is what the Midwest City detectives have learned from the Dewey George Moore case.

Evidence planting is a serious charge. And it's virtually impossible to prove that you didn't do it. I know, because I've been accused of evidence planting myself. For years, rumors about the hair and fiber evidence used to convict Dewey George Moore have swirled around Oklahoma City. The only person who spoke on the record was Janie Bates, a former OCPD crime lab employee, who, according to Pressen's appellate brief, said that she had heard talk of planted evidence in the Moore case. Could those rumors have been started by Joyce Gilchrist in order to cast suspicion on Janice Davis? Some people think they were.

John Wilson called the Dewey George Moore investigation "the kind of case you get once or twice in your career." Janice Davis almost single-handedly solved a high-profile murder case and helped win a death penalty conviction for Bob Macy.

Wilson believes, and others agree with him, that Joyce Gilchrist was jealous of the fame and approval that Davis earned with her work on the Dewey George Moore case. The two women were highly competitive. Gilchrist rarely got along with her female colleagues, but her relationship with Davis was particularly spiky. Gilchrist worked on the Moore case as Davis's subordinate and was not called to testify.

"Janice Davis was doing a great job and getting her picture in the newspaper and that's what Joyce wants" is how John Wilson explains it. "So, from that point on, Joyce starts making unbelievable cases."

Janice Davis wasn't going to take this sitting down. First she wrote a memo to OCPD brass saying that Gilchrist was incompetent and they needed to get rid of her. Nothing happened. So Davis wrote a letter to James Starrs, a forensic scientist and professor at George Washington University in Washington, D.C.

"The letter said, do something about this woman," Starrs said. "She's gone completely beyond the pale, she's doing things she shouldn't do, she's saying things she can't say." The letter stated that there was nothing that could be done about Gilchrist internally, because she was already very powerful within the department, and previous attempts to bring her behavior to the attention of authorities in Oklahoma County had failed.

Starrs decided to conduct his own investigation, the results of which he wrote up in *Scientific Sleuthing Review,* a forensic science journal that he publishes. He also wrote an article for the *Journal of Forensic Science.*

According to Starrs, Gilchrist's forensic work and testimony were "just awful." She was one of the worst forensic scientists he had ever seen, and her work on death penalty cases was particularly troubling to him.

In October 1987, Davis married Gene Lyhane, an older man she had met hunting raccoons. She quit the police department and lived with Lyhane on his cattle and wheat farm in Perry, Oklahoma. On August 25, 1988, Janice Davis committed suicide. Several people told me that Davis left a suicide note, but Macy's office got possession of it. It's not uncommon to keep suicide notes private, but in this case it might at least answer some questions as to the reason for her suicide, and possibly lay the suspicions and rumors to rest.

"We all knew Joyce and Janice didn't get along," Bob Bemo said. "We just figured it was a catfight between two women."

Their rivalry continued even years after Davis died. In 2001, Gilchrist blamed Davis for allowing her membership in the American Academy of Forensic Sciences to lapse back in 1987.

When Davis left the crime lab, Gilchrist "percolated to the top," as one defense attorney put it. She became the senior forensic chemist, unchallenged in the crime lab, and enjoyed a special relationship with Bob Macy and the detectives. With her chief rival out of the way, Gilchrist began her long and troubled reign as "queen of the crime lab."

CHAPTER FIVE

REVERSED CONVICTION

AFTER PROSECUTING AN AVERAGE OF TEN DEATH PENALTY CASES A YEAR during the mid-1980s, Bob Macy suffered a handful of high-profile reversals. Several of his death penalty convictions were overturned by the Oklahoma Court of Criminal Appeals. These reversals were based on several different grounds, ranging from procedural technicalities to prosecutorial misconduct. The case of Curtis Edward McCarty, in particular, would cast a shadow of doubt over the death penalty in Oklahoma County.

On December 10, 1982, eighteen-year-old Pam Willis was murdered and raped. Her naked body lay on the floor of her apartment. A kitchen knife was stuck in her chest up to the handle. She had also been strangled with a rope. A sheet covered her head. Pam was the daughter of Jim Willis, a former OCPD officer who was then working for the Oklahoma Bureau of Narcotics and Dangerous Drugs Control—a state agency that eventually became part of the Oklahoma State Bureau of Investigation (OSBI). At his daughter's funeral, Willis promised that he would never rest until he found her killer.

If my daughter were raped and murdered, it would be very hard to stop me from killing the suspect myself, much less keep me out of the investigation. Jim Willis conducted himself very admirably, considering the circumstances.

For more than two years, the murder went unsolved. Then police arrested Ricky Andrew Terry on March 12, 1985. Law enforcement sources said that after they had investigated thirty-five suspects, Terry was arrested when police found a witness who had previously eluded them. They would not name the witness. A month after Terry's arrest, the charges against him were dismissed and Curtis Edward McCarty was arrested. Macy said that a reexamination of the hair evidence was crucial to the decision that McCarty was the suspect.

McCarty had been one of the original thirty-five suspects. Using microscopic hair comparisons, Joyce Gilchrist had initially excluded McCarty as the killer. Nearly three years later, after a confidential informant (presumably Terry) named McCarty as the suspect, Gilchrist got a second batch of hair samples from McCarty, which she matched to those found at the crime scene. This indicates that Gilchrist was not performing her microscopic hair comparisons in an objective fashion, but was instead trying to give the detectives the results that they felt they needed in order to solve the case and get a conviction.

This practice, according to several people I spoke to, was not uncommon in Joyce Gilchrist's crime lab.

"What Joyce tended to do, frankly, was to include people who were the suspects," said Brian Wraxall, an independent forensic scientist who has worked on numerous Oklahoma County cases, for both the prosecution and the defense.

Homicide detective Bill Cook had given Gilchrist the nickname "Black Magic" because she was able to get results that no other chemist could. When Cook and other homicide detectives gave Gilchrist hair samples from a suspect, they would often let her know that this was the person they wanted to arrest.

"The detectives would be looking over her shoulder, asking, 'Is it our guy?'" said one source. Once Gilchrist matched the suspect's hair sample to known hairs from the scene, the detectives would be convinced they had the right guy.

In this case, they were probably right. Curtis McCarty was a nasty character. He had been arrested as a material witness in the 1983 murder and molestation of seven-year-old Janelle Fowler. During questioning McCarty had named David Todd Osborne as the suspect and led police to the seven-year-old's dead body inside an unused gravel and sand washer. In return for his cooperation, the charges against McCarty were dropped. Osborne eventually pleaded guilty. McCarty had also pleaded guilty to the second-degree rape of a teenage girl in Cleveland County in October 1985. And he had allegedly threatened to kill Jim Willis.

McCarty went on trial for the murder of Pam Willis in March 1986. In his opening statements, Macy said that McCarty and an unknown accomplice killed Willis after selling her LSD. Macy said that McCarty and the other suspect used two different kitchen knives, following a sexual assault on the victim. He stated that McCarty confessed the killing to one friend and "told her things only the killer would know."

When Joyce Gilchrist testified, she not only matched sixteen head hairs and one pubic hair from the crime scene to the defendant's, but also stated that since one of McCarty's head hairs was found in the victim's chest wound, he had to have been at the scene when the crime was committed.

On direct examination, prosecutor Barry Albert asked Gilchrist if she had "an opinion as to whether Mr. McCarty was physically present during the time violence was done to Miss Willis."

"He was, in fact, there," Gilchrist replied.

It was already established that McCarty had been at the victim's home several times, including the night before the murder.

On cross-examination, McCarty's defense attorney, Claude Sumner, asked Gilchrist, "For all you know, the hairs you testified about, including those you say are consistent with the defendant, were left in that house days before or possibly even weeks before the incident."

Gilchrist replied, "It's incorrect."

"So you don't know, do you," the attorney continued, "whether any of these hairs are actually associated with the events in this case, is that right?"

"That is incorrect," Gilchrist said.

These answers would come back to haunt Joyce Gilchrist. The unnamed cosuspect could have contributed these hairs. As long as he remained unidentified, Gilchrist could not say that he was not the donor. And even if all the hairs did belong to McCarty, he could have deposited them during a previous visit to the victim's apartment. Any pubic hairs taken from pubic combings of the victim that Gilchrist matched to McCarty's could have been deposited by him during consensual sex the night prior to her murder. Before going to trial, the prosecution should have at least attempted to produce one other participant in the crime, even if they had to give him immunity. This is the only way that Gilchrist's hair comparisons and the statement about the hair in the wound could have been corroborated. Even if the hair is a match—and the only way to really prove that is through mitochondrial DNA testing—hair evidence doesn't prove anything except that the donor of that hair came into contact with the victim, the crime scene, or someone who could have cross-transferred hairs to either the victim or the crime scene.

In addition to the hair evidence presented at trial, one of McCarty's fingerprints was found on a vase at Willis's house. The fingerprint also could have been left during McCarty's previous visit. Other evidence included semen from vaginal swabs of the victim and a stain on the floor near her body that matched McCarty's blood type and secretor status. And the rope found around Willis's neck was the same type used by Air Refiners Inc., where McCarty had worked in 1981.

McCarty's former girlfriend testified that he had admitted killing Willis. Cindy Parks said that "it had something to do with a drug deal." (McCarty had sold Willis LSD two days prior to her murder.)

"He said she was asleep in her bed and he slashed her throat," Parks testified. She also said that McCarty worried about leaving fingerprints at the crime scene because he had taken off a glove to smoke a cigarette.

After more than twelve hours of deliberation, the jury convicted McCarty of first-degree murder.

"One down and one more to go," Jim Willis said once the verdict was announced. Prosecutors were still saying an unknown accomplice was involved with McCarty.

"I think there is a strong possibility that we will identify John Doe," Bob Macy said, "and when we do we'll have him up here facing a death sentence, too."

The second suspect was never identified.

At one point during his police interrogation, McCarty admitted to being in Willis's apartment on the night of the murder but claimed that Ricky Terry had killed her. Was Rick Terry the unnamed cosuspect? Why wasn't he arrested and charged along with McCarty? Did

Bob Macy cut a deal with Terry—not charging him in the Willis murder in return for his giving up McCarty? Macy didn't answer these questions at trial, preferring instead to first prosecute McCarty and then hold out the possibility that he would find the unnamed cosuspect and prosecute him as well. All the serological evidence presented at trial seemed to implicate McCarty. Was there any evidence at all against Terry—or anyone else?

During the penalty phase, jurors heard testimony that McCarty was involved in the Janelle Fowler murder. David Todd Osborne, who had already pleaded guilty to that murder, testified that it was McCarty who had beaten the seven-year-old to death with a baseball bat.

"I saw him swing and hit her," Osborne said. "I saw him swing again. He was freaking out."

Macy had stated publicly that he believed McCarty was only an accessory in the Fowler murder. Osborne testified that Macy had agreed to review his case in exchange for testimony in the McCarty penalty phase. Macy had Osborne's guilty plea in his pocket. And he wanted to establish a "continuing threat" aggravator against McCarty. While Macy might have promised Osborne that his case would be reviewed, nothing ever came of it. How did Janelle Fowler's parents feel when they heard that Curtis McCarty—whom Bob Macy had released—was their daughter's killer? Did Macy believe Osborne was the killer, or McCarty?

After three hours of deliberation, the jury imposed the death penalty.

Gilchrist's testimony concerning hair evidence had gone virtually unchallenged until 1987, when Bob Ravitz hired John Wilson of the Kansas City Police Crime Lab as an expert witness. When Wilson first heard what Gilchrist was saying in court, he insisted on seeing the transcripts. When he read them, he felt "nauseated."

"Gilchrist made preposterous statements under oath," Wilson

told me. "She either didn't know what she was doing, or she didn't care."

Wilson's first case as a defense witness against Gilchrist was the capital trial of Alvin "King" Parker, who was accused of killing an Oklahoma City cop in 1985. Wilson, himself a police department employee, wasn't sure he wanted to handle the case. Upon reexamining the evidence in the Parker case, Wilson found that several of the hairs that Gilchrist had matched to the defendant's were not, in fact, his (years later, the FBI would confirm Wilson's findings). And Gilchrist exaggerated the value of the hairs that did match, saying they definitely came from Alvin Parker, to the exclusion of anyone else.

After Wilson testified against Gilchrist in the Parker case, she accused him of tampering with evidence that she had sent him for reexamination in the capital murder trials of Curtis McCarty and James Lucas Abels, who was charged with the 1984 rape and murder of Ramona Rutledge. According to Wilson, the only complaint she had was that a slide had been broken in transit. The evidence itself had remained mounted and intact.

Wilson was no hack for the defense. He was, and still is, an employee of the Kansas City Police Department. Usually when he testifies, it's for the prosecution. But he told me that he had "never testified for a prosecutor like those prosecutors I saw in Oklahoma City." Kansas City prosecutors would never accept the kind of testimony that Gilchrist gave, "under any circumstance."

Wilson registered a formal ethics complaint against Gilchrist with Pauline Louie, president of the Southwestern Association of Forensic Scientists (SWAFS).

"Ms. Gilchrist is at odds with the entire forensic community," Wilson wrote. "[She] persists in rendering scientific opinions from the witness stand which in effect positively identify the defendant based on the slightest bit of circumstantial evidence."

Gilchrist had defended such testimony by saying it was her opinion.

"Apparently," Wilson wrote, "Ms. Gilchrist believes that by adding the word 'opinion' she can make any statement, regardless of how preposterous."

Wilson charged that "Gilchrist misrepresents factual data upon which all forensic scientists base their exams and conclusions." He claimed that she had falsely testified that she was a member of the American Academy of Forensic Sciences, which she was not. He enumerated other false and misleading statements Gilchrist made under oath. He questioned her competence as a forensic scientist. And he argued that Gilchrist continually "expresses opinions that are not justified by the results of examination and is in essence 'cheating' when she does so."

The Southwestern Association of Forensic Scientists conducted an investigation of Gilchrist's work and held a hearing in which she was given a chance to respond. While the SWAFS board found that Gilchrist "should distinguish personal opinion from opinions based on facts derived from scientific evaluation," they did not recommend that Gilchrist be expelled, censured, or disciplined. In conclusion, the SWAFS board clearly let Gilchrist know that she should no longer offer her personal opinion concerning the guilt or innocence of the defendant. And they acknowledged that "undue pressure can be placed upon the forensic scientist to offer personal opinions beyond the scope of scientific capabilities."

This was a clear warning to Bob Macy and his prosecutors.

Following his ethics complaint and the SWAFS response, Wilson expected that the OCPD would conduct its own investigation into Joyce Gilchrist.

Nothing happened. There was no internal affairs investigation, no formal warning or censure, and virtually no mention of the controversy in the Oklahoma City press.

The *Oklahoman* did not mention this first Gilchrist controversy until SWAFS had concluded its investigation. Then the newspaper ran a brief article headlined: GROUP DECLINES TO DISCIPLINE CHEMIST.

It was the Tulsa *Tribune* that broke the story statewide. In a four-part series published in October 1987, the *Tribune* (now defunct) took an in-depth look at the Gilchrist controversy. Following a two-month investigation, Joan Biskupic, now a national reporter for *USA Today,* wrote a series of articles about the controversy swirling around Joyce Gilchrist and hair evidence.

Macy told the *Tribune* that "Gilchrist is one of the finest chemists I've ever seen." He went on to say that one of the reasons he liked using her so much was that "she's one [chemist] who's willing to give an opinion [in court testimony]."

"Part of the problem I've had with forensic experts is that they're too cautious," Macy continued. "I can get them up here in my office and say, 'What's your opinion?' And they say, 'Well, there's absolutely no question in my mind, the guy did it.' And then they get in the courtroom and they won't say that."

Barry Albert, who had already tried several capital cases with Macy, told the *Tribune* that any chemist who would positively state guilt based on forensic evidence "would be out of line, because the state of the art is not sufficient to make that kind of identification."

Macy and Albert also disagreed about John Wilson's qualifications. Albert defended Wilson's reputation, saying, "He has impeccable qualifications, education, experience, training."

While Bob Macy didn't attack Wilson by name, he did by implication. "Generally, people who come from the outside are not qualified," Macy said. Captain Harold Campbell of the OCPD said that as long as Macy's office was satisfied with Gilchrist, "I'm satisfied with her."

After the *Tribune* articles were published, Wilson never came back to testify in Oklahoma County. Two OCPD detectives called Wilson's supervisor at the Kansas City Police Department, complaining that he had testified against their forensic scientist. After that phone call, Wilson was told that he could no longer work on private cases.

"They never brought up the fact that I was right," Wilson said of the OCPD detectives. "They never questioned my competence. They just didn't want me down there."

Wilson suspected, and a source inside the Oklahoma County DA's office confirmed to me, that Macy was behind the phone call to the Kansas City Police Department.

Bob Ravitz had a hard time finding forensic chemists willing to testify for the defense, because they all knew what had happened to John Wilson. At that time, the only scientists who performed microscopic hair comparisons were working for crime labs affiliated with law enforcement.

In each of the three cases where Wilson testified against Gilchrist, the defendant was initially convicted (Alvin Parker, Curtis McCarty, and James Lucas Abels). Yet all three convictions were reversed on appeal. Parker's sentence was reduced to life imprisonment, Abels pleaded out to life, and we will see in a moment what happened to McCarty. These reversals vindicated Wilson's opinion of Gilchrist's work, but they didn't happen until years later.

"Basically, everyone ignored me because they liked what she was doing down there," Wilson said. "The prosecutor loved that stuff, the police department didn't have any problem with it, so it was a big vicious circle."

More than two years after McCarty's trial, the Oklahoma Court of Criminal Appeals overturned his convictions and granted him a new trial because of Gilchrist's improper testimony and statements made by Bob Macy and Barry Albert.

"The unprofessional conduct of Mr. Macy and Mr. Albert during closing argument should make conscientious prosecutors cringe," Judge Ed Parks wrote in the court's two-to-one ruling. "A complete statement of the facts is unnecessary, because the record is replete with error."

The court found that Gilchrist had delayed submitting evidence to the defense and that she had testified beyond the scope of the science. Gilchrist had begun her forensic examination in the Pam Willis case on December 15, 1982. She obtained the second group of hair samples from McCarty (the ones she matched to the crime scene hairs) on January 16, 1986. McCarty's lawyers filed a discovery motion five days later, requesting all scientific and technical reports, as well as hair, fiber, fingerprint, and serology samples for independent evaluation by John Wilson. He didn't receive the hair slides until March 17, the day the McCarty trial began. Wilson examined the slides and mailed them back to Gilchrist the next day. The Court of Criminal Appeals called Gilchrist's delay "inexcusable."

Not only did Gilchrist not give the defense enough time to examine the evidence, but she then used the delay that she herself had created as a means to discredit Wilson's findings. Gilchrist testified that Wilson did not have adequate time to perform a competent forensic examination.

Gilchrist's forensic report was, in the words of the court, "at best incomplete, and at worst inaccurate and misleading." Wilson had testified that her report reflected that none of the pubic hairs found on the victim were consistent with McCarty's. Gilchrist had matched another evidentiary pubic hair to McCarty's. She admitted at trial that she had failed to include that hair in her forensic report. "This significant omission," the court wrote, "whether intentional or inadvertent, resulted in trial by ambush."

The court found that Gilchrist's testimony concerning hair evidence was "in error." Gilchrist herself had testified that forensic science had not advanced to the point where a person could be positively identified through hair examination. "We find it inconceivable why Ms. Gilchrist would give such an improper opinion, which she admittedly was not qualified to give." While John Wilson attempted to refute Gilchrist sworn statements, the court recognized "the devastating impact of improper identification testimony by a police forensic expert."

David Autry, McCarty's appellate attorney, had argued that Gilchrist "in effect told the jury that Mr. McCarty had murdered Pamela Willis" and the question of guilt or innocence should be left to the jury. The court agreed: "An opinion as to the defendant's guilt or innocence is solely a question for the trier of fact."

Gilchrist's statement that McCarty was at the scene during the commission of the crime was "an improper expert opinion, because it was beyond the present state of the art of forensic science and certainly beyond Gilchrist's personal knowledge," according to the court. "We hold that such personal opinions beyond the scope of scientific capabilities have no place in a criminal trial."

The ruling also strongly criticized Bob Macy for statements made during closing arguments. The court found that Macy commented on facts not in evidence, expressed his personal opinion of the guilt of the accused, told the jury that it had a responsibility to convict on the basis of the prosecutor's personal sense of justice, and requested sympathy for the victims.

"The combined effects of the improper prosecutorial comments were so prejudicial as to adversely affect the fundamental fairness and impartiality of the proceedings," wrote Judge Parks.

"The evidence against the appellant cannot fairly be termed overwhelming, and we cannot conclude that the multitude of errors was harmless beyond a reasonable doubt," the court concluded. "This court will not stand idly by, 'wringing its hands' expressing nothing more than a 'ritualistic verbal spanking' and an 'attitude of helpless piety' in denouncing the deplorable conduct of prosecutors such as we have found in this case."

While they stopped short of accusing Macy and Albert of the intentional use of false or misleading evidence, the court warned: "We will not hesitate to reverse a conviction where an appellant establishes that (1) certain testimony was in fact misleading, (2) the prosecution knowingly used said testimony, and (3) the testimony was material to guilt or innocence."

After the McCarty decision came down, Macy dismissed it as a dispute over the death penalty. "It's a well-established fact," Macy said, "that Judge Parks and I have serious philosophical differences with respect to death penalty litigation."

In an editorial headlined MORE JUDICIAL NITPICKING, the *Oklahoman* opined: "Another convicted killer has won a new trial because of an Oklahoma Court of Criminal Appeals majority that seems more interested in finding reasons to reverse than in upholding the death penalty." The newspaper echoed Macy's reaction, saying that Judge Parks's decision "continues the nitpicking that has become so tiresome to citizens who wonder if a death sentence will ever be carried out in Oklahoma." And it said that a "number of district attorneys doubt [Judge Parks's] commitment to that particular law, based on what they say is his record of siding with defendants."

"I don't think I did anything wrong," Gilchrist said following the McCarty decision. "I never give my personal opinion in court. My opinion is always based on the evidence."

In a later interview with Captain Byron Boshell, Gilchrist explained her delay in providing evidence to McCarty's defense team by saying that she had to examine more than three hundred pieces of evidence, including reference samples from forty-two people. "I was also under a lot of pressure to complete other cases and had numerous trial obligations during this same time period," she said. Concerning her testimony about hair evidence, Gilchrist said, "Based upon the unusual characteristics that I observed in the foreign hairs from the crime scene, which were consistent with the characteristics observed in McCarty's reference sample, I felt I could make a strong association with him being at the crime scene."

In 1989, McCarty had a second trial. During this trial Gilchrist stated that a pubic hair found on the victim's chest was consistent with McCarty's. When asked why she had initially noted that the hair did not match McCarty's, Gilchrist stated that this was due to a typographical error made by her secretary on a report that she failed to notice prior to signing it.

Once again, McCarty was convicted of first-degree murder. The jury deliberated for seventeen hours and at one point reported an eleven-to-one deadlock. After voting for the guilty verdict, they only deliberated for two hours and twenty-five minutes before giving McCarty the death penalty. Prosecutors said that McCarty had an accomplice, who still was not identified.

Six years later, McCarty's second conviction was overturned and remanded for resentencing because the jury had not been told that they could give life without parole. Life without parole had become law in 1987, but District Court Judge Jack Parr denied a defense request that the jury be given that option during the penalty phase.

In the resentencing hearing, McCarty got the death penalty again.

When the FBI began to reexamine Gilchrist's hair and fiber evidence in several problematic cases, the McCarty hair slides could not be found and had been missing for at least a year. In June 2000, Gilchrist informed Captain Byron Boshell that she could not find the McCarty evidence. She was not sure if the DA's office had ever returned it following McCarty's retrial. Boshell asked her to document all the evidence she knew to be missing. A month later, Boshell himself went into the evidence room to examine the state of evidence storage. He observed a box of evidence. It was wide open, with no top. Inside the box were a white sweater-type shirt, a pair of jeans, and several unsealed envelopes. Attached to one of those envelopes was a court sheet with McCarty's name. This was the evidence that Gilchrist had said was missing. "This blatant disregard for evidence is unacceptable," Boshell wrote the next day, stating that Gilchrist would be instructed to secure all the evidence in that room.

Boshell and OCPD forensic chemist Laura Schile photographed the McCarty evidence and the rest of the evidence in the storage room. The photos show a complete shambles—open boxes of evidence, sacks and envelopes strewn on the floor, files damaged by water rot and animal infestation, biohazard bags with their seals broken.

"Don't get me wrong, I don't know if Eddie McCarty is guilty or not guilty," Chris Euhlberg, McCarty's appellate attorney, said. "But there is not enough physical evidence that any intelligent person looking at the evidence can say he did it absolutely, no question about it."

Euhlberg argues that there is no evidence that a second suspect was involved, and that Bob Macy used the John Doe theory in order to account for hair, and possibly semen, evidence that did not match McCarty's.

"Bob Macy was convinced from early on that McCarty was guilty and he did everything he could to prove it," Euhlberg said. "Any evidence that McCarty didn't do it was ignored. Some was disregarded, some was explained away, some was hidden."

The McCarty case is a mess. His prior exclusion as a suspect by Gilchrist's hair examinations really troubles me. And even if his hairs do match the evidentiary hairs found at the crime scene, they could have been placed there innocently (or at least not as a result of his murdering and raping Pam Willis). McCarty's confession to his girlfriend is powerful evidence, but it should have been corroborated. Why couldn't Macy get the snitch (presumably Ricky Terry) to testify?

There is a window of time and opportunity during which a case can be successfully solved and prosecuted. If it's not done right during this time, there will always be questions, whether legitimate or not, as to the suspect's guilt. I fear this is what happened in the McCarty case. Mitochondrial DNA tests on the evidentiary hairs would determine whether or not they were McCarty's, but that still does not prove guilt beyond a reasonable doubt.

When the OSBI reinvestigated all of Gilchrist's felony cases, the McCarty case was one singled out for further DNA examination by the attorney general's office. The DNA tests in the McCarty case were not completed at the time of this writing. Whether or not they confirm McCarty's conviction, the errors in the case remain.

McCarty is in prison, where he should be. And he will not be executed until the DNA tests, and possibly other appellate procedures, are conducted and affirm his conviction.

The person I feel sorry for is Jim Willis. He is convinced that McCarty killed his daughter. Yet he also believes there is another suspect, who has yet to be prosecuted. He must feel that his daughter's murder has only been half-solved.

Legal loopholes are a frustrating part of law enforcement. Defense attorneys use them all the time to get guilty suspects acquitted or released. As infuriating as overturned convictions on technicalities can be, they are the only way, short of criminal charges, to penalize misconduct on the part of cops and/or prosecutors.

The problems with Macy's prosecution and Gilchrist's lab work and testimony in the McCarty case go far beyond legal loopholes. Regardless of the apparent guilt of the defendant, such behavior cannot be ignored, particularly in a death penalty case. The closer I looked at McCarty and other Oklahoma death penalty cases that had problems that Bob Macy and others were calling legal technicalities, the more I realized how misdeeds with the investigation and prosecution of cases, when they go unpunished, allow a pattern of behavior that can often result in even more serious miscarriages of justice.

BLINDSIDED BY SCIENCE

JOYCE GILCHRIST WAS ONE OF THE FIRST FORENSIC CHEMISTS IN THE country to use DNA to help convict a suspect. In 1987, Hayward Reed was charged with rape and kidnapping. Gilchrist sent a sample of Reed's blood along with semen from the crime scene to Lifecodes, a New York City laboratory, on December 27, 1987. Speaking for the DA's office, Barry Albert promised that if the DNA sample did not match the defendant, he would be exonerated. Albert also said that DNA evidence was so powerful that it might satisfy the burden of proof all by itself. The Lifecodes test cost around $2,000.

At that time, there were still questions about the reliability and accuracy of DNA evidence. It had been used in only a handful of cases, and in the Hayward Reed case, Oklahoma County was on the cutting edge of technological progress in criminology.

The DNA tests came back as a match to Hayward Reed. The evidence was irrefutable. Reed was convicted and sentenced to ninety years. Gilchrist proposed that the OCPD develop its own DNA lab. She said it might take years for the lab to have the ability to perform

DNA tests itself, but it would be worth the expense and the effort. Everybody in the DA's office and OCPD seemed eager to develop this technology, as it promised to be more powerful than any evidence that had ever before been introduced in a courtroom.

Joyce Gilchrist's proposal quickly gained support from the political leadership. A city sales tax was levied in 1988 to help pay for the DNA lab. The tax raised $295,000 for equipment. Although the OCPD had gotten a head start, over the next few years it lagged behind the OSBI in the development of DNA technology. The Oklahoma state legislature approved a bill funding the establishment of an OSBI DNA lab, and by 1994 the OSBI lab was accepting casework and performing DNA tests.

In January 1995, Gilchrist promised that the DNA lab would be up and running "within a few months."

Three years later, in the summer of 1998, the OSBI's DNA lab was fully operational, and the OCPD sent evidence there for analysis. Since the OSBI lab had RFLP (restriction fragment length polymorphism) technology, Gilchrist suggested that her lab develop the more sensitive PCR (phosoglutomase) technology. Unfortunately, most of her expenditures and training had already been for RFLP.

More than ten years had passed since Gilchrist's DNA project had begun, and there was very little progress. OCPD detectives, eager to take advantage of quick and easy DNA testing within their own building, began to complain. City politicians, aware of how much money had already been spent, also grew concerned.

In June 1999 a formal complaint was filed with the city manager concerning the fact that hundreds of thousands of dollars had been spent and the police department still didn't have an operational DNA lab. In her response, Gilchrist claimed that her casework and managerial duties at the crime lab had kept her from devoting enough time to the DNA project. Gilchrist had been promoted to supervisor in 1990; four years later, she was officially relieved of her casework duties (although she continued to perform tests for a handful of detectives). Her only responsibility was to manage the crime lab and oversee the DNA project.

Gilchrist wrote to Deputy Chief Bob Jones, telling him that she expected the DNA lab to be operational in the fall of 1999. "I more than anyone else realizes that the time has long past [sic] when this lab should have been ready. But circumstances out of my control caused these numerous delays." Gilchrist complained that while the OSBI "has numerous people and unlimited financial resources for their project, the OCPD only has me."

"Everything was lip service," said Melissa Keith, one of the OCPD chemists who worked under Gilchrist. "Bottom line, Joyce never put in the time to get the lab operational."

By the summer of 2000, seventy-three inmates had been released from prison nationwide due to DNA evidence. Three of them were death row inmates in Oklahoma, including one from Oklahoma County. On June 1, 2000, Governor Frank Keating signed a law allowing DNA testing in certain felony cases on appeal. Oklahoma defense attorneys were clamoring for DNA tests in several cases that Gilchrist had worked on.

For years, the defense bar in Oklahoma City had been complaining about Joyce Gilchrist, yet they had been unable to prove absolutely that she was wrong. Barry Scheck's Innocence Project was now providing financial, legal, and logistic support for postconviction DNA tests. Oklahoma defense attorneys whose clients were on death row wanted any serological evidence submitted to DNA tests. Hairs that Gilchrist had matched to those of suspects could now be tested using the highly sensitive mitochondrial DNA to determine, once and for all, whether they truly did match. Blood and semen samples on which Gilchrist had performed presumptive ABO typing and electrophoresis examinations could now be tested for DNA, and the identity of their donors could be proven as definitively as science allowed.

That summer, Gilchrist said she would review the physical evidence in all the death row cases she worked on, to determine whether there was enough evidence to perform DNA analysis. She also said that the final decision of whether or not to perform these tests would be up to the state attorney general. And she promised that the DNA lab would be up and running "soon after the beginning of the fiscal year." By this time, the cost of DNA tests had gone down considerably. It now cost $250 to $450 to have DNA samples analyzed at an outside lab. The OCPD lab would be even less expensive, Gilchrist claimed, and would be able to produce results overnight.

None of the crime labs in Oklahoma, including OCPD's was federally accredited. At the OCPD lab, there were no established procedures or manuals for lab work, safety, training, or evidence handling. There was no proficiency testing nor any quality control standards. The lab did not have a formal procedure for peer review, and while some of the other chemists conducted informal peer reviews, Gilchrist never allowed anyone else to look at her work. There were also serious personnel problems under Gilchrist's management. (Even Gilchrist's staunchest defenders admit that she was not a particularly good administrator.)

"The lab has been supervised by someone who does not fully understand what it is to supervise and manage a laboratory," an OCPD chemist said at the time. "There has just been a complete, total lack of either knowledge or concern."

"Gilchrist's whole supervisory technique seemed to be based on only emotions, vengeance, vendettas," said chemist Elaine Taylor. "You never knew what to expect from her. So the only choice, if you wanted to stay in this career field, was to keep your mouth shut and do what she told you. It was like walking around on eggshells all the time."

As lab director, Captain Jessica Cummins acted as Gilchrist's direct supervisor. Cummins performed Gilchrist's job evaluations, but she was not able to judge her scientific work because she didn't have the forensic background or training.

"Supervising the OCPD crime lab was a nightmare," Cummins said.

It grew worse when Gilchrist filed a sexual harassment complaint against Major Garold Spencer, a former lab director who became chief of investigations. According to Gilchrist's complaint, Spencer had touched and caressed a female civilian brought in to teach a class at the OCPD. Once Gilchrist had brought the complaint to Cummins's attention, she was required by federal law to report it.

"The sexual harassment charge opened up a whole new bag of worms," Cummins said. While Gilchrist's charge against Spencer was being investigated, recommendations Cummins had made for changes in the crime lab were put on the shelf. Cummins asked to be transferred, and eventually traded positions with Captain Byron Boshell, a onetime homicide detective and one of the most respected officers in the OCPD. When Boshell took over, Major Spencer asked him to look into the problems with the DNA lab, and Gilchrist's conduct in general.

Boshell walked into a crime lab that was rife with conflict and exposed to a severe credibility risk. He had to discover exactly what had gone wrong with the lab. And he would have to prove it.

Boshell was a homicide dick, not a forensic scientist. He needed a qualified outsider to evaluate the DNA lab. Boshell hired Roger Kahn, a forensic scientist from the Ohio State Crime Lab, for the evaluation. While Kahn praised some of Gilchrist's efforts, he found that "a great deal of work remained to be completed." Kahn was concerned by the lack of documentation. Gilchrist was not documenting her DNA validation studies or even writing down the results. Kahn reported that Gilchrist was unqualified to become a DNA analyst. She needed a master's degree and/or three years of casework experience, and she had neither. It would take at least two years for Gilchrist to become qualified.

The DNA lab could not wait that long. Kahn recommended that the OCPD hire an experienced DNA analyst "as soon as possible" or else the DNA project "might not happen at all."

Boshell reduced Gilchrist's responsibilities so that she could focus on the DNA project; meanwhile, he went looking for an experienced analyst.

Kahn also reported to Boshell that he was hearing negative things about Gilchrist in the forensic community. He had met with chemists from the OSBI, who told him that Gilchrist "seems uninterested in working with them," when he recommended that she do a three-month internship in their DNA lab. He also stated that the OSBI chemists "mentioned that there had been a series of ethical problems with her forensic work." And he said that he himself had met with a well-known hair expert at the FBI who had "voiced concern about Ms. Gilchrist" and Kahn's own involvement with her laboratory. Kahn worried that he and Boshell might be "naive to a serious problem" with Joyce Gilchrist. He was not alone. Gilchrist's reputation in Oklahoma County had fallen so far so quickly that in trials and court motions, OCPD chemists were being impeached by defense attorneys simply because Gilchrist had trained them.

"As long as Joyce Gilchrist is affiliated with our lab," one chemist told Boshell, "we will have no credibility. Not just within our community or our state, but nationwide.

"Everybody knows of her reputation," the chemist continued. "The FBI does not trust her work. Most people feel that she is unethical."

Following Kahn's recommendation, Boshell hired an experienced and qualified DNA analyst. Laura Schile had worked as a forensic chemist and DNA analyst for the Texas Department of Public Safety. In the field of DNA technology, Schile had more experience and technical knowledge than Gilchrist.

Laura Schile joined the OCPD crime lab on January 5, 2000. From the beginning it was apparent that Schile was going to move into a senior position in the DNA lab, perhaps even become supervisor. Even before Schile started work, Gilchrist complained about her. Schile had requested a laptop computer and thirty reference samples to conduct DNA validation studies. When Gilchrist heard about this, she said she hoped Schile "did not think she was going to start operating the instruments when she arrived." Boshell noted that Gilchrist "did not like the idea of Laura Schile having input in the plans to get the lab operational."

"Based on Joyce Gilchrist's inability to work with her peers in the past," Boshell promised to ensure that Schile had "a fair opportunity to work in the DNA lab."

Once Schile started working at the crime lab, Boshell placed her in charge of the DNA project. Gilchrist was "to support the effort and assist Ms. Schile until the lab is fully operational." Gilchrist and Melissa Keith, a chemist, were to work as "understudies" to Schile. Once the DNA project was off the ground, Gilchrist would return to her supervisor's position over both the DNA and the serology labs. When Boshell told Gilchrist about these changes, she got upset and refused to go along with them.

Boshell asked Schile to perform an audit on the equipment Gilchrist had purchased for the DNA lab and determine what equipment could be used and what had expired or become obsolete. At first, Schile was reluctant, afraid that it might show Gilchrist in a bad light. Boshell convinced Schile to perform the audit. She went through all of Gilchrist's purchases over the past five years. In

Schile's estimation, Gilchrist had purchased $50,000 worth of useless equipment.

Boshell called Gilchrist's expenditures "excessive, premature and/or inappropriate." Some equipment had been bought with the intention of performing one type of DNA testing and discarded or rendered unusable when the decision was made to perform different tests. Other equipment and materials became outdated due to advances in technology or outlived their shelf life before they were ever used.

"Tens of thousands of dollars in supplies were purchased," Boshell wrote, "and it resulted in no DNA lab."

Gilchrist later explained that she had been following the OSBI's recommendations.

Following Schile's audit, Boshell asked Gilchrist what she needed to purchase for the DNA lab. Gilchrist suggested additional pipettes (glass tubes used for transferring liquids). Boshell found that request quite odd. Laura Schile had just documented that the lab had far too many pipettes. "There are only two reasons for such a statement," Boshell concluded. "Either she wants us to continue to spend money inappropriately or she really does not understand the DNA lab operation."

On February 11, 2000, Boshell discovered that the crime lab was destroying rape evidence after only two years. (The Oklahoma statute of limitations for rape is seven years.) He ordered that this practice cease immediately and began an investigation. On two separate occasions, Boshell asked Gilchrist under what authority she had destroyed rape evidence. The first time she said that Bob Macy told her to do it. Later she said that Captain Wilhelm (a former chief of detectives who had retired in 1989) had given her the go-ahead.

Boshell asked Gilchrist to produce the letter that Wilhelm wrote authorizing her to destroy evidence. She could not find it. Gilchrist told Boshell that when she started destroying rape evidence after two years, she had not known that there was a seven-year statute of limitations for rape.

"The rape kits, as a rule of thumb, were destroyed after two years and Joyce stated to us that it was by direction of Mr. Macy," Elaine Taylor told Boshell. "I never saw anything in writing. She was my immediate supervisor so I believed the only thing I could do was to follow her orders or else pay the consequences." Taylor said that Gilchrist told her she had "a blanket okay from Mr. Macy to destroy rape evidence."

Gilchrist decided what evidence was to be destroyed and told the other chemists to perform the evidence destruction. Often the destruction of rape and other evidence was not documented. So they never knew what evidence had been destroyed and what evidence they still had, or should have had, in storage.

At one point chemists Melissa Keith and Kyla Marshall decided that they would no longer destroy rape evidence despite Gilchrist's orders. So they repackaged it and stored it elsewhere. They did this on their own and did not tell Gilchrist what they had done. Both of them were concerned that rape evidence was being destroyed in cases that were still open or pending.

Laura Schile had previously asked Gilchrist to show her the letter that authorized the destruction of rape evidence. Gilchrist yelled at Schile and never showed her any letter. In fact, no letter from either Macy or Wilhelm existed. Macy himself told me so, and I was able to confirm it with other sources in the DA's office.

Dale Reed, an evidence officer, stated that Gilchrist advised him to destroy rape and other evidence by burning it on a creek bank. Reed said that Gilchrist told him the crime lab had always disposed of evidence in this manner. He informed a member of the city's Risk Management Unit about this practice and was told to discontinue it.

In addition to the destroyed rape evidence, the OCPD discovered that all the case files for the years 1980, 1981, and 1990 were missing. (Many of those files remain missing to this day.) Case files should be treated like evidence, because they are the only records of the criminal investigation. Without the case file, there's no way to retrace the steps of what was done in the laboratory, particularly if the physical evidence has been destroyed or consumed by prior testing.

Boshell also discovered that blood evidence, some of it possibly HIV-infected, was being disposed of by pouring it down the sink. He instituted a policy that would follow OSHA standards by disposing of blood in biohazard bags.

The problems with missing, misplaced, or inappropriately stored evidence were so bad that on October 10, 2000, Boshell ordered the temporary closing of the crime lab to find, document, and repackage evidence and then to implement new procedures. "This laboratory operated for many years without any policies and procedures, making it susceptible to judicial problems," Boshell wrote. "We should identify our weakness and problems before they are exposed in the courts. We will thus minimize a public relations incident and be doing what is right."

During the cleanup and repackaging, more evidence contamination was discovered. Chemist Kyla Marshall found several boxes of evidence from cases dating between 1980 and 1986. The evidence was moldy and water-damaged. Because it had not been properly stored, much of this evidence was irreparably contaminated.

When confronted with photographs and documentation about the mishandling of stored evidence, Gilchrist said that she had heard some of the evidence in the basement storage area had been damaged by water, but she never went down to look at it or have the evidence repackaged.

"Whose responsibility would it be to go in and take the evidence and dry it to salvage it?" Boshell asked.

"Well, since we really didn't have any procedure in place, I don't know that I could name anybody in particular," Gilchrist replied.

Evidence was still missing in several high-profile cases that Boshell knew about, only because the cases had recently been reversed or were pending appeal. David Bryson had been convicted of raping a legal secretary in downtown Oklahoma City. Joyce Gilchrist had performed a saliva swab on a marijuana pipe, which she matched to Bryson's blood type and secretor status. After DNA tests showed that he was not the semen donor of the rape evidence taken from the victim, Bryson's conviction had been overturned and he was given a new trial. When Bryson's defense attorney asked for all the evidence in the case, neither the saliva swab nor the pipe itself could be located.

"I feel we should be open and forthright with this case," Boshell wrote Gilchrist, urging her to locate all the evidence and send it to Bryson's attorney. "Our interest is with the scientific value of the evidence and the test results, not with whether Bryson is successfully prosecuted."

After Boshell gave Gilchrist this memo, he told her in person that he was deeply concerned about missing evidence and asked specifically about the Bryson case. She told him that the evidence must have been thrown out, although she did not remember. Boshell asked Gilchrist to tell him exactly what evidence was missing in which cases. She stated that in addition to the Bryson evidence, there was also missing evidence in the Robert Lee Miller/Ronnie Lott double homicide/rape case, and the shirt and jacket of murder defendant Bigler Jobe Stouffer had been lost. Boshell instructed Gilchrist to make a report on all cases with missing evidence.

Gilchrist reported back that the saliva slides in the Bryson case were probably not missing, but that she had used up all the samples during her testing. She also stated that it was possible the remaining extracts had been destroyed. Three days later, she informed Boshell that Stouffer's jacket had been located, but his shirt was still missing.

"We have really no idea," one chemist told Boshell, "as far as a lot of the older cases are concerned, what evidence we have or don't have."

When Boshell conducted a formal interview with Gilchrist concerning these and other problems, he was able to elicit the following information:

Q [BOSHELL]: *Were you aware that evidence was deteriorating in the storage area?*

A [GILCHRIST]: *Yes.*

Q: *Were you aware that boxes were rotting and breaking open?*

A: *Yes.*

Q: *Were you aware that the boxes were not properly sealed?*

A: *Yes.*

Q: *OK. Did you ever take steps to routinely go and protect that evidence? Was it one of situations where it has been this way and there is nothing to be done?*

A: *Well, I made suggestions and recommendations to our captain, I think it was Captain Hill at the time, prior to that it was Major Upchurch. But we didn't get anything done.*

Q: *OK. Did some of this evidence become important in appeals and new trials, where we would have to go back and dig this evidence out and reexamine it?*

A: *Yes, I believe so.*

Q: *Were some of these cases with evidence in these improper conditions part of death penalty cases?*

A: *I believe there were, yes.*

Boshell had a serious problem on his hands. He began looking into the history of allegations against Gilchrist, particularly concerning her testimony and lab work in death penalty cases. He studied the reversals by appellate courts in which her work and testimony was criticized. He also looked into the charges made by John Wilson and the investigations by professional associations. When he contacted Max Courtney, a member of the Southwestern Association of Forensic Scientists, Courtney told Boshell that he felt Gilchrist "may have received poor training in her early years and was too prone to support the prosecution." Boshell also spoke to Kimberly Wasse of the American Association of Forensic Sciences. Wasse told Boshell that Gilchrist was not an active member of the association. When Boshell asked if Gilchrist had ever applied and been rejected for membership, Wasse told him that information would require a subpoena.

Gilchrist brushed off John Wilson's criticism by saying that since those cases all got convictions "the jury didn't find his testimony credible." She blamed all her problems on a group of defense attorneys who "wanted to get me out of the business because I was hurting them in court." During this period, Gilchrist charged, "Nobody in this department said a word or came to my defense about anything."

When asked about the problems resulting from her hair testimony, Joyce Gilchrist responded, "One judge said as an expert I was allowed to give my opinion based on the evidence, and my educational experience."

Boshell asked Gilchrist if she knew of any other chemist who had similar problems.

"I don't know that anybody has had similar problems," Gilchrist said. "My situation is unique, because of the defense attorneys' attitude toward me. And their attitude was that because of who I am, being a black female, I shouldn't know what I know, I shouldn't have the intelligence that I have, I shouldn't be able to defend myself against them in the courtroom based on the results of my analysis, because they would ask me questions I am sure they did not know the answers to but they didn't think I knew the answer to, and I did."

"So you think race plays a role in this?" Boshell asked.

"I really do, I really do."

One of the major concerns with Gilchrist over the years was the fact that she never submitted her lab work for peer review. Boshell asked her, "Do you feel that peer review is important in the Forensic Laboratory?"

"Ah, yes," Gilchrist replied.

"Were peer reviews conducted on a routine basis?"

"No."

"Why are peer reviews important?"

"So that we can know that everyone is operating on the same page, doing the same basic standard procedures, and if there are any discrepancies or mistakes that can be brought to one's attention before report results go out of the lab."

"Are peer reviews also designed to prevent mistakes in the lab?"

"Yeah, I just said that."

"Did you subject your casework to peer review?"

"Well, not my casework to peer review, I did not."

"Do you feel the failure to have peer reviews conducted could place the laboratory in jeopardy?"

"Yes."

In late March 2000, Gilchrist was transferred to the Equine Laboratory. Shortly after her transfer, Gilchrist filed a grievance against Boshell, stating that she had "been falsely accused and unfairly treated" and that Boshell's actions had caused her "undue duress, pain and suffering." The same day, she sent a memo to Police Chief M. T. Berry, who had been her supervisor at the crime lab and a friend from their days at Central State University. "I will do whatever I have to in order to survive this assault on me," Gilchrist wrote the chief. "I have never lied about anything in a court of law, nor have I ever withheld any evidence or information from an attorney." Gilchrist blamed the defense attorneys for all her troubles and claimed she had received death threats.

"Joyce Gilchrist was the most blame-layingest, finger-pointing woman I ever saw in my life," Major Garold Spencer told me. "In every case where something was found wrong with something Joyce did, she had other people or other reasons why it happened. In many cases, the people that she would blame were either long retired or dead. It was amazing how her reasoning would center around things you couldn't verify."

Summing up his interviews with Gilchrist, Boshell noted that "there were numerous occasions in which she responded to questions in a misleading manner."

After she had been transferred to the Equine Laboratory, Gilchrist was found in the DNA extraction room, rummaging around in the cabinet drawers. She was not wearing gloves, even though she should have known that touching anything in the room bare-handed would result in contamination. Chemists had just spent a week decontaminating the room. Once Gilchrist was observed there, the extraction room had to be decontaminated all over again.

On September 25, 2000, the compressor in the crime lab's evidence freezer broke down and the temperature rose from minus twenty-three degrees Fahrenheit to room temperature. Laura Schile was working in the crime lab when the freezer malfunctioned. Her first reaction was to try to save as much evidence as she could. She and the other chemists retrieved the evidence from the freezer. Some of the blood evidence had been improperly packaged in paper envelopes, and much of it had been caked in ice because the freezer had never been properly defrosted. When the freezer thawed, the ice melted and the resulting water mixed with the blood evidence, thoroughly contaminating it. Not all of the evidence was lost. Schile and her coworkers dried out the wet evidence and recataloged it, recording every single piece of evidence to maintain chain of custody and make sure that it was not potentially contaminated or compromised. Then they repackaged the evidence so that if the freezer broke down again, it would not become water-damaged.

The freezer failure and resulting contamination could have been prevented. At least a year earlier, Gilchrist had asked Elaine Taylor, Kyla Marshall, and Melissa Keith to destroy some rape kits. The evidence was so frosted over that the chemists had to hack the envelopes out of ice in order to get them out of the freezer. They notified Gilchrist about the problems with ice buildup, yet nothing was ever done about it.

In the summer of 1999 the temperature in the freezer had been rising. Gilchrist called a repairman, who told her to move several boxes of evidence away from the freezer. He also told her that the freezer should be defrosted. Too much ice had formed and the freezer could no longer self-defrost. The boxes were moved, but Gilchrist never defrosted the freezer. When interviewed by Boshell, Gilchrist said she didn't remember anybody telling her that ice buildup was causing problems with the freezer. And she said she didn't remember talking to the freezer repairman about defrosting the freezer.

After documenting all of these problems, and more, on January 16, 2001, Boshell sent a memo, along with several hundred pages of supporting documents, to Chief M. T. Berry, Major Garold Spencer, and Deputy Chief Bob Jones.

"To say the serology lab was mismanaged is an understatement," Boshell wrote in his cover letter. "It was grossly mismanaged!"

Boshell made several recommendations, including that Gilchrist be removed from lab duties, that Laura Schile be placed in charge of the lab, and that the OCPD review all of Gilchrist's cases where the defendants were awaiting execution.

"If we fail to take action," Boshell concluded, "we very well may find civil action being taken against the city, the laboratory and the civilian and sworn personnel involved."

The Boshell memo and its five hundred pages of attachments read like a novel—"The Decline and Fall of Joyce Gilchrist."

And it was only just beginning.

CHAPTER SEVEN

DNA DOESN'T LIE

AT THE SAME TIME THAT PROBLEMS WITH THE CRIME LAB AND THE DNA project were coming to a head, Joyce Gilchrist's testimony in a prior death penalty case would come back to haunt her.

Elaine Scott was a student at the University of Oklahoma. She volunteered at the Pilot Recreation Community Center, working with disadvantaged youth in a poor Oklahoma City neighborhood. On January 7, 1991, Scott was working at the center with its director, Carolyn Ross. At approximately 1:35 P.M. Ross took her lunch break, leaving Scott alone in the office. On her way out, Ross ran into Alfred Brian Mitchell, an eighteen-year-old black male who lived nearby. Ross told Mitchell that Scott could help show him the center's library. Then she left the building.

A few minutes later, Allen Biggs, a contractor hired to fix the center's leaking roof, came by to check on his work crew. Mitchell met Biggs at the door and told him the center was closed. Biggs had the impression that Mitchell did not want him to enter the building. The roofing crew returned to the center at approximately 2:20 and spent forty minutes cleaning up. They did not enter the office where Scott had been working.

When Carolyn Ross returned to the center at 2:50 P.M. she noticed that Scott's car was gone and the building had been left unlocked. When she entered the office, she found Elaine Scott's almost naked body on the floor, lying facedown in a pool of blood. Scott had been struck with a golf club and a wooden coatrack, causing massive head trauma—her skull was crushed and splinters from the coatrack were embedded in her brain. She had also been stabbed five times in the neck with a compass. Her nose, one of her front teeth, and two ribs were broken. There were cuts and bruises all over her body. Her car and purse had been stolen.

Shortly after being called to the crime scene, police spoke to two of Alfred Brian Mitchell's acquaintances who said they had seen him near the center around the time of the attack. Mitchell had told one of the witnesses that he had been at the center earlier but left because a couple of guys were giving the girl working there a hard time. The police found Mitchell at home, where he lived with his mother. He had recently been released from a juvenile detention center, after having served three years for the rape of a twelve-year-old girl.

At this point, police considered Mitchell a witness. They took him to the center, where he showed crime scene officers where the men he had seen might have left fingerprints. Then police took Mitchell to several homeless shelters to see if he could identify the men. When this proved unsuccessful, the police asked Mitchell to give them the sneakers he had been wearing that afternoon and to come back the next morning for further questioning.

That next morning Mitchell came to the station, where he waived his Miranda rights and spoke to the detectives. After four hours of questioning, Mitchell voluntarily surrendered blood and hair samples. While they still had him in custody, the officers were informed that Mitchell's sneakers matched bloody footprints found at the crime scene. The interview became an interrogation. Mitchell admitted being present at the crime scene but said that someone else had killed Scott. He was arrested and charged with first-degree murder.

"In this business, you see a lot of bad crimes," Bob Macy told the media shortly after Mitchell's arrest, "but this has to rank as one of the worst. Here was a girl who dedicated herself to helping underprivileged kids, and she is bludgeoned to death. This should never occur in a civilized society."

Macy blamed the state Department of Human Services for Scott's death, because it had released Mitchell some two weeks prior to the murder. He also said the killing may have had some "sexual motivation." Meanwhile, his assistant prosecutors were saying that the motive was robbery. Semen had been found inside and on the victim's body, as well as the sheet used to carry her from the crime scene. The sexual assault evidence was being sent to the FBI for DNA testing.

Three weeks after his murder arrest, additional charges of rape and anal sodomy were filed against Mitchell. Assistant DA Don Deason said that Joyce Gilchrist had needed the time in order to perform forensic tests. In that short a time frame and using OCPD facilities, Gilchrist could only have done preliminary blood typing and electrophoresis. The FBI DNA test results had not come back yet.

Before going to trial, Mitchell's lawyer, Jim Rowan, had offered to plead his client out to murder but not rape, if the victim's family asked Bob Macy not to seek the death penalty. According to the Scotts' civil attorney, "Rowan was sure that Mitchell would admit to everything except the rape. Brian keeps insisting he didn't rape Elaine. However, Mr. Rowan did say that if Mitchell knew he would be getting life without parole in this deal, he may then admit to the rape."

Mitchell was saying that he didn't rape Scott but would admit doing it if it would save his life.

Three witnesses placed Mitchell inside the Pilot Center around the time of the murder. Another witness described a black male leaving the center in Scott's red Ford. Two witnesses who knew Mitchell identified him near the center and in the proximity of Scott's stolen car shortly after the crime occurred. Scott had previously told one of these witnesses that she was afraid of Mitchell.

At trial, Joyce Gilchrist testified that bloodstains matching Scott's ABO type were found on the defendant's sneakers and sweatpants. The bloody footprints at the crime scene had also been matched to Mitchell's sneakers. Blood matching Mitchell's type was found on Scott's blue jeans and panties. And fiber taken from her fingernail matched a black wool jacket he had been wearing.

In addition to the fiber and blood evidence, Gilchrist testified that sperm and semen samples taken from the victim's body were consistent with both Mitchell's and Phillip Taylor's, the victim's boyfriend. Taylor swore that he and Scott last had sex eight days prior to her murder. Michael Harjochee was also reportedly having sexual relations with the victim at the time. Gilchrist testified that a viable semen or sperm sample would be present within a female's body for up to twelve hours after intercourse. She further stated that she would not expect eight-day-old semen to be found.

Gilchrist testified that DNA tests performed by the FBI had been "inconclusive." The same samples were then sent to a private lab where chemists "were able to associate them" with Mitchell, Gilchrist stated.

Mitchell took the stand in his defense. He testified that he had masturbated in Scott's presence while she was still alive, but that he had not had any sexual contact with her. He also denied killing her.

The medical examiner found no trauma to the victim's anus or vagina. He did find areas of bruising around both hipbones, which he determined were caused by some form of blunt trauma, perhaps as the result of a sexual assault, perhaps not.

During the trial, Ann Scott, the victim's mother, left the courtroom for a break. The defendant's mother was standing in the hall. Ann Scott went up to her and said, "Your son has made victims of both of us."

Bob Macy had not been able to try the Mitchell case himself as he was in the hospital for emergency surgery. His assistants Steve Deutsch and Don Deason handled the prosecution. Macy appeared in the courtroom for closing arguments as a spectator, still wearing bandages and drainage tubes.

Mitchell was found guilty of murder, rape, anal sodomy, armed robbery, and car theft. Following the penalty phase, the jury gave Mitchell a death sentence, plus 170 years on the other felony charges.

Three years later, Mitchell's conviction and sentence were upheld by the Oklahoma Court of Criminal Appeals, despite the court's concerns about Gilchrist's testimony. The court noted that while the Oklahoma County medical examiner and an independent expert, Brian Wraxall, had found no sperm on the vaginal or anal swabs taken from the victim, Joyce Gilchrist had found sperm on both. They dismissed this as differing opinions among professional experts, not a dispute over verifiable scientific fact. "This court," wrote Judge Charles Chapel in the five-to-zero decision, "cannot distinguish between Gilchrist's veracity and that of other experts."

The judges did note that during closing arguments both Deutsch and Deason had claimed that Gilchrist and Wraxall had come to the same conclusions regarding the rape evidence. "This was incorrect," Chapel wrote. "However, every misstatement of fact does not amount to impermissible argument." Chapel went on to say that Mitchell's appellate attorneys had "not shown, and the record does not reflect, that this statement was purposefully made in bad faith to mislead or prejudice the jury."

Following an evidentiary hearing that focused on Gilchrist's testimony, Judge Ralph Thompson of the U.S. District Court overturned Mitchell's rape and anal sodomy convictions. Thompson's opinion, issued on August 27, 1999, found that Gilchrist had clear knowledge of DNA evidence that exonerated Mitchell of the rape charges, yet she withheld this evidence from the defense and lied about it in her testimony. According to the judge, she had given testimony that was "misleading," "entirely unsupported by the evidence," and "without question, untrue." Prosecutors Deutsch and Deason were spanked for "blatant withholding of unquestionably exculpatory evidence" that was "absolutely indefensible." And the judge called parts of their closing arguments "absolutely untenable."

The sexual assault evidence that Joyce Gilchrist presented at trial had serious problems. She compounded those problems with her testimony in the evidentiary hearing. At trial, Gilchrist testified that she had found six sperm on the vaginal swab taken from the victim but was unable to identify the donor.

Gilchrist testified that she found ten sperm on the rectal swab and determined that the donor had the same blood type as both Mitchell and the victim's boyfriend, Philip Taylor. She said that "blood, semen and sperm found on the sheet in which the victim's body had been transported from the crime scene were consistent with both Mitchell and Taylor, as were semen stains on the victim's panties." For none of this evidence did she take the next step and determine whether the donor was Mitchell or Taylor.

Finally, she testified that "a viable semen or sperm sample would be present in a woman's body for up to twelve hours after intercourse if she were up and moving around." The jury had been told that Taylor had not had sexual relations with the victim for eight days prior to her murder.

Was Taylor telling the truth when he said he had not had sex with the victim for eight days before her death? Gilchrist apparently never performed the test that would have answered that question, but a federal court would describe Taylor's testimony as "questionable." What was the effect of that testimony? If Taylor's last sexual contact with Scott had been eight days before her murder, then any semen of a similar blood type would have to have been donated by Mitchell. Then where does Harjochee fit in? He was one of the witnesses who placed Mitchell near the crime scene. Could he have had consensual sex with the victim shortly before her death? These questions were never answered by the investigating detectives. They showed a reluctance to thoroughly investigate the victim's sex life. Perhaps they thought they were being gentlemen. Whatever their motivations, the detectives did the victim and her family a great disservice by not fully investigating the circumstances surrounding her death.

And it happened to help the state's case, at least for a while. The belief that Scott had not had sex with her boyfriend for more than a week prior to her killing led the jury to believe that Mitchell must have been the donor of the sperm and semen that Gilchrist had been unable to positively identify. What the jury didn't know was that DNA testing had already eliminated Alfred Brian Mitchell as the donor of some of those semen stains.

Gilchrist had sent eleven items of evidence to FBI Agent Michael Vick for further examination. Vick was unable to find DNA on much of the evidence. Still, he was able to exclude Mitchell, and include Taylor, as the donor of the semen found on Scott's panties (we can assume that Scott changed her panties at least once in eight days). Since Taylor was not the suspect, Vick did not perform further tests to absolutely confirm that the semen was Taylor's. Gilchrist later used this to support her testimony that the tests were "inconclusive," despite the fact that she was clearly referring to the tests concerning Mitchell. Vick's written report was not entirely clear. It confused both Brian Wraxall and the Court of Criminal Appeals. However, Gilchrist's own handwritten notes proved that she knew the DNA was not Mitchell's prior to her testimony at trial.

During discovery in preparation for the evidentiary hearing,

Mitchell's lawyers asked for and received notes written by Gilchrist during her phone conversations with Agent Vick about the DNA test results. These notes show that she had known Vick's DNA tests contradicted her preliminary conclusions that had failed to exclude Mitchell as the semen donor. Vick had told her that the semen on the panties matched Taylor's, that no DNA was present on the rectal swab, and that the only DNA on the vaginal swab was consistent with the victim's.

One note, dated 4-10-91, said, "Match—Taylor (Panties)." Another note, dated 5-3-91, said, "Panties—c/w Taylor [c/w means consistent with]."

"The results thus completely undermined Ms. Gilchrist's testimony," Judge Thompson ruled.

Here's what Gilchrist said regarding the DNA evidence during the trial:

Q [DON DEASON]: *Ms. Gilchrist, do you know whether the FBI DNA analysis was able to associate any of this evidence to the defendant in this case?*
A: *No, they were not able to.*
Q: *Would it be correct to say the results were inconclusive?*
A: *Yes.*

On cross-examination, Gilchrist testified:

Q: *You testified that this FBI report received from Michael Vick at the FBI DNA lab was inconclusive, right?*
A: *In reference to [Alfred Brian Mitchell], yes.*

"When she testified at trial," Judge Thompson found, "Gilchrist knew the semen on Ms. Scott's panties was not consistent with both Petitioner and Taylor. She knew the semen was at least a preliminary match for Taylor *and* that [Mitchell's] DNA had *not* been found on the panties. Thus, the DNA test results were far from inconclusive."

Mitchell's defense attorney had not known about Gilchrist's notes during trial because she had not turned them over on discovery. When asked why she did not turn over the notes, Gilchrist stated that she was not asked for them, and she did not turn over anything unless she was "under a court order to do so." Judge Thompson found this a clear discovery violation.

"I didn't withhold anything," Gilchrist said shortly after the ruling. "As far as I know, everything was turned over to the assistant DA. Now, if it wasn't sent over to the defense attorney, that's out of my hands."

Prosecutors Deutsch and Deason "labored extensively at trial to obscure the true DNA test results and to highlight Gilchrist's test results," according to Judge Thompson.

The prosecutors had supported Gilchrist's testimony by telling the jury that the FBI tests were "inconclusive" because of "low molecular weight and degraded sample of DNA." Judge Thompson wrote that "this statement is entirely unsupported by the evidence and misleading." During the evidentiary hearing, Gilchrist admitted that electrophoresis testing she performed prior to the trial excluded Mitchell as the donor of the samples later found consistent with Taylor and Scott. However, she neglected to say this at trial. In fact, she stated that her testing revealed that both Mitchell and Taylor could have been the donors when her own electrophoresis testing had already eliminated Mitchell.

While Judge Thompson overturned the rape and anal sodomy convictions, he still upheld Mitchell's death penalty. The judge found that the "horrific nature of the assault on Ms. Scott" met the "heinous, atrocious or cruel" aggravator, Mitchell's prior conviction on rape charges satisfied the "continuing threat" aggravator, and the jury was justified in finding the "killing to escape prosecution" aggravator. Even without the rape and sodomy charges, he decided that "this is an appropriate case for the death penalty," and his overturning of the rape and sodomy convictions did not affect the death sentence.

In addition to the case under review, Judge Thompson also cited several other cases in which Gilchrist had been criticized by the Oklahoma Court of Criminal Appeals for testifying "to a conclusion which was not scientifically supported" and submitting a report that was "at best incomplete, and at worst inaccurate and misleading."

Shortly after Judge Thompson's ruling, Gilchrist was expelled from the Association of Crime Scene Reconstruction for giving testimony that misrepresented evidence.

On August 13, 2001, the Tenth Circuit Court went even further, overturning Alfred Brian Mitchell's death penalty, while upholding his conviction for murder. In a three-to-zero decision, the judges denounced prosecutors for deliberately misleading jurors and hiding exculpatory evidence.

"We simply cannot be confident that the jury would have returned the same sentence had no rape and sodomy evidence been presented to it," the court wrote, calling the state and district courts "wrong as a matter of law" in not vacating Mitchell's death penalty in their previous opinions, since they had already noted the problems with Gilchrist's testimony and the prosecutors' questions and remarks supporting it.

Judge Thompson had been convinced that the prosecutors could have gotten the death penalty without the sex charges, so he let Mitchell's death sentence stand. The Tenth Circuit Court was not convinced and overturned the death sentence.

The Tenth Circuit decision recounted the facts surrounding the rape and sodomy evidence, then concluded, "Ms. Gilchrist thus provided the jury with evidence implicating Mr. Mitchell in the sexual assault of the victim which she knew was rendered false and misleading by evidence withheld from the defense. Compounding this improper conduct was that of the prosecutor [whose] . . . conduct in this case strikes a heavy blow to the public's trust."

One of the prosecutors had stated that "Brian Wraxall and Joyce Gilchrist confirm each other's testimony that there was semen and sperm found inside the vagina of Elaine Marie Scott." This statement was untrue and the prosecutor should have known that.

In closing arguments during the guilt phase, a prosecutor said that Mitchell had killed Scott in order to escape punishment for raping her. "After he was through with Elaine Scott, after he had his way with her, knowing that she knew him, knew who he was, the fact that she was afraid of him before, he murdered her, he beat her to death, because she was the only living witness to the crime that he had committed."

The court pointed out that "sexual assault charges are by their nature highly inflammatory and prejudicial" and that there was a "qualitative difference in terms of culpability" between a suspect who rapes and kills to silence his victim and one who kills in a fit of rage. "Had the rape and sodomy charges not been before the jury," the court found, "the state would have been unable to infuse the murder with prior sexual abuse or to argue that Mr. Mitchell killed the victim in a premeditated plan to avoid arrest and prosecution." Both the guilt and the sentencing phases of the trial "would necessarily have had an entirely different focus and character."

Clearly, there was a sexual element to this crime. Mitchell's sperm and semen were found on Scott's clothing and body, but that evidence fit his testimony that he masturbated in her presence. Maybe he did it after he killed her, which is sick and disgusting—but it's not rape or anal sodomy. In Oklahoma, sexual assault requires penetration. And the state did not prove the crimes with which Mitchell was charged that so inflamed the public and the jury and helped get him the death penalty.

"The case was bad enough without the rape," Jim Rowan said. "Apparently Macy and his prosecutors felt they had to make it better with sexual misconduct."

The murder of Elaine Scott was a horrible crime, and Mitchell clearly did it. Based on the evidence the prosecutors had, they could have gotten a righteous conviction and quite possibly the death penalty using the "heinous, atrocious or cruel" and "continuing threat" aggravators. Why did Macy and his prosecutors insist on prosecuting the sexual assault charges when the evidence contradicted them?

When Gilchrist got the phone call from Michael Vick, why didn't she just walk down the hall to the homicide bureau and tell the detectives that the semen wasn't Mitchell's? She shouldn't have been surprised by the results. Her own electrophoresis tests had already excluded Mitchell as the semen donor before she even sent the samples to the FBI.

While Gilchrist also testified to hair, blood, and fiber evidence at the trial, the bulk of her testimony regarded the semen and sperm evidence supporting the sexual assault charges. She didn't seem to be too worried about proving the murder, just the rape and anal sodomy. None of the blood evidence was DNA tested. Why did Gilchrist send the semen stains out for DNA testing but not the blood found on Mitchell's sneakers and sweatpants? If she could have positively identified that blood as coming from Elaine Scott, the murder case would have been a slam dunk.

The Tenth Circuit decision came when Gilchrist was already on paid administrative leave and under investigation by the FBI and a multiagency task force. A week after Mitchell's death penalty was overturned, Gilchrist began her administrative hearing. In a little more than a month, she was fired.

"Mitchell was one case that was very significant in prompting people in Oklahoma County to finally come to grips with the idea that they had to do something about Gilchrist," said Pat Ehlers, a federal public defender.

When interviewed by Captain Byron Boshell about the Mitchell case, the only mistake Gilchrist would admit making during her testimony was that perhaps she had been sitting too close to the microphone.

"I totally disagree with [Judge Thompson]," Gilchrist told Boshell. "During the trial, I testified consistently that based on my analysis, I could not exclude either the boyfriend or the defendant as being the donor of the semen. I testified to the work I performed, which was performed correctly. I cannot change the results of my work based on the conclusions of the FBI's report. This seems to be what Judge Thompson wanted or expected me to do. I realize he makes his own determinations and it would not be possible to challenge his opinions, but if called again I would testify the same way."

Gilchrist refused to accept the fact that the FBI's DNA tests were more accurate, more definitive, and more probative than her own presumptive testing. She also felt that Judge Thompson "was wrong in placing total blame for errors solely on me. I merely analyzed the evidence and testify [*sic*] to my results."

When Boshell asked about her dismissal from the Association of Crime Scene Reconstruction, Gilchrist said she had received a letter from the organization, but she couldn't read it. "The print was bad," she said. "[T]hat was about the same time all this other stuff in the lab was going on, [and] I didn't feel that was the most important thing for me to focus on at the time." She didn't tell anybody because she received the letter right before Christmas and quickly forgot about it.

If Alfred Brian Mitchell had been righteously tried and sentenced, whether to death or life without parole, Bruce and Ann Scott would hopefully be able to move on. Instead, they wait for Mitchell's retrial, praying that he will eventually be executed.

The Scotts are angry at the judges who overturned Mitchell's sentences. They call Jim Rowan "slime" and "sleazy." And they are very bitter about the way legal technicalities have kept justice from being served. "Joyce Gilchrist was straightforward and honest," Bruce Scott said. "I don't think she lied about anything. Of course, I don't know how good a chemist she was."

To these parents of a murdered child, the only fact that matters is that Alfred Brian Mitchell was responsible and should be punished. If he is not executed, they are afraid he might someday get out of prison and kill again. Their daughter was murdered shortly after he had been released from a juvenile detention center.

"If Mitchell is ever released, somebody else will have to sacrifice their daughter, because we've already given our only one," Ann Scott said. Still, the Scotts know there will never be any closure for them.

"My daughter is dead," Bruce Scott said. "Every time I pass her picture, I am reminded of her. Nothing—not even executing Alfred Brian Mitchell—[will] bring her back."

I asked the Scotts if they could ever consider forgiving Mitchell.

"There was a time," Ann Scott said, "that I could forgive him for what he did to me. But I could never forgive him for what he did [to] my daughter."

"Only God can grant him forgiveness," Bruce Scott said. "I just want to hasten the meeting."

CHAPTER EIGHT

A ROBBERY GONE WRONG

IN A CRIME WITH TWO SUSPECTS, PARTICULARLY A MURDER COMMITTED during a robbery attempt, it is common for police or prosecutors to get one of the suspects to roll. In return for a signed statement and testimony at trial, the cooperating suspect will usually get special consideration, like a reduced sentence. The death penalty is a useful investigative tool in cases like this. Faced with the prospect of lethal injection, suspects are often eager to provide evidence. In this way, the death penalty works without even having to use it.

Bob Macy did not like cutting deals on high-profile murder cases, however. If there were two suspects involved and Macy could prosecute both of them, he would. And if he thought he could get the death penalty for both, he would try. In one drive-by shooting case, he won separate death penalty convictions for both the shooter and the driver. In another case, he convicted two men in separate trials of shooting a convenience store clerk (he argued in each trial that the defendant was the shooter—only one shot was fired).

One case stands out, not so much for the questionable circumstances under which Macy prosecuted two suspects for a murder that could have been committed by one killer, or for the problems with the evidence presented by Joyce Gilchrist (although both factors were present in this case) but because my investigation brought me into contact with Jim Fowler, who, more than any other person, made me begin to reexamine my opinion concerning the death penalty.

Shortly before 4:00 A.M. on July 3, 1985, Carrie Lee Wever arrived for work at Wynn's IGA supermarket in Edmond, Oklahoma. Wever was a sixteen-year-old high school student who worked part-time making doughnuts in the supermarket bakery. When she entered the store with her mother, who wanted to buy cigarettes, they didn't see any employees. Carrie started looking for her coworkers. Eventually she went into the back storeroom. There she saw three men lying on the ground in a semicircle—the floor was slick with what looked like blood. She recognized them as Rick Cast, John Barrier, and Chumpon Chaowasin. At first Carrie thought it was some kind of prank.

"Come on, Rick," she said, nudging Cast with her foot, "the joke's over. Let's get to work."

Carrie turned and started to walk out of the storeroom. When she didn't hear the men getting up, she realized they were dead.

The three men had been herded into the back storeroom during a robbery. Cast, the thirty-three-year-old night manager of the store, and Chaowasin, a forty-four-year-old Asian graduate student who worked as a stocker, had both been shot in the back of the head with a shotgun. John Barrier, a twenty-seven-year-old manager trainee, had been stabbed and beaten to death.

The quiet town of Edmond, part of Oklahoma County, reacted with shock and horror.

"This isn't supposed to happen in Edmond," said one store employee.

Kirk Kemper, a friend of both Cast and Barrier, who had come to the supermarket that morning to find the entire shopping center sealed off by police, said, "They were damn good people. I don't understand it. It seems the sorry people never get killed."

No one was more outraged than Bob Macy himself, who lived in Edmond at the time and shopped at that very grocery store. Summoned by the Edmond Police Department, Macy arrived at the supermarket while the crime scene was still being processed and the bodies had yet to be removed.

"It's a horrible crime; a totally needless crime," Macy told reporters. "If they had executed Roger Dale Stafford, this wouldn't have happened."

Stafford was awaiting execution for the killing of six people in the Sirloin Stockade steak house (at the time, Oklahoma's worst mass murder), and three other murders. While Macy hadn't prosecuted Stafford, he was impatient to see the man die. (Stafford was finally executed on July 1, 1995.)

If the local residents, and even law enforcement professionals, were shocked by the crime, its motive was simple—robbery. A total of $2,700 in cash and checks were missing from the cash register and a register tray in the grocery's office. The safe, in the same office, had not been opened.

"We teach our employees to cooperate with robbers in every way," manager Jack Smith said. "Lives are more valuable than anything we have in our store."

Yet something went wrong, and all three employees were killed. Wynn's management announced a $10,500 reward for information leading to the arrest of the suspects responsible for the murders.

Around 8:00 P.M. on July 3, Roger Collins called in a tip to the Edmond police crimestopper line. Collins told police that he knew who had committed the robbery and murders at Wynn's IGA, and that he knew the location of the murder weapon. Collins was brought into the police station and interviewed by detectives. He told them that his roommate Billy Ray Fox had admitted involvement in the crime to his two other roommates, Chris Glazner and Roger's brother, Jimmy Collins. When police interviewed Glazner and Jimmy Collins, they said that at approximately 2:30 the previous morning, Fox and Mark Fowler had borrowed two shotguns from them. When Fox returned around seven that morning, he brought back one of the shotguns, saying, "I fucked up, man. I killed some people." Fox and Glazner then went into the living room and turned on the television, where they saw a news bulletin concerning the Wynn's IGA murders. Fox said, "That's what it's about. I killed two of them. Then I killed the third one. I hit him over the head with a gun." Fox apologized for breaking the shotgun that his roommate had lent him and said he would replace it. He also said that Fowler had stabbed the third victim. He asked his roommates to vouch for him as an alibi.

Shortly after midnight on July 4, the nineteen-year-old Fox was arrested as he approached his pickup truck outside his residence. When he saw police coming toward him, he handed a companion a wad of cash. In the bed of Fox's truck, police found bloody splinters from the broken stock of a shotgun, along with the gun's forestock and two spent shell casings. A T-shirt was found in the cab of the truck that had bloodstains consistent with a knife being wiped clean on it. Later the next morning, Fox told police where to find a white purse that contained checks taken from Wynn's IGA. He also told them where he had hidden a knife that was later proved to be consistent with Barrier's wounds. The shotgun barrel was found hidden beneath some debris in Fox's backyard.

Fox had worked at the Wynn's IGA as a night stock clerk from December 1983 until he was fired in January 1985. He did not have a criminal record. After the robbery and murders, he had gone on a shopping spree at Quail Springs Mall, buying clothes and jewelry.

Twenty-year-old Mark Fowler was arrested the same night at his girlfriend's apartment, where they had just finished throwing a party with beer and steaks taken from the supermarket. Fowler still had a wad of cash on him when police took him into custody. Three years prior, he had been convicted of car theft and credit card fraud and sentenced to eighteen months in prison. He also had pleaded guilty to five counts of forcible oral sodomy that took place while he was in county jail.

During taped police interrogations following their arrests, both Fox and Fowler admitted they were at the scene but blamed each other for the murders. Both of them said the plan had been originated by Fox. Fowler was to enter the store, pretending to be a shopper, and signal to Fox, who would be waiting outside, when the employees were in the back room. Fox, who thought he could get into the safe, would then enter the store unnoticed and take the money. From there, the two suspects' stories went in different directions. Fox said that Fowler forced the three employees into the back room at gunpoint. As Fox gathered money from the cash registers, he heard a gunshot and headed toward the storeroom. When he arrived there, he heard another shot. Then he saw Fowler beat Barrier with the shotgun.

Fowler told police that Fox had been carrying the shotgun. The employees recognized their former colleague. "I haven't seen you in a while, Bill," Fowler remembered one of the employees saying. Fox then herded them into the back storeroom. Fowler said he stayed outside the storeroom until he heard two shots. When he entered the storeroom, he saw the bodies on the floor.

"I freaked out, man," Fowler told police. "It was over with. Them people were gone. There was no reason for them people to die. Kinda like I got set up in this deal."

Mark's father, Jim Fowler, is the son of a law enforcement official and a devout Catholic. Jim Fowler believed that criminals should pay for their crimes. But in this case he was torn between his sense of justice and love for his son.

Mark Fowler admitted helping to plan and carry out the robbery but claimed that he hadn't killed anybody. Jim believed him. He knew his son would go to prison. He just wanted to save the boy's life.

When an accomplice in an armed robbery that results in murder can be reasonably eliminated as the killer, and he agrees to testify against the other suspects, it is common practice to reduce the sentence sought against the cooperating witness. If life without parole is sought for the other suspects, you might cut a deal for life with the possibility of parole. In a death penalty crime, this is very powerful leverage to ensure a conviction, not just against the killer but also against the cooperating suspect, who will plead out and therefore avoid a trial. Even if the law gives the prosecutor the power to charge every suspect with the death penalty, it's counterproductive, even unjust, to seek the death penalty against each suspect. When a cosuspect is used as a witness for the prosecution, the state has an eyewitness to the entire crime, including its planning and execution.

In most states, the act of engaging in felony that results in murder is grounds for first-degree murder. In California, this is called the "felony murder rule." Oklahoma has a similar law. If a suspect is involved in the felony, he can be charged with the murder, even if he was not directly responsible for it. The California law was often used as an inducement for accomplices to roll on their cosuspects. In the case of Fox and Fowler, Bob Macy used it to get two death sentences for a single crime.

Even if Mark Fowler was involved in the death of John Barrier, a plea deal with Fowler would have ensured a death sentence against Billy Ray Fox. Most of the evidence pointed against Fox as both the instigator of the robbery plot and the killer of at least two of the victims. If Macy had cut a deal with Mark Fowler, he could have saved himself a lot of trouble. Yet he never seemed to consider it.

Initially Fox and Fowler were going to be tried separately. Two weeks before Fox's trial was to begin, both his trial and Fowler's, which was to start immediately after Fox's, were delayed because Joyce Gilchrist was late in finishing her forensic testing and sending it to the defense on discovery. Once Joyce Gilchrist did finish her lab reports, Macy asked for the trials to be joined. Macy said that hair evidence was "real important" because it placed both defendants in the back storeroom.

Because the two suspects had mutually antagonistic defenses, it would make sense to try them separately. But Bob Macy wanted one trial.

"It really doesn't make much difference from a legal standpoint which one did what because they're both guilty on all counts of murder in the first degree if they were there and participated in any way. Or even if they knew in advance that this was going to happen," Bob Macy said.

Macy argued that a joint trial would save time and money. And he said that if the trials were held separately, the second trial might have a change of venue because of publicity surrounding the first. Judge David Cook ruled that Fox and Fowler would be tried together.

"The defendants are entitled to a fair trial, not a perfect one," Judge Cook said, setting their trial date for less than a month later.

In an editorial, the *Oklahoman* applauded Judge Cook's decision: "One of the glaring flaws in our criminal justice system is the amount of nitpicking over minute legal technicalities which contribute to inordinate trial delays and, on appeal, often result in reversals of trial court verdicts or orders for new trials."

Whether or not a defendant in a criminal case is going to be tried individually or with an alleged accomplice is hardly a minute technicality. By refusing to sever the cases, Judge Cook severely handicapped both Fowler's and Fox's ability to present effective defenses.

After being told the defendants would be tried together, Fowler's and Fox's attorneys had less than a month to prepare a new defense. The only defense available to each defendant was that the other had committed the killings. While state law required only that they knowingly participate in a felony that resulted in death in order to be convicted of murder in the first degree, there was a chance that, if their trials had been severed, one of the defendants would have been able to effectively argue that he was not directly responsible for the killings and maybe get a life sentence instead of death.

At the time, life without parole was not available in Oklahoma. Under a straight life sentence the inmate could be eligible for parole after a period of as short as seven years. The Oklahoma Pardon and Parole Board would never release an inmate convicted of participating in a brutal murder after only seven years. However remote, that possibility did exist, according to the law. This was a situation that Macy worked to his advantage in pursuing the death penalty. An Oklahoma jury had to choose between the death penalty and what they knew could be only a seven-year sentence (Macy and his assistant DAs had pounded this issue into the public consciousness through a series of speeches and media comments). The Wynn's IGA murders had happened almost in his own backyard. Macy wanted two death penalties, and he was determined to get them.

Billy Ray Fox was defended by Opio Toure and Tim Wilson. Mark Fowler's lawyer was Jim Rowan, then with the public defender's office. This was Rowan's first capital case. Jim Rowan has gone on to become an experienced capital trial attorney. Yet when he defended Mark Fowler, according to one observer, "Rowan didn't know shit from apple butter."

The defense attorneys agreed on what they called "a mutual nonaggression pact." Even though both defendants had already blamed the other in taped statements to the police, their lawyers decided not to offer any evidence, testimony, or arguments that the other defendant was responsible for the killings. This way, Macy's tactic of trying Fowler and Fox together effectively cut the legs out from under their defense.

Statements by both Fowler and Fox had already placed them both at the crime scene with the intent of robbing the store.

"We decided," Macy said later, "that we could successfully prosecute both of them without using their statements to police."

If Macy did use the defendants' statements, he would have had to include their claims that the other had been the killer. Without the statements, Macy needed to link both defendants to the murders themselves. Not only were Fowler's and Fox's defenses antagonistic, but most of the evidence pointed toward Billy Ray Fox as the killer. Fox's statement (reported thirdhand by his roommate) that Fowler had stabbed Barrier was the only evidence linking Fowler to any of the murders. In order to get the death penalty for both defendants, Bob Macy would have to place the two of them in the back room at the time the murders were committed.

Enter Joyce Gilchrist.

Gilchrist had been able to find hair evidence that, according to her analysis, not only put both suspects in the back storeroom when the murders were committed but also put them "in close contact" with the victims at that same time. This was 1986, before Gilchrist had been contradicted by defense experts or criticized by appellate courts for giving such testimony.

At trial, Gilchrist testified that four scalp hairs consistent with Fowler's were found on Barrier's shirt. Another scalp hair that Gilchrist matched to Fowler's was found inside a spring that had broken off the shotgun and lodged beneath Barrier's body. Gilchrist matched a bloody hair stuck to a ring on Barrier's finger to Billy Ray Fox's.

As a result of this hair evidence, Gilchrist concluded that in her opinion, "Mark Fowler and Bill Fox were in contact with John Barrier prior to death."

As Macy had indicated before the trial, the hair evidence was crucial to placing both defendants at the murder scene. But did it prove that both men were responsible for the killings?

The defense hired Skip Palenik, a forensic scientist from Chicago, as an expert witness. Palenik examined the hairs that Gilchrist had matched to both defendants'. At trial, Palenik testified that the unknown hairs found on Barrier's body that Gilchrist had matched to Mark Fowler's "could be from the suspect or the victim equally." Palenik also disagreed with Gilchrist's conclusion that the hair found on Barrier's ring came from Billy Ray Fox. Gilchrist admitted that her hair analysis had been rushed.

In addition to Gilchrist's hair testimony, Macy presented a blood expert who testified that examinations showed blood present on the clothes worn by both defendants on the night of the murders. These tests, the expert admitted, were presumptive and not conclusive. Not only could he not link the blood to any of the victims, but he could not even determine conclusively whether the blood was human or animal.

Tom Bevel of the OCPD testified as an expert in blood spatter analysis. Bevel reconstructed the crime scene following the state's theory that both Fowler and Fox had been present in the back storeroom and involved in the murder. Fox was alleged to have shot Case and Chaowasin and beaten Barrier with the shotgun. Fowler was alleged to have stabbed Barrier nine times. (The knife had been found in Fox's possession and the T-shirt with bloodstains indicating that it had been used to wipe the knife clean was found in his pickup truck.) On cross-examination, Bevel conceded that it was possible, although not probable, that one person could have committed all three murders. He also said that he had based much of his analysis on the presumptive blood tests on the defendants' clothing that was not conclusive as to the origin or even the nature of the blood.

Blood spatter analysis is a very complex forensic science. A small miscalculation or misreading of the evidence can result in a severely flawed crime scene reconstruction. Because the science relies on fluid dynamics and trajectory, a series of complicated equations is necessary to come up with a final analysis that is, even when done correctly, only a theory and not a scientific fact. While blood spatter analysis can be useful in crime scene reconstruction during an investigation or at trial to show a more vivid picture of how the crime occurred, it cannot be used to prove guilt, as Macy did in this trial.

Other than Skip Palenik, the defense called no other witnesses during the guilt phase of the trial. In what they described as a "tactical move" Wilson and Toure declined to make a closing argument. In his closing argument, Rowan abrogated the "mutual nonaggression pact," telling jurors that Fox alone was responsible for the murders.

After two hours of deliberation, the jury found Fowler and Fox each guilty on three counts of first-degree murder. In retrospect, Fox's defense attorneys admitted that they had not expected an acquittal.

"We knew this is where we were going to be," Tim Wilson said after the verdict. He said that the next day, during the penalty phase, was when "the real struggle begins."

Jim Rowan had a little more fight in him, but he also knew that the real challenge would be to save his client's life.

Just before Macy went into the courtroom for closing arguments during the penalty phase, he saw Billy Ray Fox's dad in the hallway. Sam Fox was a local firefighter. He and Macy had become friends over the course of the trial, even though Macy was seeking to execute Fox's son.

"I'd rather you not go in there," Macy told Sam Fox. "I'm going to say some pretty bad things about your son."

"You've got a job to do," Fox replied. "Go in there and do it."

Defense witnesses testified that when he wasn't high on drugs, Billy Ray Fox was a shy, polite, and hardworking young man. A former girlfriend cried as she described breaking up with Fox "because he was changing, he was getting into drugs."

Sam Fox took the stand and pleaded for his son's life.

"I love my son. I know he's done wrong and needs to be punished. The only thing I could ask is not to put him to death."

"Let the carnage end. Choose life," Jim Rowan urged the jury when his turn came to argue on behalf of Mark Fowler.

During his closing arguments, Macy told the jury to ignore any mitigating circumstances: "Why these defendants are what they are may be a good field of research, but it's no mitigation or justification for what they did."

"If this isn't a crime that deserves the death penalty," Macy said in conclusion, "I don't know what is."

Following a deliberation of three hours, the jury gave Mark Andrew Fowler and Billy Ray Fox the death penalty.

Shortly after Fowler and Fox were sentenced to death, a mail carrier walked into the Edmond Post Office and shot fourteen of his coworkers dead and wounded seven others. Bob Macy was at this crime scene, too, but he wasn't able to prosecute Patrick Henry Sherrill, who concluded one of the worst mass murders in this nation's history by shooting himself to death.

In 1994, Jim Fowler's son Jimbo died in a motorcycle accident. Mark and Jimbo had both been adopted. Their adoptive mother died when both boys were teenagers.

"Mark knew his biological mother had abandoned him," Jim Fowler said. "Then the only mother he knew died."

Jim Fowler had remarried in 1980. Immediately after Mark's conviction Jim and Ann Fowler could not bring themselves to visit him at McAlester.

"You can't imagine"—Jim broke down sobbing—"how you feel when your baby boy has been convicted of something like that and you feel so shameful, it just kills you."

Jim and Ann Fowler came to accept the fact that their son had been involved in a homicide and sentenced to death. They began to visit Mark regularly and got involved in his appeals process, both hoped that once the case got out of the state courts, Mark might have his sentence reduced.

The Court of Criminal Appeals upheld both Fowler's and Fox's convictions in separate decisions. However, in the Fox decision the court noted that while Joyce Gilchrist had "admitted that an individual could not be positively identified by hair evidence . . . she went on to testify that '[in] her opinion . . . Mark Fowler and Bill Fox were in contact with John Barrier prior to death." The court noted that this opinion lacked scientific weight, but since Skip Palenik had been called as a witness by the defense, there was no reversible error.

Sometimes Gilchrist would qualify her statements about hair, saying only that she could not exclude the defendant; other times she would testify that hairs were an absolute match. Many who have studied her testimony over the years have been unable to determine why she would testify differently in different cases.

David Prater, who handled the DA's internal investigation of Gilchrist, said that in some cases Gilchrist would be asked by the prosecutor whether she could say the hairs were a definite match, and she would answer no. In other cases, however, she would not be asked these specific questions by the prosecution, and she would not add any qualifiers to her statements.

Years later, when Captain Byron Boshell asked Gilchrist about the problems with her testimony in the Fowler and Fox case, she blamed Bob Macy.

"I did give my opinion," Gilchrist said, "based on the results of my examination of the evidence that both defendants (Fox [and]

Fowler) were in direct contact with the victim. Although it was deemed inappropriate conduct by the Court of Criminal Appeals, I was merely responding to the prosecutor's questions."

In January 2000 the Tenth Circuit Court upheld Fox's and Fowler's convictions. In a concurring opinion, Judge David Ebel criticized Macy for improperly linking Fowler to Fox's confession but stated that there was still "strong independent evidence of Mr. Fowler's participation in the crimes." Therefore, Macy's error "though improper, did not render the trial fundamentally unfair."

After the Tenth Circuit affirmed Fowler's and Fox's convictions, the U.S. Supreme Court declined to hear their case.

With all their appeals exhausted, Fowler and Fox now waited for their execution dates. Attorney General Drew Edmondson asked the Court of Criminal Appeals to set the executions on the same day, to "save the victims' families from having to endure this trauma twice." The court declined and gave them separate dates, two days apart. Mark Fowler was scheduled to die on January 23, 2001. Billy Ray Fox would die on January 25.

Did Mark Fowler deserve the death penalty? It's hard for me to judge because of my conversations with Jim Fowler and the sympathy I feel for him. Trying to be as objective as possible, I would have to say that the evidence doesn't prove Fowler was directly involved in the murder, and although his involvement in the robbery might have constituted a murder committed during the act of a felony, this seems to me to be a narrow reading of the law. The investigating detectives could have corroborated (or disproved) Fowler's claim that he did not directly participate in the murders. Using Gilchrist's hair evidence and Bevel's crime scene reconstruction, the detectives might feel that they did prove Fowler's involvement. I am not convinced. They could have offered Fowler a polygraph and used those results (pass or fail) as a way to help Bob Macy decide whether or not Fowler should be tried for first-degree murder. A polygraph could have helped determine Fowler's intent—whether he planned to participate in the robbery without any thought of murder, or whether he had gone into that supermarket ready to kill. If he could convince me that he did not have intent to kill, I would recommend to a DA that Mark Fowler be charged with armed robbery and as an accessory to murder.

While awaiting his clemency hearing, Mark Fowler said that he hoped the governor would reduce his sentence to life without parole.

"We would have been happier than hell if he had been given life without parole," Jim Fowler said. "I told people, goddamnit, if I ever get Mark off death row, I'll kill him myself."

More than two hundred of Mark Fowler's family, friends, and supporters showed up for his clemency hearing. Because of space limitations, only sixty-two were allowed inside the room. At the hearing, some of Oklahoma's top Roman Catholic clergymen pleaded for Fowler's life.

"I am totally sorry for my role in this tragedy," Mark Fowler said when his turn came to speak. "I never, ever planned to be part of a murder."

Family members of the murder victims got the last word.

"In my heart, I can't forgive these boys," said Frank Cast, brother of Rick. "After the executions, maybe I can start to forgive them."

By a vote of four to zero, the board denied Fowler clemency. Fox did not seek a clemency hearing.

Jim and Ann Fowler spent the entire last week at McAlester visiting Mark.

"One day we were kept waiting for about an hour and a half," Jim remembered. When Mark finally showed up on the other side of the visitors' window, Jim was angry. He asked where Mark had been.

"Pop, I've just received the last rites of the church and made my last confession and took communion."

Jim remembers the look on Mark's face was "beautiful." There was a glow coming from him. "It passed over us and we felt better because he felt better."

Fowler's last confession was private. Previously, his uncle Father Greg Gier, a Catholic priest, had asked Mark point-blank whether he had killed anybody and Mark said no. Jim believes his son was telling the truth.

"You don't lie on your deathbed," Jim said. "If you have any fear of God at all, you're going to come clean."

Mark had told his father that he didn't want him to watch the execution, but Jim felt that, in truth, Mark wanted him there.

"No son is going to ask his dad to watch the state kill him," Jim said. Mark had told his father that the guards and administrators at the prison didn't like him. But Jim found out this wasn't true. "He had made some friends with the people who worked there, he hadn't caused them any trouble, but it was their job to kill him," Jim said.

"I said, 'Boy, if you were dying from any other cause, cancer or AIDS or a car wreck or anything, I'd be beside you,' " Jim told me. "I would not abandon him. I would not leave him there to go through that moment of his life alone."

Although witnessing his son's execution was the most painful moment of his life, Jim Fowler said that he would "do it again tomorrow, because Mark needed us. And I don't think I could look myself in the mirror again had I not gone down there."

When he told me this, I said it was very brave.

"It's not brave. It's what parents are for."

On the day of Mark's execution, Jim and Ann Fowler visited with him all day. For his last meal, Mark had a cheeseburger, a bacon cheeseburger, two orders of onion rings, a grilled chicken sandwich, and a cherry limeade.

Jim told his son that there were two hundred people outside the prison holding a candlelight vigil for him. Earlier that day, seven people had been arrested outside the offices of the Oklahoma Pardon and Parole Board for protesting the execution.

Before he said good-bye, Mark asked his father to put his hand on his head in the witness viewing room so that he would be able to recognize him through the glass. At 5:00 P.M. Mark made some last telephone calls. Then he was led into the execution chamber.

Jim and Ann Fowler sat in the front row of chairs. When the blinds came up, Jim saw his son lying on the gurney. Jim put his hand on his head. So did every other family member.

"Mark looked back and when he saw that, he settled down," Jim said.

Asked if he had any last words, Mark began to recite the Hail Mary. His family prayed along with him. Mark kept repeating the Hail Mary as the drugs rushed into his veins. Then he was silent. His head slumped down. His eyes closed. At 9:07 P.M. Mark Andrew Fowler was pronounced dead.

"In a way, Mark's death was beautiful," Jim said. During the fifteen years he waited to die, Mark had a chance to make his peace with everyone, particularly his family. "There was not one stone unturned. Not one 'I love you' that went unsaid."

Two days later, Billy Ray Fox was put on the gurney. When asked if he had any last words, Fox said, "No." He smiled at his family members, then his eyes went glassy. He looked up at the ceiling and his head slowly drooped. Billy Ray Fox was declared dead at 9:06 P.M.

Mark Fowler and Billy Ray Fox were both executed before the scandal surrounding Joyce Gilchrist broke. After the Gilchrist grand jury was convened, Fowler wrote a letter to the Office for U.S. Attorneys, offering to testify. He never heard back from them.

Before Mark was executed, Jim Fowler promised his son that he would devote the rest of his life to fighting the death penalty. Jim serves on the board of the Oklahoma Coalition Against the Death

Penalty and is involved in several lobbying campaigns to change Oklahoma statutes concerning the death penalty. He regularly participates in vigils and protests against state executions.

"I am against the death penalty forever more," Jim said. "That's a promise I made my son."

To speak with Jim Fowler and see the anguish and grief in his eyes is to see another side of the death penalty. Jim Fowler did nothing wrong, yet he is a victim.

A very warm, sincere, and friendly man, Jim Fowler has a sense of humor that has survived all the tragedies of his life. His love for his son is very evident, yet he never makes excuses for what Mark did. Several times when I spoke to him, he referred to Mark in the present tense, as if he were still alive. The pain Jim felt was still with him when we spoke. It will be with him always. Yet he is never bitter. He accepts what happened with grace and humility, as much as he wishes that it never occurred.

I hope that if something half as terrible happened to my family, I would be as brave as Jim Fowler. He has a courage that is rare and beautiful. It is the same courage that I have seen in Dorthy Moxley, whose fifteen-year-old daughter was killed, and her murder went unsolved for twenty-three years. It's not the courage of street brawls or gunfights; it's a moral courage—the ability to withstand the worst that can happen and not give in to hatred or despair.

Without trying to convince me that capital punishment was wrong, Jim Fowler made me look at it from a different perspective—that of a parent whose child faces death. The parents of the condemned follow each step of the trial and appellate process, all the way up to the day when their child is executed. The death is planned in great detail and well in advance. For the parents, the grief is drawn out over years and lasts a lifetime. There is no closure for Jim Fowler or any other family member of someone who has been executed. It remains a nightmare that never ends.

After I spoke to Jim Fowler, I wondered how I would react if my son were facing the death penalty. Would I be able to handle the anger, shame, pain, and grief? Before I had children myself, it was easy for me to say that the parents of criminals were to blame for the way their children turned out. I had ideas about what kind of behavior I would or would not tolerate as a parent. Now I realize that no matter what you do, no matter how hard you try, your children will become their own individual selves. All you can do is guide them, support them, and love them.

As parents, we try to keep our children safe, teach them responsibility, and help them become good people. And if they go wrong, we don't love them any less. I know that I would never abandon my son, no matter what he might do. I would forgive him, as Jim Fowler forgave Mark. And if I could forgive my own son, why can't I forgive someone else's son? That, for me, is the question at the core of the death penalty. It is a punishment of revenge, as final as any judgment can ever be, leaving no room for compassion or forgiveness.

When I was a cop, I only had compassion for the victims of crime. I could not allow myself to feel anything but contempt for those who were responsible. Jim Fowler helped me realize that it was possible to feel compassion even for criminals—which is right and necessary, yet only makes the rendering of justice more difficult.

CHAPTER NINE

HELPLESS VICTIMS

FOUR MONTHS AFTER HIS SON WAS SENTENCED TO DEATH, JIM FOWLER'S mother was raped and murdered in her Oklahoma City home.

The body of eighty-three-year-old Anna Fowler was found in her home on September 3, 1986. Fowler lived alone in a house on a corner lot in the Military Park neighborhood. The suspect had broken in through the back porch. He confronted Fowler in the kitchen, where there was a brief struggle. Then he took her into the bedroom, where he raped her and killed her by asphyxiation. Four of Fowler's ribs were broken. A piece of cloth was found near her body that could have been used as a gag. The motive appeared to be rape and not burglary. The house was not ransacked. Fowler's wedding band was still on her finger. Her purse was open and still contained twenty-nine dollars in cash, as well as her credit cards. Semen stains recovered from the crime scene later showed that the suspect was a type A secretor. Negroid hairs indicated that the suspect was black.

After the Fowler murder, the Military Park neighborhood experienced several other burglaries, rapes, robberies, and assaults. Then another elderly woman was found dead.

On January 11, 1987, the body of ninety-two-year-old Velma Cutler was discovered. She had been raped and murdered several days earlier in her home directly across the street from Anna Fowler's. After attempting to enter through several windows, the suspect broke in through the back door. Once inside the house, he raped Cutler and asphyxiated her. Cutler's ribs and her left arm were broken. A knotted sock found nearby could have been used as a gag. Once again, rape seemed to be the motive. The house had not been ransacked and there was no evidence of robbery. Semen stains indicated the suspect was a type A secretor. Several Negroid hairs were found.

One could safely assume that the Fowler and Cutler homicides were connected. The similarities in MO, as well as the blood and hair evidence, indicated that they were committed by the same man. The fact that the suspect was black and both victims were elderly white women who lived alone contributed to an atmosphere of fear among the neighborhood's white residents, many of them widows who lived alone.

Military Park was once a middle-class family neighborhood. As years went by the neighborhood became run-down and rife with crime. People moved out, but the older folks couldn't afford to leave or refused to give up their homes. This had to be a factor in the outrage of the public and the press. Maybe there was a hint of guilt also, that decent people let their aging parents live in a neighborhood that was no longer safe.

There is a brutality that goes beyond blood and broken bones in these two murders. The helplessness of the victims, raped and murdered in their own homes, where they should have been safe, added to the shock and outrage over these horrible crimes.

The media coverage was intense. So was the pressure to catch the killer. A task force of fourteen police officers swarmed all over Military Park, looking for a suspect. Black males seen in the neighborhood were stopped and interviewed by the police. After the Cutler murder, task force detectives began carrying mobile blood-typing kits, which they used to test the blood of men they had stopped. Undercover officers spent several nights hiding near the Cutler and Fowler houses, hoping that the suspect would return to the scene of the crime. One detective canvassing door to door was telling residents that the Fowler and Cutler murders were "carbon copies."

As long as the killer went free, the whole neighborhood remained on edge.

The task force assembled a list of 173 suspects. They interviewed forty men. At least twenty-three who submitted to the blood tests matched the ABO type of the suspect. One of them was Robert Lee Miller, an unemployed heating and air-conditioning worker who lived nine blocks from the Fowler and Cutler homes. Miller had been interviewed in the field twice before, first after the Fowler murder, then again once Cutler's body was found. His only prior record was a short jail term for unpaid tickets. On February 21, 1987, Miller was stopped for a third time. Detectives gave him a preliminary blood test and found he had the same blood type as the suspect. Miller was asked to come to the station. He agreed.

Detectives Jerry Flowers and Bob Woods asked Miller if he could help them solve the murders. Miller replied that he had special powers, sometimes he had visions. In fact, Miller said, he could see through the killer's eyes.

During the twelve hours that followed, Detectives Woods, Flowers, and Shupe performed an interrogation that is at the same time bizarre and terrifying. The videotape of the interrogation would be funny if one forgets that the man being interrogated was suspected of murder, and the detectives questioning him were intent on giving him the death penalty.

The detectives accused Miller of raping and killing both Fowler and Cutler. He repeatedly claimed that he was innocent. At one point, the interrogation was halted and Miller gave additional blood and hair samples. Once the interrogation was over, Miller was arrested and charged with two counts each of first-degree murder, rape, and burglary. He was also charged with rape by instrumentation for allegedly using a knife in the Cutler assault.

The day after Miller's arrest, Bob Macy said he would seek the death penalty. Macy wanted "to let the public know this man is in custody and the danger has been removed."

Miller was examined by a psychiatrist in order to determine whether he was competent to stand trial. These tests were ordered by Ron Evans, Miller's public defender. The psychiatrist, Dr. Larry Prater, determined that Miller was not mentally ill but would be a threat if released from custody without treatment.

In the preliminary hearing, Detective Flowers testified that Miller wanted to see a psychiatrist because he wasn't certain whether or not he had committed the murders. Testifying in his own defense at the prelim, Miller said he went to see Dr. Prater, "so that I can prove my innocence to everyone."

Robert Lee Miller is a strange man. Nearly everybody I spoke to told me that, and it's obvious from watching the video of his interrogation. But there are no indications that he is violent. I don't see how the detectives came to the conclusion so quickly that they had a serial homicidal rapist in front of them. Miller's demeanor throughout the interrogation shows no aggression whatsoever. He was so unthreatening the detectives did not search him when he came to the station. During the interrogation, he pulled out a pocket knife to demonstrate what kind of weapon the suspect might have used in the homicides. The detectives took the knife from him, but at no time did they perform a complete search to make sure he didn't have any other weapons. And they were clearly never in any physical danger themselves.

Prosecutors and the press were eager to blame Miller for all the other crimes occurring in Military Park. Miller had been a suspect in the killing of Ethyl Kaiser, the eighty-five-year-old widow of the Kaiser ice cream fortune. Miller talked about the Kaiser case during his interrogation, but he was eliminated when the police developed another suspect. Miller was also called "a very strong suspect" in the murder of Exie Lee Wilkerson, a seventy-five-year-old woman shot at a Christian Science Reading Room.

The MOs in the Kaiser and Wilkerson murders had little in common with the Cutler and Fowler cases. When Miller repeatedly mentioned the Kaiser homicide during his interrogation, this was one indication that he knew little about the Fowler and Cutler cases.

While those other accusations didn't stick, Miller was eventually accused of breaking into the home of Izabelle Lendvay early on Thanksgiving Day in 1986. The Lendvay charge was the only case in which there was any kind of a witness, although it wasn't actually an eyewitness. A nun had been watching from across the street and saw a black male attempt to break into the Lendvay home. She told another nun to call the police and described what she saw while the other nun was on the phone with emergency services. The nun who made the phone call did not witness the attempted break-in; yet she was the witness brought in to testify at trial.

The main evidence used to link Miller to the Fowler and Cutler murders included his blood type and secretor status, several hairs found at the Cutler scene, and his statements to detectives during the interrogation.

Three weak cases were bound together to make them more powerful than if the jury had considered them in isolation. It is unlikely that any one of the cases standing alone would have resulted in a conviction. And joining the three cases made it easier for Macy to ask for the death penalty.

The Fowler and Cutler crime scenes were processed by two different chemists. Janice Davis had worked the Fowler scene, while Joyce Gilchrist handled Cutler's. By the time the case went to trial, Davis had left the OCPD; she came back to testify. In their testimony, Davis and Gilchrist both stated that Miller's blood type and secretor status matched the semen stains found at their crime scenes. (Gilchrist also testified that a bloodstain from the Lendvay attempted break-in matched Miller's blood type, although further determinations, including secretor status, were impossible because the stain was dried.) Davis testified that after electrophoresis tests on the Fowler semen stain, she determined that 13 percent of the black population (or one in eight black males) could have been the donor. Davis didn't find any hairs that were microscopically similar to those of Robert Lee Miller. She stated that all the Negroid hairs found at the Fowler scene were fragments too short for meaningful comparison.

Electrophoresis tests, which identify blood enzymes and proteins and are distinct from ABO typing, found that Cutler and Miller shared the same PGM (1) marker. (Electrophoresis isolates different blood polymorphisms and their subtypes.) By comparison, Fowler had PGM (+2). Therefore, PGM (1) enzymes found in the Cutler semen stains could have been contributed by the victim, but those same enzymes from the Fowler evidence must have belonged to the suspect. Further enzyme testing showed that Cutler and Miller had a different PGM subtype, but Gilchrist testified that these subtypes were not retrievable from semen stains. Therefore, Gilchrist said she could not further narrow down the blood evidence based on electrophoresis of the semen stains.

Blood samples and semen stains from Miller were sent out to Atlanta, where Dr. Moses Schanfield performed allotyping, a form of identifying genetic markers in blood that is no longer used. In his testimony, all Schanfield could state with any certainty was that his analysis of the semen stains at the Cutler scene showed that Robert Lee Miller had the same allotype markers as the suspect, as well as 33 percent of the black male population. His tests from the Fowler scene were inconclusive.

Gilchrist had already determined that the blood characteristics shared by both Miller and the suspect belonged to 12 percent of the black male population. In order to make those numbers more convincing, Gilchrist took Schanfield's 33 percent figure and stated that one in thirty-six black males would have the same characteristics shared by both Miller and the suspect. Gilchrist got her math wrong—she multiplied twelve by three, rather than dividing, which would have resulted in 4 percent or one in twenty-five, not one in thirty-six. Even worse, she confused two separate tests that could not be used together to further reduce the possible donors. Allotyping, blood type, and enzyme markers are all exclusive; Gilchrist should not have combined them to make her numbers stronger.

Regarding hair evidence, Gilchrist testified that three scalp hair fragments and one pubic hair fragment were found on Cutler's neck. Although these fragments, according to Gilchrist's own testimony, were too small and damaged to make forensic comparisons, she noted that she saw "points of similarities" between Miller's hair and the evidentiary hairs. Three more scalp hair fragments were taken from Cutler's bedsheet. Gilchrist identified two of these as "consistent with Robert Lee Miller" despite the fact that they were fragments and without the disclaimer that they were too short and/or damaged to make forensic comparisons. Another scalp hair fragment found on the pillow was not suitable for forensic comparison but also "showed points of similarity of characteristics of Miller's hair."

Out of all the hair evidence that Gilchrist analyzed and testified about, she could not match a single full hair to Miller's. But that's not the impression she left with the jury. Joyce Gilchrist might have seen "points of similarity" with Miller's hair, or with any other black man's hair. And without explicitly stating it, she left the jury with the impression that these were Miller's hairs. What she should have said, and what Janice Davis said in her hair testimony, was that she could not include or exclude Robert Lee Miller based on any of the hairs available for comparison.

Gilchrist also testified that two Negroid scalp hairs from the Cutler scene were not consistent with Miller's. One hair was recovered from a sock beneath the covers on Cutler's bed. The other was a fragment found on the top sheet. She stated that she had eliminated eleven possible suspects by comparing their known hair to the hairs that she found suitable for forensic comparison. While Gilchrist could not determine to whom these hairs belonged, she could be certain that they were not Miller's.

Gilchrist then testified that two animal hairs found on the sheet used to remove Cutler's body were consistent with those from a rottweiler named Bear with whom Miller had frequent contact. Gilchrist admitted that animal hair comparisons were even less conclusive than those of humans, and also stated that she could not determine the species (I think she means breed) of dog. "I can't identify the species of a rabbit or the species of a horse," Gilchrist said at trial. "Certainly the breed of horses I can just say what kind of animal, you know, it is. That's it. And that's all I'm doing here. I'm not identifying any dog. I'm just saying it's consistent with Bear."

Again, Gilchrist offered qualifications of her evidentiary findings and then went on to testify as if she weren't bound by them. "The possibility of some other dog having the same characteristics as Bear—the dog Bear and the hair—in this case are the same as the possibility, you know, as far as I can say about a human's hair." (When she said this, she had just stated that animal hairs are not as determinative as human hairs.)

Her method of determining whether or not these animal hairs came from the dog in question was to compare them to known hairs from Bear and two other rottweilers. Macy later argued that 90 percent of the population could be excluded as possible suspects because they didn't come into contact with a dog like Bear.

By the time of Robert Lee Miller's trial in 1988, Gilchrist had already been publicly criticized for her testimony regarding hair evidence. Miller's attorney tried to introduce John Wilson's complaint and the resulting warning from the Southwestern Association of Forensic Scientists in order to impeach Gilchrist's credibility. Judge Charles Owens would not allow it.

Right across the hall from the courtroom where Robert Lee Miller was on trial for his life, Hayward Reed was being tried for rape and kidnapping. In the Reed case, Joyce Gilchrist had sent a blood sample from the defendant and the semen stain recovered from the crime scene to Lifecodes, a New York City laboratory specializing in the then-infant science of forensic DNA. Lifecodes's test results showed that one in sixty million people might share the same genetic characteristics as the rapist, and that Hayward Reed was one of them. Joyce Gilchrist presented this evidence at trial, which helped convict Reed, who was sentenced to serve ninety years.

Before the Miller trial, defense attorney Ron Evans asked Barry Albert about DNA tests and was told they were too expensive. Also, Evans had heard Gilchrist testify in another trial that DNA testing was cost-prohibitive. When he finally contacted Lifecodes, Evans discovered that the lab charged $300 per stain tested, in addition to a witness fee of $2,500 plus expenses.

Miller's defense had already spent $2,900 to have Brian Wraxall test the blood and semen evidence, and there was no more money in the budget for further tests or expert witnesses, so Evans offered to pay for DNA testing out of his own pocket. He moved for a continuance of the trial to do so, but Judge Owens denied his request. Later in the trial, when Evans was trying to cross-examine Gilchrist about why DNA testing was not done in the Miller case, the judge sustained assistant DA Ray Elliot's objection to that line of questioning. The lawyers approached the bench, and Evans said all he wanted to do was find out why the state didn't perform DNA testing in the Miller case.

Macy responded: "Your honor, this is a process which became available in only the fairly recent past. There is one laboratory in the United States that does it. It is financially prohibitive for us to submit all our cases to have that kind of testing. It's not practical. It is not a test that's available to us."

Macy was arguing that DNA was cost-prohibitive in this case, where a man was on trial for his life. Meanwhile, across the hall, Barry Albert was trying a rape case with DNA evidence that Joyce Gilchrist had sent out for testing.

Macy also complained that the defense attorney was "making it look like we haven't done our job."

When Evans protested, the judge threatened him with a fine and/or jail time for contempt.

Evans requested that he be able to ask Joyce Gilchrist whether DNA testing could have been done in the Miller case (a question she had already answered in the affirmative out of court). Then Evans wanted to ask her why the semen stains from both crime scenes were not submitted to DNA testing. The judge refused to let him question Gilchrist about DNA.

Joyce Gilchrist was only one part of the prosecution's case. The other major piece of evidence presented by Bob Macy and his assistant Ray Elliot was a nine-hour videotape of the twelve-hour interrogation of Robert Lee Miller. They played the videotape for the jury and had Detective Jerry Flowers testify about the interrogation.

Prior to showing the videotaped interrogation to the jury, Judge Owens stated that in those tapes, Miller "expressly denies" committing the crimes, and they are "certainly not a confession, and not admissions of anything except that he's seen this person in his dreams or visions."

During an early part of the interrogation, Miller said that he sometimes had dreams and visions that demons were out to get him. Flowers wrote a note to Detective Bob Woods, telling him to get a hold of the homicide detectives and have them start videotaping the interview. "I felt as though Mr. Miller was going to say something that might only the killer would know," Flowers testified.

A close examination of the videotape and the trial transcript shows that Miller knew very little about the crimes.

Miller's responses to the detective's direct questions were rambling and incoherent. He talked about people who were trying to get him, steal his tools, beat him up, frame him for a crime. At several points when the detectives asked him questions about the Fowler and Cutler murders, he responded with his own personal beefs with other people. When pressed about details of those specific crimes, he would talk about the Kaiser murder, or something else that happened in the neighborhood.

The detectives asked Miller to look through the eyes of the suspect and tell them what he saw. Miller's answers—when he gave answers—were either derived from rumors that were rampant around the neighborhood (some of them accurate, others not) or based on information he got from the newspapers and television, or they were simple guesses, often following the prompts of the detectives interrogating him. For example, the detectives asked Miller what the killer had left behind. He described a series of personal items and clothing. When he said "underwear," the detectives said, "Tell us more about the underwear."

"Tell us more" was a cue that meant you've got it right. If Miller guessed wrong, they would say "What else?" That was a cue meaning you haven't got it right yet, guess again.

When they asked Miller where the killer found Anna Fowler, he mentioned just about every room in the house, including the kitchen. After a break, they resumed the interrogation by saying, "Earlier, you were telling us that she was in the kitchen." Miller suggested maybe she was eating dinner, washing dishes, cleaning up, putting food away. The detectives jumped on the fact that Miller had mentioned the possibility that Fowler had been putting food away when the suspect confronted her.

Cutler's vagina had been torn during the attack. Until a week prior to trial, the detectives believed that a knife was used. Then the medical examiner established that it was a blunt instrument (possibly the suspect's penis) that had caused the trauma. During the interview, the detectives still thought it was a knife. When Miller said something about the killer using a knife in the victim's vagina, the detectives keyed in on this detail—which wasn't true. This isn't an example of "something only the killer would know." It's something only the detectives would know.

The detectives invoked God and tried to ward off Satan. "Get back in that corner, Satan!" Detective Woods shouted several times, waving his hand as if to dispel evil spirits. Woods took a Bible out of his pocket and told Miller to keep his hand on it in order to bring him visions. At one point Flowers put Miller's hand on the Bible and told him he couldn't lie to God.

"My Father, Lord in Heaven, God of all Gods," Miller said, "let them know I did not do this and if I did, let me speak now."

When they weren't praying together silently, much of the interrogation consisted of the detectives trying to get Miller to say something, anything. It's not that he was uncooperative, he just didn't know anything. Maybe he was genuinely trying to help solve the murders, maybe he wanted to be in a warm place for a few hours, where he would be fed and given cigarettes. But if I were a detective investigating a double homicide/rape, I would have kicked him out of the interview room after about five minutes.

Using the interrogation tape and transcript, Bob Macy and Ray Elliot argued that Miller knew several facts that only the killer would know. None of these "facts" stand up as proof of personal and independent knowledge of the crimes. And the prosecutors didn't talk about all the times that Miller guessed wrong. He had said that the victims weren't very old; that one of them had been shot; that the other had been stabbed; that the suspect had taken several valuable items; that they had been severely beaten. These wrong guesses clearly show that Miller did not know anything more about the crimes than anyone else who lived in Military Park at the time. Detective Flowers explained these discrepancies away by claiming that Miller was just trying to "muddy the waters" with false information.

An accurate written transcript of the interrogation would be impossible to produce. The audio on the tape is frequently inaudible, and Miller has a tendency to mumble. The detectives took full advantage of this. During the trial, Flowers testified that Miller had referred to the killer as "I" or "me" seven times. No certified transcript has been made of the interrogation, and not even the police transcript, filled with countless inaccuracies, was provided to the jury in order to confirm Flowers's statement.

One defense attorney I spoke to called Jerry Flowers "a maniac" and said the interrogation tape "looks exactly like a *Saturday Night Live* skit. It's just nonsense." But, he said, if you present it to an Oklahoma County jury, show it to them just once, and tell them it's a confession, they'll see it that way.

"The Miller interrogation was pathetic," said Jamie Pybas, a defense attorney with the Oklahoma Indigent Defense System who specializes in capital appeals. "Unfortunately, that's the kind of stuff that gets people sent to death row in Oklahoma."

In his closing argument, Macy called the interrogation "a classic confrontation between two very skilled police officers and a very streetwise Cajun criminal."

After several hours of interrogation, the detectives asked Miller to take them to the crime scenes. Miller showed them the Cutler house but could not find the Fowler house, even though it was directly across the street. Then Miller took them to the Lendvay house, where the attempted break-in had occurred. Miller remembered the Cutler house because it had been sealed with crime scene tape until just prior to his interrogation. The detectives said that Miller pointed out several items, including the point of entry, glass from a broken window stacked inside a trash can, the breaker box where the electricity had been turned off, and pry marks on a window where the suspect might have attempted another point of entry. All of these observations, according to Detective Shupe, were things only the suspect would know. Some of them had not been previously noted by detectives or forensic investigators. It could be that Robert Lee Miller was simply more observant than those who were investigating the crimes.

At trial, Steven Dale Hall, a convicted felon in custody, testified that shortly before the Fowler murder, Miller told him he was tired of being broke and was going to rob an old lady in the neighborhood.

Detectives stated that Miller wore the same brand and size of Fruit of the Loom jockey shorts as the suspect, who left the elastic waistband of his underwear at the Fowler crime scene.

Miller took the stand in his own defense.

"I told them I had a vision from the Lord," Miller said, explaining why he spoke to the detectives. "An angel came to me. I assume it was my grandmother warning me someone was trying to frame me."

"Did you do any of these things they've got you accused of?" Evans asked Miller.

"No, I didn't, sir."

Then it was Bob Macy's turn to cross-examine the witness. Macy went through several of the details from Miller's interrogation, often switching from third to second person in describing the suspect.

Q: *You said that after killing Mrs. Cutler you laid her back in the bed and covered her up. How did you know that, Mr. Miller?*
A: *I did not know that. I just—I told the detectives from the get go that I didn't know if any of it was true but I will try to help them.*
Q: *You stated that the second rape/murder was worse than the first, that he sexually abused her. How did you know that?*
A: *From the nightmares I had, from hearing these horrible things.*
Q: *Your nightmares or theirs, Mr. Miller?*

Sometimes Miller corrected Macy.

Q: *You said that the killer tried to slip up behind Mrs. Fowler in the kitchen but she seen you and there was a fight and he drug her into the bedroom. How did you know that?*
A: *I didn't say that he seen—she seen me. I said that from the nightmare I had that she seen the person and they had a fight.*

Macy hammered away at Miller, but from the transcript it seems that the witness held up pretty well. How it looked in court is something else entirely.

Q: *In the final tape you told Jerry Flowers the killer doesn't like white girls but he wants to have sex with them. Mr. Miller, are you talking about the killer or are you talking about Robert Lee Miller, or are Robert Lee Miller and the killer one and the same person?*
A: *I'm not talking about myself. From the things that I had gathered from the murders, I just assumed that the killer didn't like white women. But I'm not, you know, prejudiced in any kind of way.*

I'm—I treat everybody equal, no matter what race, creed or color. Some of my best friends are white people.

Q: *Mr. Miller, after what you did to those old ladies, don't you think it's natural you'd have nightmares?*

A: *No, I wouldn't, sir.*

MR. MACY: *Pass the witness.*

A: *I don't know why I had the particular nightmare at the time because, you know, I was just a little shook up because the police were coming up to me like they were—you know, I was one of the criminals or something, you know.*

MR. MACY: *I have no further questions of this witness, Judge.*

Ron Evans did not ask his client any further questions on redirect.

At the end of the trial Bob Macy delivered, in the words of Lee Ann Peters, an OIDS lawyer who represented Robert Lee Miller on appeal, "what perhaps was one of the most outrageous first-stage closing arguments ever given in Oklahoma County."

Macy attempted to demonstrate the mathematical impossibility of Miller's innocence. He said that if you took all of the people in the state of Oklahoma and divided them by sex, then race, then blood type, then age, then approximate height, then people familiar with the Military Park neighborhood, then those who wear a baseball hat at night, then those who carry a knife, then those who have dirty, brittle hair that breaks easily into little pieces, then those who have regular contact with a dog whose hair was microscopically consistent with Bear the rottweiler's and wear Fruit of the Loom jockey shorts—they would find that only one person shared all of these characteristics: Robert Lee Miller.

After ninety-five minutes of deliberation, the jury convicted Robert Lee Miller on all seven charges. During the penalty phase, a young couple testified that one morning while they were delivering newspapers in the Military Park neighborhood, they were robbed by a black man wearing a bandanna over his face and an "Indiana Jones"–style hat. Nine months after the robbery, when the couple saw Robert Lee Miller on television and identified as the suspect in the Fowler and Cutler murders, they believed he was the man who had robbed them.

Another witness testified that someone had attempted to break into the house where he lived with his seventy-four-year-old grandmother not far from the Cutler and Fowler houses. Joyce Gilchrist testified that two hairs taken from the windowsill of that house were microscopically consistent with Robert Lee Miller's.

During their closing arguments in the penalty phase, Macy and Elliot argued that the murders were "heinous, atrocious and cruel," that they were committed to avoid prosecution, and that the probability existed that Robert Lee Miller would commit future acts of violence. The jury agreed. After two hours of deliberation, they gave Miller two death sentences. On the other charges, Miller got 725 years.

Once the verdict was read, Miller said, "I want to ask a special prayer for the jurors, for they know not what they've done."

After having watched a jury condemn his own son to death row, Jim Fowler attended Robert Lee Miller's trial, where he saw the man convicted of raping and killing his mother sentenced to death. As he exited the courtroom, Jim Fowler saw a man with a stunned look on his face sitting by the aisle. It was the defendant's father. Jim placed his arm on Mr. Miller's shoulder and said, "I know exactly how you feel." Mr. Miller looked up at Jim Fowler, yet said nothing. When Robert Lee Miller was sent to death row, he was kept segregated from Mark Fowler, because of fears that Mark might retaliate against Miller for killing his grandmother.

"I don't know what the death penalty solves," Jim Fowler told the press later that day. "He's off the street. He's not going to hurt anybody anymore. Let that be the end of it. There's got to be a better answer than killing people."

Detectives Jerry Flowers, Bob Woods, David Shupe, and Bill Citty, as well as Joyce Gilchrist, all received certificates of achievement for their work in the Cutler and Fowler cases.

"The detectives will tell you that they are proud of the Miller case, particularly the interrogation, because they got a conviction," Bob Ravitz told me. Ravitz believes that after the interrogation, the detectives went to Joyce Gilchrist and told her to check Miller's known hair against the unknowns recovered from the Cutler crime scene because they had just got a confession from him.

"Why would the detectives do this?" I asked Ravitz.

"Because they knew Joyce would take care of Miller."

One ex–homicide detective confirmed that was possible. "Joyce would have gotten that information if she asked for it," Bob Bemo told me. "And she probably did."

Lee Ann Peters handled Miller's appeal. During the research for this book, I read scores of appeal briefs, and Peters's brief in the Miller case stood out. It was clear, elegantly written, and convincing. Instead of relying on legal minutiae, or throwing out hundreds of unrelated and inconsequential arguments, Peters's brief simply argued that her client was an innocent man, railroaded by cops, chemists, and prosecutors who felt they had to convict and execute someone, anyone, for the Fowler and Cutler murders.

Peters examined the evidence, including the Fruit of the Loom jockey shorts. The waistband found at the Fowler crime scene was obviously longer than a similar waistband taken from Robert Lee Miller's underwear. In their closing arguments, Macy and Elliot had both explained this discrepancy by saying that the waistband was completely stretched out. Peters measured the two waistbands herself and found that the crime scene waistband could be stretched out from twenty-nine to fifty-three inches. The waistband taken from Robert Lee Miller's shorts could be stretched out from its original twenty-four inches to only forty-two inches.

The strongest argument in Peters's appeal was the fact that there was another suspect in the Fowler and Cutler homicides. This man had pleaded guilty to two similar rapes of elderly women. These victims had not died, but in every other way these crimes were identical to those for which Miller had been convicted. Peters argued that this man, Ronnie Lott, was an even better suspect than Robert Lee Miller.

The appeal was denied, but the Robert Lee Miller case wasn't over yet.

CHAPTER TEN

THE WRONG MAN

WHEN ROBERT LEE MILLER WAS ARRESTED, BOB MACY ANNOUNCED THAT "the danger has been removed."

Shortly before the trial, Ron Evans, Miller's defense attorney, told one of the detectives, "You've got the wrong man."

"If we've got the wrong man," the detective replied, "then how come the crimes have stopped?"

In fact, the crimes had not stopped. In March 1987 seventy-four-year-old Grace Marshall was raped by a black man. Marshall, who was white, lived alone in Military Park, not far from the Fowler and Cutler homes. Outside her house, the cover of the fuse box had been torn off and all the breakers turned off. The suspect had broken in the back door, gagged the victim with a piece of cloth, and told her he would kill her if she told anyone. After raping her, the suspect took forty dollars from the victim's purse but did not steal anything else.

Two months later, another elderly white woman was raped by a black man in the same neighborhood. Elenor Hoster was seventy-one years old and lived alone. Sometime around 3:00 A.M. on May 7, she was awoken by noises that sounded like someone was trying to break into her home. Hoster got her gun and went downstairs. There was a man in her house. He took the gun away from her and struck her in the head with it. Then he forced her upstairs where he raped and anally sodomized her.

Hoster's arm was broken during the attack. The suspect took her gun and forty-seven dollars in cash, but he left her credit cards and the jewelry she was wearing, including a gold Omega watch and a diamond ring. Outside the house, an electrical breaker that controlled the kitchen appliances had been turned off. A small wire that led to a nonfunctioning alarm had been cut.

A fingerprint found on Hoster's storm window was matched to Ronald Clinton Lott, an Oklahoma resident who had a record for violent crime in Kansas. Lott was arrested on May 20, 1987. He still had Hoster's gun in his possession. He was charged with two counts each of rape, burglary, and robbery, and single counts of anal sodomy and illegal possession of a firearm.

Lott's name had come up several times in the Fowler and Cutler investigations. On January 20, 1987, just after the Cutler homicide, Lott had been stopped in the street and interviewed by police officers but not given a blood test. At that point in the investigation, they were not yet performing mobile blood tests.

In August 1987, Lott's preliminary hearing in the Marshall and Hoster cases was conducted in the same courtroom and on the same day as Miller's hearing, which stretched out over several weeks, because preliminary hearings were held only on Fridays.

Barry Albert presented the state's case in both preliminary hearings. At one point, he told the judge, "This is déjà vu." Except for the fact that Fowler and Cutler had been murdered, the cases were almost exactly the same.

The deaths of Fowler and Cutler may have been unintentional. Both victims had been gagged and their chests were crushed. The medical examiner could not determine the exact cause of death in either case. They had been asphyxiated, but the ME was uncertain whether that was the result of the gags or pressure upon the chest or throat.

On September 1, 1987, Lott pleaded guilty to burglary, rape, and illegal possession of a firearm. He was sentenced to serve two twenty-five-year terms, to run concurrently. Eight months later, Robert Lee Miller went on trial.

Lott was clearly a problem for the prosecution in the Miller case. Gilchrist testified in the Miller trial that she had eliminated Lott because his hairs didn't match the Cutler crime scene hairs that were "found suitable for forensic comparison." In addition to Lott, she said she had eliminated ten other possible suspects with the same hairs. Two Negroid hair fragments taken from Cutler's bedsheet were the only hairs that Gilchrist had matched to Miller's. There was also a full Negroid hair that she had not been able to match to Miller's. Was she saying that this hair didn't match Lott's, or that of any of the ten other possible suspects? Her testimony is unclear, and Evans did not get her to clarify it on cross-examination.

As we will see shortly, Gilchrist was actually looking at two of Ronnie Lott's own hairs when she said they didn't match, if she even compared Lott's samples to the evidentiary hairs. Miller was already in custody when Lott surrendered hair and blood samples following his own arrest for the Marshall and Hoster rapes. If anything, Gilchrist should not have matched the hair fragments to Miller's. Why did she? Had she already determined that Miller was the suspect? Gilchrist did not compare the crime scene hair fragments to Miller's known samples until after his interrogation and arrest. The detectives said that during the interrogation, they came to believe that Miller was the suspect. After several hours, the interrogation was stopped so that Gilchrist could take hair and blood samples from Miller.

"I think if you catch Gilchrist earlier on, before the charges are filed, and she'll flip over and say it's Lott," John Wilson said. "But it's too late at that point."

Even with the hair exclusion, Gilchrist apparently felt that she needed more proof that Lott wasn't the suspect in the Fowler and Cutler cases. She sent samples of Miller's and Lott's blood, along with semen stains from both crime scenes, to Dr. Moses Schanfield for allotyping tests in September 1987. By this time, Lott had already pleaded guilty and Miller was waiting to go on trial. In her cover letter to Schanfield, Gilchrist wrote, "Due to apparent similarities, the following referenced blood needs to be examined."

Schanfield found that Miller and Lott both had the same allotypes, along with 33 percent of the black male population. He apparently considered Lott excluded, however, not because of his own allotyping tests but because Lott's PGM subtype never turned up in any serological tests. He could have said the same thing about Miller, as his PGM subtype, which was different from Lott's, also did not turn up. Gilchrist had said at trial that PGM subtypes were not detectable in semen—her own tests in other cases proved this statement to be false (as we will see in the next chapter). She had claimed that the PGM subtype markers degraded too quickly for her to identify them.

"If we had been able to get to the crime scene fast enough after they died," Assistant District Attorney Richard Wintory told me, "we would have been able to see the difference between Miller and Lott."

Either way, Schanfield's allotyping tests did not exclude Lott. Yet, because of the way that he had written his report, Gilchrist and the police were able to say that the tests had excluded Lott.

After Schanfield's results came back, one of the detectives called him in Atlanta and asked, "Are you saying that Lott didn't do it?"

"No," Schanfield replied, "that's not what I'm telling you."

But that's precisely what Gilchrist and the detectives took Schanfield's written report to say. The report was not clear—that's why the detectives had called him. When the OCPD didn't hear what they wanted to from Schanfield, it didn't change the way they interpreted his written report.

"The detectives were confused about the serological evidence," Brian Wraxall said, "so they just went ahead prosecuting Miller."

While working on Miller's appeal, Lee Ann Peters spoke to Schanfield herself. After their conversation, Peters felt that "an evidentiary hearing on this matter would show that Ronald Lott cannot be positively excluded as the murderer." Her request for an evidentiary hearing, along with Miller's appeal, was denied.

"Obviously, the police were concerned the wrong man had been charged," Peters wrote in her appellate brief. (Assisting Peters was Bob Thompson, a former OCPD homicide detective, now an investigator for the public defender's office. Thompson worked the Miller case for six years and was instrumental in helping him win his freedom.) Peters found that even before Lott had been arrested, "police suspected the rapist may have been the same man who raped and killed Mrs. Fowler and Mrs. Cutler." Peters stated that an OCPD sergeant told the investigating detective in the Marshall case that "he was particularly interested in any similarities" between the Marshall rape and the two homicides (the Hoster rape had not yet occurred). Robert Lee Miller was already in custody at this time.

When Lee Ann Peters checked the detectives' suspect list, there were 173 names. Twenty-one of them had been eliminated by blood or hair. Number twenty-two was Robert Lee Miller, who could not be eliminated, according to the lab. Number twenty-three was Ronnie Lott. Lott's name was penciled in; all the other names had been typed. Apparently, he was eliminated after the original suspects had been investigated and after Miller had already been arrested.

One of the detectives working the Marshall and Hoster cases notified one of the Fowler and Cutler detectives about the similarities between the two cases. That detective told Gilchrist, who then sent Lott's blood, along with Miller's, to Schanfield for allotyping.

Gilchrist sent Schanfield's written report to the defense on discovery. Yet she withheld her cover letter, according to Peters's brief. Was she afraid of the defense's knowing why she had sent Lott's blood, and no one else's except for Miller's, out for further comparisons?

Before the trial, Miller's defense team had hired Brian Wraxall to reexamine the serological evidence. Wraxall's tests basically confirmed Gilchrist's and Davis's results: Miller had the same blood type and secretor status as the suspect, along with about 30 percent of the population. Since the body fluids from the crime scene were semen stains, they were mixed with the victims', so the victims' PGM markers could show up when the stains were tested. That's one reason why both Wraxall and the OCPD lab weren't able to further narrow down the serology evidence. If Wraxall had been given Lott's blood sample, he would have come to the same conclusions about Lott.

One difference between the two men's blood could be distinguished by DNA. While DNA technology was in its infancy at the time of Miller's trial, there was ample time, opportunity, and, despite the claims of Macy and his prosecutors, money for DNA tests. The state and county spent hundreds of thousands of dollars prosecuting Robert Lee Miller in both his trial and his subsequent appeals.

The prosecution withheld all information about Lott from Miller's trial defense, except for Lott's field interview from January 20, 1987; his name on the list of 172 possible suspects; and the serological report by Dr. Moses Schanfield.

During the trial, Ron Evans focused on another possible suspect, not Ronnie Lott. Barry Albert said that he had told Evans about Lott, and the similarity between the two cases. Evans insists that Albert never told him this. Some people say that Albert begged off the Miller case because he thought Lott might be the real suspect.

Lee Ann Peters was working for Bob Ravitz's public defender's office at the time. Ravitz gave Peters funds to have DNA tests performed by Brian Wraxall. When Peters asked for the semen evidence from the Fowler and Cutler cases, she was told that all the evidence had been lost or destroyed. Brian Wraxall went back to look at the evidence that he had examined prior to the trial. When Miller's defense team first sent Wraxall the bedclothes from both crime scenes, he had cut out pieces containing what appeared to be semen stains. He did this because Gilchrist had been late in sending him the physical evidence. There wasn't much time before trial, and the crime lab wanted everything back as soon as possible. So Wraxall took the stains, performed some presumptive tests, determined that they were semen, then took enough of a sample to perform his own tests and sent the rest back to the OCPD. When he conducted his own blood typing and electrophoresis tests, Wraxall held back some samples in case he needed to retest them.

The semen samples were not the only evidence missing. In 2001, Byron Boshell discovered that the two hairs Gilchrist had matched to Miller's at his trial were missing from the OCPD crime lab. The hairs and bloodstain from the Lendvay attempted burglary were also missing. Boshell later determined that the Lendvay bloodstain had been destroyed, along with two other hairs from a burglary victim that Gilchrist had matched to Miller's during the penalty phase. The rape kits from the Marshall and Hoster cases had also been destroyed.

The scraps of evidence that Wraxall had saved contained sufficient DNA for him to compare to Miller's in January 1995. Wraxall's results proved what Miller had been saying from the beginning. He was innocent. The tests proved that the semen samples from both crime scenes did not belong to Miller. Instead, the DNA matched Ronnie Lott's.

"Luckily, I kept all that stuff," Wraxall told me. If he hadn't, Robert Lee Miller might have been executed for a crime he didn't commit. (Gilchrist later complained to Ray Elliot in an official memo that "Wraxall retained portions of the evidence *without* our knowledge or approval.")

When the test results became public, Bob Macy argued that the evidence "does not prove [Miller] didn't kill either of those women."

Bob Ravitz asked Macy to drop the charges against Miller. Macy refused.

"It doesn't prove an innocent man was convicted," Bob Macy said. "All the evidence we convicted Miller with is still valid."

Macy promised to try both Miller and Lott for the murders. Yet there had never been any evidence indicating that two suspects were involved.

One homicide detective told Bob Ravitz that if the DNA excluded Miller, he wasn't involved in the crime. Ravitz asked him why.

"We all knew they were single-suspect killings," the detective said. "No question about it."

After the DA's office received Wraxall's report, Macy asked the scientist for all his notes and reports. Wraxall complied, and Macy sent everything to a lab in New York for further testing. Wraxall's findings were confirmed. Still, Macy refused to drop the charges against Miller. He was transferred from death row and held in county jail pending a retrial.

In February 1996, Macy's office dropped murder charges against Ronnie Lott. Ray Elliot, who had assisted in Miller's prosecution, said there was not enough evidence to corroborate the DNA results linking Lott to the murders.

"At this point, we are not saying he didn't do it, and we're not saying he did," Elliot said, referring to Lott. "We're saying that we don't have sufficient evidence to proceed."

What else did the prosecutors need? Were they trying to develop more evidence against Lott, or were they trying to find evidence against Miller? At this point, it looked like Macy was only interested in prosecuting Miller. Even though he had dropped the charges against Lott, Macy was planning to proceed with Miller's retrial.

A preliminary hearing was held in August 1996 to determine whether Miller should face a retrial. Macy and his prosecutors presented the videotaped interrogation and transcript as their evidence. As for the DNA evidence, Macy argued that it only proved Miller didn't rape the victims; it didn't prove he didn't kill them.

Miller's defense was simple. He was innocent. He took a polygraph examination and passed it.

"You've got to believe at some point in this process that his innocence will work as a defense," said Tim Wilson, who represented Miller at the preliminary hearing.

Six months after the preliminary hearing, Special Judge Larry Jones decided that there was not enough evidence to try Robert Lee Miller and dismissed the murder charges against him. Jones said that Miller's statements to police were not an admission of guilt.

Wilson said that Miller got "about eight hundred wrong things and thirty right things."

Prosecutor Ray Elliot countered that Miller got some things wrong because "he did so many of these crime scenes he's getting them confused."

Macy promised to appeal Judge Jones's ruling, and Miller was kept in jail. On appeal, District Court Judge Karl Gray ruled in favor of the prosecution and ordered Miller retried. Gray said that in the videotaped interrogation Miller said "things which only the perpetrator would be aware of."

Days after Gray's decision, Macy refiled murder charges against Ronnie Lott. Macy had waited to refile Lott's charges until he knew he could still prosecute Miller. Apparently, Macy feared that filing against Lott while Miller was still in limbo might be taken as an admission that Lott, and not Miller, was the murderer.

Tim Wilson appealed to the Oklahoma Court of Criminal Appeals, which decided to let Miller's retrial proceed.

On January 22, 1998, Judge Charles Owens severed the attempted break-in charges in the Lendvay case from the Fowler and Cutler murders.

That same day, Bob Macy dismissed the charges against Robert Lee Miller, and he walked out of the Oklahoma County Courthouse a free man. Miller had spent nearly eleven years in custody, seven on death row. Leaving the courthouse, Miller said that he had forgiven the prosecutors and the police.

"They could never pay me for what happened," Miller said. "You can't turn back the hands of time."

Bob Macy still wouldn't admit that Miller was innocent. He and Ray Elliot stated that the only reason they had dropped the charges was that they had insufficient evidence to proceed with Miller's retrial, because the judge had severed the Lendvay charge from the murder cases.

"We still feel and have always felt we have evidence to present to a jury that would convince them beyond a reasonable doubt that Mr. Miller is guilty," Ray Elliot said. "We don't feel at this time we were left with enough evidence to present to a jury."

Later that year, Ray Elliot was elected district court judge.

Two months after Miller's release, Ronnie Lott was charged with the Fowler and Cutler murders (the statute of limitations on the rape charges had expired). While Lott was awaiting trial, Bob Macy sent hairs from the Fowler and Cutler crime scenes for DNA comparison with Miller's. He was still hoping to link Miller to the murders.

The most convincing evidence that Robert Lee Miller was innocent came from Ronnie Lott himself. Before Lott went on trial, Ray Elliot offered him two life sentences in return for testimony that Miller was his accomplice. Lott refused. He was facing the death penalty, and Lott wouldn't lie about Robert Lee Miller's involvement.

When the DNA evidence showed Miller hadn't raped Fowler or Cutler, Macy claimed that Miller still could have killed them. When he couldn't prove that charge, Macy and his assistants said that Miller was an accomplice in the break-ins and robberies. When they couldn't prove that, they argued that Miller was Lott's lookout.

To this day, Oklahoma County prosecutors refuse to admit that Robert Lee Miller is innocent. While charges against him have been dropped, they have officially been dismissed without prejudice, meaning that whenever it wants to, the Oklahoma County DA's Office can prosecute Robert Lee Miller for being an accomplice to murder, rape, and burglary.

"Gilchrist compared Ronnie Lott's hair to a fragment too short for us to do DNA on and excluded Lott as a possible contributor of that hair," Wintory said, explaining why his office feels they still have a case against Miller. Wintory said the hair that she used to exclude Lott was one that she couldn't match to Miller's.

Wintory told me that the DA's office performed mitochondrial DNA testing on hairs from the Fowler crime scene (which Janice Davis processed). According to Wintory, one hair matched Ronnie Lott's, and another hair matched Robert Lee Miller's. None of the hairs from the Cutler scene, which Gilchrist analyzed, were long enough for even mitochondrial DNA testing. That's funny, because at trial Janice Davis testified that all of the hairs recovered from the Fowler scene were too short for meaningful comparison. And while

Gilchrist had mostly hair fragments, she was somehow able to match them to Miller's. The one full hair she couldn't match to anybody, not even Lott. Does that mean there's a third suspect—or is it Joyce Gilchrist's hair?

And what about the hair that Wintory said was matched by DNA testing to Miller's? If the Oklahoma County District Attorney's Office has evidence that places Miller at the crime scenes, why isn't it prosecuting him?

"If I could convict Miller for being present at the crime scenes, I would," Wintory said. He admits that there is no evidence of criminal conduct by a second suspect at either crime scene. The houses weren't robbed or ransacked. There is no evidence indicating anyone other than Lott was involved in the actual rapes and murders.

In the information filed against Lott, Bob Macy, who was still DA at the time, charged Lott with the murders of Anna Fowler and Velma Cutler "with malice." A pair of alternative charges also included in the information charged that Lott had committed the murders "aided and abetted by Robert Lee Miller." In these alternative charges, Macy claimed that Miller had killed both women by "strangling and/or smothering" them to death.

In his formal review of cases in which Joyce Gilchrist was criticized, Captain Byron Boshell asked the criminalist if she still considered Robert Lee Miller a suspect in the Fowler and Cutler murders (at the time, Miller had been released from death row and Ronnie Lott was awaiting trial). She asked Boshell, "My own personal opinion or based on the evidence?"

"Based on the evidence," Boshell said.

"Based on the evidence, yes."

Gilchrist told Boshell that she still considered Miller a suspect because of "human and animal hairs" that she recovered from the Cutler crime scene.

While the Oklahoma County prosecutors retain the legal right to prosecute Miller as Lott's accomplice, no one expects that they will. Meanwhile, Miller remains in legal limbo.

"Wintory's never going to prosecute Miller," Bob Ravitz said. "But if he's talking to somebody in the media, he'll say Miller was there."

Even David Prater, a former DA, says, "If you've got the evidence, try him. Or else shut up."

In early November 2001, Ronnie Lott went on trial for the Fowler and Cutler murders. Richard Wintory would prosecute. By this time, the Joyce Gilchrist scandal had reached full pitch. Lott was represented by John Albert, Barry's son. Albert planned to attack Gilchrist's credibility in hopes of discrediting the DNA evidence against his client, which identified Lott out of thirty-two billion people as the semen donor in both cases. Albert argued that Gilchrist had commingled the evidence from the Fowler and Cutler murders and the Marshall and Hoster rapes, which could have resulted in false-positive results identifying Lott as the rapist. As the trial approached, nearly half of Albert's prospective witnesses were expected to impeach Gilchrist's credibility. Boxes of documents concerning Gilchrist, including the internal investigation and termination hearing that preceded her firing, were submitted by Johnny Albert and then sealed by Judge Virgil Black.

Gilchrist herself was listed as a witness for both the prosecution and the defense. The Lott case was shaping up to be the first major legal battle over Joyce Gilchrist after her termination. John Albert was eager to impeach her. Other defense attorneys were watching the case closely, hoping that Albert might win a breakthrough that they themselves could then follow. Oklahoma County law enforcement was reeling. Bob Macy had retired. Blood was in the air. However, the evidence against Ronnie Lott was overwhelming, and soon even the contamination argument would be taken away from Albert.

On November 11, only a few days after the Lott trial began, Dr.

Larry Balding, the deputy state medical examiner, stated that his office had saved slides from vaginal swabs taken during the autopsies of Anna Fowler and Velma Cutler. The slides contained sperm cells. They had been stored at the medical examiner's office for almost fifteen years. Joyce Gilchrist had never touched them. (During one of her several meetings with Richard Wintory around that time, Gilchrist had told him, "The only way I could have come up with that evidence was if I went to prison and jerked off Ronnie Lott myself.")

When Dr. Balding mentioned that he had these slides, Richard Wintory reacted with surprise and jubilation. Did Wintory not know about the slides until his examination of Dr. Balding? Hadn't he preinterviewed his witness? Had he never tried to find rape evidence where Gilchrist was not a link in the chain of custody?

The newly discovered evidence halted the trial, at least temporarily, while the slides were sent out for DNA testing. The tests were expected to take a few days. In the meantime, both the prosecution and the defense awaited the results.

"The gauntlet is down. Gilchrist is either guilty or vindicated in this case," Richard Wintory and John Albert said in a joint statement.

The DNA tests on the newly discovered slides showed, once again, that Lott was the rapist. His DNA matched that found on the slide taken from Anna Fowler. The tests performed on the Cutler slides were inconclusive.

Joyce Gilchrist said she felt "vindicated" by the DNA results and thanked prosecutors Richard Wintory and Greg Mashburn for their loyalty and support. How did this finding vindicate Gilchrist? She had identified Robert Lee Miller as the suspect through her hair comparisons and blood tests.

Lott's attorneys asked for a mistrial, arguing that the jury would think "Mr. Lott did it and we're a bunch of jerks because we tried to ruin the good name of Mrs. Gilchrist to protect our client," Perry Hudson of the defense team told Judge Black.

"It's not their fault. It's not our fault. It's just the truth," Wintory responded. "The truth is, Joyce Gilchrist did not plant any evidence and Lott was willing to drag Joyce Gilchrist's name through the mud and to let Robert Miller languish on death row for his crime."

Bob Macy and Richard Wintory wanted, and still would like to see, Robert Lee Miller in prison for these crimes. And even though Ronnie Lott let Miller take the rap initially, he refused to save his own life by implicating Miller.

Judge Black declared a mistrial and scheduled a new trial for Ronnie Lott to begin two weeks later.

I sat in on part of that trial, watching a detective testify to crime scene evidence. When the photographs of one of the victim's bloodied and bruised body were shown, Ronnie Lott covered his face and shook his head.

Richard Wintory introduced the bedclothes from both victims as evidence and displayed them in court. These were the same bedclothes that Lee Ann Peters had been told were missing or had been destroyed when she hired Brian Wraxall to perform DNA tests in the Miller case.

Now that he was trying Lott for the murders, Wintory called the Miller interrogation "gibberish, nonsense and disjointed."

After deliberating for one hour, the jury returned a guilty verdict on both murder counts.

Anna Fowler's children testified during the penalty phase. Harold Fowler and Libby Temling testified for the prosecution, urging the jury to execute their mother's killer. Their brother, Jim Fowler, had seen his own son die, and an innocent man almost get executed for his mother's murder.

"I am the oldest son of Goldie Fowler," Jim told me, "and I

wanted to get up on the stand and tell the jury that I thought life without parole was by far a more extreme punishment."

Shortly before he was about to appear as a witness, Fowler was called into the judge's chambers. There he was told that he could state his name, his relationship to the victim, and what kind of punishment he would like to see.

"Richard Wintory didn't want me or anybody else to give the jury the idea that perhaps life without parole would be a more suitable punishment," Fowler said. He recognized that there are statutory limitations on the testimony of family members of murder victims during the penalty phase of a trial. However, throughout both trials of the men accused of his mother's rape and murder, Fowler was treated as a pariah by the prosecution, because of his son.

The jury gave Lott the death penalty.

I asked Jim Fowler if he would witness Ronnie Lott's execution.

"If he didn't have anybody else to be there for him, I would."

CHAPTER ELEVEN

OVER A BARREL

WHILE THE TRIAL AND INCARCERATION OF JEFFREY TODD PIERCE WAS NOT a death penalty case, a close look at the investigation and trial shows what was wrong with the Oklahoma County criminal justice system. Eventually, it would be the case that ended the careers of both Bob Macy and Joyce Gilchrist.

S. B., a twenty-seven-year-old white female, was living with her roommate Karen Cooper in a furnished apartment in the Woodlake Apartment complex in Oklahoma City while she did marketing and promotional work for R. J. Reynolds. On May 8, 1985, she left her apartment to go to work around 10:00 A.M. Walking toward her car, she saw a white male standing outside. He looked at her, then quickly disappeared into the bushes. The man had blond hair and wore a bandanna around his head. He wore a T-shirt and jeans. He had black gloves on his hands.

Later that morning, S. B. returned to her apartment to get some supplies. As she entered, she noticed that a window had been broken and her belongings were in disarray. While she surveyed the damage, a white man came out of another room in the apartment and grabbed her. He threatened her with a knife. She fought back but was quickly overpowered.

The man pushed her facedown onto the floor. He held a pillow over her face and told her that he would kill her if she looked at him. Then he demanded oral sex. She saw a meat fork on the ground and reached for it. Her assailant took the fork and stabbed her in the arm. Then he pushed her back down to the floor, where he raped and anally sodomized her.

Following the assault, the suspect forced the victim to take a shower. He pushed her into the bathroom, still holding a pillow over her face. While she was in the shower, the suspect left her apartment. She later told police that nothing had been taken from her apartment except a bar of soap, a bottle of laundry detergent, and the return address from a checking deposit slip.

At first glance, this looks like a rape of opportunity. The suspect had broken into the apartment intent on committing burglary. When an attractive young woman unexpectedly returned, he took advantage of the situation. Because the only items missing were laundry detergent, soap, and an address from a checking deposit slip, it is not out of the question that the suspect was a transient who was looking specifically for these items in order to clean up. He could even have taken a shower before the victim returned. The address torn from the checking deposit slip might have been taken in order to send money to her later. (It might sound strange, but I once had a case where a burglar sent money to his victim after he was back on his feet.)

S. B. called the police, who arrived at the scene at 12:40 P.M. She told the police the man who raped her was wearing a leather belt with a large oval buckle, faded blue jeans with fringe on the bottoms, a tan T-shirt, and white leather running shoes that looked "new and expensive." He wore a red bandanna tied like a headband and black leather gloves. The suspect was "very clean in both his clothing and his personal hygiene." S. B. told police that she thought her assailant was the same man she had seen outside her apartment that morning.

Jeffrey Todd Pierce was a twenty-four-year-old laborer employed by Can Do, a contracting firm that did landscaping and yard work for the Woodlake Apartments complex. He had been working on the grounds around the victim's apartment that morning. When the police responded, Pierce was returning from his lunch break with his colleagues, where he had cashed his paycheck and bought a pair of diamond earrings as a birthday present for his pregnant wife (May 8 was her birthday). Pierce saw a patrol car sitting in the parking lot and figured there must have been a burglary in the complex. The apartment manager told him that a woman had been beaten. S. B. was waiting in the patrol car, about to be taken to the hospital. Because Pierce was similar in appearance to the suspect, police asked him to step closer to the patrol car. He stood some twelve to thirty feet away (the distance is a matter of some dispute). Inside the car, an officer asked Burton if Pierce was the man who had attacked her. S. B. said she didn't think so. S. B. stated that Pierce's hair appeared lighter in color than her attacker's and Pierce was wearing a blue T-shirt, not a brown one. He also was not wearing a belt, a bandanna, or gloves.

At the hospital, medical technicians performed a rape examination, during which vaginal and anal swabs, as well as an apparent semen stain on the victim's thigh, were collected. When she returned home, S. B. called the police to ask what she should do with the clothes she had been wearing during the attack. The dispatcher told her to bag the clothing herself and bring it to police headquarters. S. B. became upset and demanded to speak to a supervisor. She wanted to make a formal complaint against the way she was being treated. (The responding officer had said to her, "Well, we've got a burglary and a rape. What do we want to do about it?" Then he let maintenance people fix the window the suspect had broken to gain entry into the apartment, before it was photographed or analyzed for possible evidence.) The OCPD sent another unit to her apartment to collect evidence. Technical investigators eventually found a number of hairs. They took photographs of a tennis shoe footprint outside the bedroom window where the suspect had gained entry.

S. B. helped generate a composite drawing of the suspect. Beneath the drawing was the following description:

"This suspect is wanted in reference to several sex crimes occurring since May 1985, in the Oklahoma City area. The suspect is a white male, 25 to 30 years of age. He is 5'10" to 6'1". The suspect is a natural blond."

Jeffrey Todd Pierce is six feet three inches tall. His dirty blond hair grows lighter in the summer. He has a prominent nose. In fact, his nose is the first thing you notice about Pierce. It is very large, broken and bent to one side. Even if S. B. didn't get a good look at her attacker's face, if Pierce had been her rapist, she would probably have said something about that nose.

S. B. didn't mention the nose until November 7, 1985, when a second composite was done, after she had complained that the hair wasn't right in the first one. Neither one of the composites shows the suspect with a prominent nose. At one point during the drawing of the second composite, S. B. reportedly told Detective Larry Koonce, "His nose was somewhat different, not large, just different. One that I would recognize if I saw it again."

Police said that the S. B. suspect was wanted for several sex crimes. These included at least twelve rapes and attempted rapes that the OCPD had been unable to solve. The S. B. rape was also linked to the 1984 murder of Judy Weichert, a thirty-three-year-old woman who had been raped and anally sodomized and stabbed twenty-two times. Weichert was found by the side of the road naked and gravely injured on the morning of June 28, 1984. Before she died, Weichert reportedly identified her attacker as "a very big white man with stringy blond hair and a big nose."

The OCPD formed a task force and investigated the Weichert murder for a year with no results. The Weichert murder was high-profile. The victim was a young, successful professional woman who was very active in the community. The fact that she had been jogging when she was attacked struck fear among many women. The public pressure to solve the Weichert case was enormous.

OCPD detective Bill Cook was on the task force of the Weichert homicide, as was Bob Horn. Early on in the S. B. investigation, Detective Larry Koonce asked Joyce Gilchrist "if she would check and see if there were any similarities between the two cases."

Sometime near the end of June 1985, Joyce Gilchrist told Bill Cook that "the suspect in the Judy Weichert homicide and the suspect in the S. B. rape were going to be one and the same." Gilchrist told him "she had positively matched four hairs found on S. B. to the hairs found on Judy Weichert." (A hair analyst can't match hairs when neither one of them comes from known sources.) One of the hairs Gilchrist matched from the Weichert scene was later found to be an animal hair recovered from a nearby fence.

As a result of Gilchrist's hair analysis, Cook and Koonce believed that one person had to be responsible for both crimes, even though the attacks were very different in nature and MO. The murder and rape of Judy Weichert was a rage-based, stalking-type attack that would indicate a connection between the suspect and the victim (even if that connection existed only in the suspect's mind). The S. B. case was a residential burglary that escalated into a rape of opportunity when the victim unexpectedly returned home.

Cook felt that if he could solve the S. B. rape, which had a living witness, he would then solve the Weichert murder. So Cook began working with Koonce on the S. B. case. Cook and Koonce sent along information on the S. B. case (and a dozen other unsolved rapes and attempted rapes) to the FBI for their suspect profile on the Weichert murder. The FBI profile had originally been requested in March 1985, before the S. B. rape had even been committed. The S. B. file was sent along to the FBI, with the explanation that forensic evidence had linked that rape and the Weichert murder.

The finished profile was sent to OCPD on September 9, 1985. Working on the assumption that the S. B. and Weichert cases were absolutely linked through forensic evidence, the profiler obviously had difficulty in working up a useful profile of a suspect in two very different crimes. In the twelve other rapes and attempted rapes that Cook and Koonce also felt could be connected, there were different MOs and even different suspect descriptions. Assuming that the Weichert and S. B. cases were connected, the FBI then reasoned that all the others in between must be as well.

The FBI profilers did the best they could with this information, coming to some very general conclusions about the suspect—that he was a white male, probably single, and maladjusted socially. In other words, the basic assumptions one could make from the evidence and experience in rape and murder investigations.

When Cook started working the S. B. case, Koonce told him that it was his "personal feeling" that the suspect was a maintenance man working at the apartment complex. Koonce's hunch was probably based on the victim's saying that she saw a man in the bushes shortly before she left that morning, and her feeling that this man was her attacker. The hunch didn't quite follow the evidence. The victim had described her attacker as "clean smelling," like he had just taken a shower. He wore new, expensive, white running shoes and black leather gloves. There was no grass or dirt collected from the victim's clothes or apartment, which the suspect would have left if he had been working outside that morning.

Cook began focusing on all blond male Can Do employees. He found out that Jeffrey Todd Pierce was working at Woodlake Apartments that day. The detectives claim that Pierce had not been on the original list of past and present Can Do employees (this claim is disputed by Pierce). Either way, the police had questioned Pierce soon after the attack, when they asked the victim whether he was her assailant. The OCPD did not take down any of Pierce's information, probably because the victim had not identified him. Still, as a possible witness, they should have recorded his name, address, and phone number.

Pierce had quit working for Can Do a few days after the S. B. rape.

On January 29, 1986, Detectives Cook and Horn visited Jeffrey Todd Pierce at home. They said they were investigating another rape at Woodlake Apartments, this one involving a black man who had raped a woman in a wheelchair (apparently they were trying to make Pierce think they weren't hot on his trail). Before they left, the detectives took Pierce's photograph, with his permission.

Cook and Horn noted that Pierce resembled the composite sketch, had a crooked nose, had quit his job shortly after the rape, "seemed very reluctant and nervous about giving hair samples," and lived in a neighborhood where other rapes had occurred. "At this point in the investigation," Cook wrote in his police report, "the only thing that looks negative about Pierce being a good suspect is the fact that his hair is dark blond."

On February 3, Detective Charles McIntyre went to Pierce's home to pick up more photographs. They wanted a picture from summertime, when his hair was sun-bleached blond (the rape had occurred in May, before his hair changed color). Pierce gave McIntyre a photograph from the wedding of his friend Joseph Fowler, the son of Jim Fowler and brother of Mark. Pierce had been Fowler's best man.

On February 8, Detective Koonce went to see S. B. in Tennessee. He asked her several questions about the man she had seen outside her apartment immediately following the attack. Two weeks later,

Koonce returned to Tennessee with three photo lineups. At several different points during the investigation, S. B. had been shown photographs of potential suspects (she looked at some seventy or eighty photos total). She had identified two different men as looking similar to her attacker. She had been shown Pierce's photograph at least once and not selected it. This time, she picked Pierce.

There is some controversy over how that photo lineup was conducted. Former homicide detective Bob Bemo, Cook's longtime partner (Cook has since died of cancer), told me that he was "kind of concerned about what Koonce did in order to get the victim to feel like this was the guy who raped her." Several people also told me that S. B.'s identification of Pierce was very tentative at first and only grew more positive with reinforcement from the police and the prosecutors. There are also claims that Koonce reinforced S. B.'s identification of Pierce by telling her that Joyce Gilchrist had matched his hairs to those found at the crime scene. Koonce wrote that S. B. had said during the February photo lineup, "I am positive, this picture of him was taken at about the same distance I saw his face when he attacked me."

Photo lineups should be presented to witnesses without any prejudice or indication toward the suspect. This not only ensures that the identification is accurate but also protects the evidence from being attacked at trial. Unfortunately, some detectives stack the deck, hoping that it will aid the witness in selecting the photograph they think is their suspect. This can be done by surrounding the suspect with photographs of other individuals who do not share distinctive characteristics (like mustaches or eyeglasses, as in the Bowen case). In a "six pack" lineup it is easy to put the suspect in slot #2; when the detective holds the photographs up for the victim to view, his or her index finger points toward the suspect's picture. Even after the witness has selected the suspect, the detective cannot reinforce the ID by telling the witness she made the right choice.

In a rape investigation, eyewitness identification is a powerful element of the case, which is even more reason for the detectives to be careful about how they present the witness/victim with any line-ups of potential suspects. And even the strongest witness identification still has to be corroborated with evidence.

On Saturday morning, March 1, 1986, Jeffrey Todd Pierce was driving to work when he was pulled over by a patrol car. He was searched, handcuffed, and taken to the station.

Detectives Cook and McIntyre sat Pierce down and gave him a McDonald's hamburger. Then Cook threw down photographs of a dead woman on the table.

"That's terrible," Pierce said. "What happened to her?"

"That's the woman you killed!" Cook replied.

"I ain't never hurt no lady," Pierce said. "I can't believe this is happening to me."

Over the next twenty hours, Pierce was interrogated by Detectives Cook, Koonce, and McIntyre. The detectives later testified that Pierce waived his Miranda rights. Pierce claims he was never read his rights. Whether advised or not, Pierce spoke freely with the detectives, confident that he would be released once he convinced them of his innocence. He voluntarily surrendered hair, blood, and saliva samples to Joyce Gilchrist. Bob Bemo told me that Gilchrist knew Pierce was the suspect the detectives wanted when she performed the hair analysis that matched him to the Woodlake Apartments rape.

Detectives Cook, Koonce, and McIntyre accused Pierce of four rapes, one murder, and a credit card theft. After executing a search warrant on his home, the detectives told Pierce that they had seen his wife packing up to leave him and that Pierce's own father believed he was guilty. They held a mock trial, in which they convicted Pierce and sentenced him to sixty years in prison. When Pierce's father arrived at the jail, Koonce told Mr. Pierce that his son was a pathological rapist.

At that time, the only evidence they had against Pierce was the victim's photo identification. Nothing else fit. Pierce had an alibi— he had been on lunch break with his coworkers, first going to a grocery store to cash his paycheck, then buying diamond earrings for his wife. He had been working the whole morning, in sight of his coworkers almost the entire time. He would have been dirty and sweaty, not clean-smelling as the victim had described her attacker. He had been wearing a blue T-shirt, no bandanna, no black gloves, no new, expensive white running shoes. He had no record for violent crimes. He had no connection to Judy Weichert, and no evidence linked him to any of the other rapes.

When Jeff's wife, Kathy, came to the police station the first day he was being held, she recognized Bob Macy standing outside the room and heard the DA say to one of the detectives, "You got that kid over a barrel yet?"

Pierce was held in custody for four days before being formally charged. After his lawyer, Raymond Burger, filed a writ of habeas corpus, the police finally charged him, not with the murder of Judy Weichert, or the three other rapes, but only the S. B. assault.

Police blamed the ten-month delay in arresting a suspect in the Woodlake Apartments rape on "misleading" information that Pierce had quit his job as a maintenance man at the complex. In fact, the police knew that Pierce was working at the complex on the day of the attack. The excuse that they were not told about Jeffrey Todd Pierce until months later is just an attempt to explain why it took them so long to find him.

Shortly after Pierce's arrest, the OCPD told the media that they believed he was also responsible for the Weichert murder. In a search warrant for Pierce's residence, Bill Cook stated that "Pierce's rare blood type, hair evidence, a knife and his resemblance to the man Weichert described as her attacker" had led him "to conclude that Jeffrey Todd Pierce had perpetrated both of these crimes." By now

Gilchrist had performed the serological tests on Pierce's blood and saliva samples. She determined that he was an AB blood type and a nonsecretor, which meant that his blood type would not be secreted in other bodily fluids like semen, saliva, tears, and sweat. What blood-type evidence could they have matched to the Weichert murder? If Pierce was a nonsecretor, then his blood type would not be evident in a semen sample. I don't believe they had any serological evidence linking Pierce to the Weichert murder, or else they would have charged him.

During the search of Pierce's residence, police found a tan T-shirt and jeans that they said matched the clothing the suspect was wearing during the attack. They did not find a bandanna, black leather gloves, or a large-buckled belt.

On March 16, Pierce was released on bail. Ten days later, his preliminary hearing was held. Prior to the hearing, Detective Koonce brought S. B. to the courthouse. In the hallway outside the courtroom, he pointed out Jeffrey Todd Pierce to her. She went on to identify him at the preliminary hearing, although that identification was still tentative. By the time she testified at trial, S. B. was positive that Jeffrey Todd Pierce had raped her.

"I will never forget his face," S. B. said.

On July 30, Joyce Gilchrist asked for and received additional hair samples from Pierce. In her examination report, Gilchrist did not specify how many hairs she had taken from Pierce, either on March 1 or on July 30. The evidentiary hairs were not mounted or photographed immediately upon receipt. Neither were the known hairs taken from Pierce.

Examining the body fluid evidence, Gilchrist found that the victim was a type O secretor. Prior to DNA testing, it was difficult to distinguish between semen stains and vaginal secretions in rape evidence. Often scientists would look for sperm in order to be certain that they were not testing a fluid that had come from the victim.

Gilchrist had one stain that seemed to have been donated by the suspect—an apparent semen stain on the victim's thigh. Testing that stain, Gilchrist found the donor was a type O secretor, just like the victim (that's not surprising, since type O blood type is the most prevalent, found in some 48 percent of the population). Further electrophoresis testing showed a PGM (1) enzyme marker. Jeffrey Todd Pierce did not have this marker. The victim did. If this was in fact a semen stain, then Gilchrist's own tests should have excluded Pierce as the suspect. Gilchrist had performed preliminary tests indicating the stain was semen. (Years later, DNA tests confirmed that it was.) That means the suspect shared the same blood type, secretor status, and enzyme markers as the victim. Since those traits were all very common, this was not unusual.

Yet Pierce did not match the evidence. While he shared two enzyme markers with the victim, his PGM marker (2-1) was different. Gilchrist admitted that she found no evidence of that marker in any of her examinations. She explained away the presence of PGM (1) by saying it originated from the victim, despite the fact that she described the stain as being semen twice in her written reports. Either Gilchrist had found no serological evidence from the suspect or her results excluded Pierce. She couldn't have it both ways. But she did.

Gilchrist claimed to have identified another source of semen—the anal swabs taken during the rape examination at the hospital. In neither the anal swabs nor the semen stain from the victim's thigh did she identify the PGM enzyme that Pierce would have contributed if he was the suspect. On both these samples, Gilchrist explained away the presence of blood typing and enzyme markers that excluded Jeffrey Todd Pierce by saying that they came from the victim. In her testimony, Gilchrist neglected to say that if she could detect Pierce's PEPA and ESD markers from the anal swabs, then she should also have been able to detect his PGM marker, which she didn't.

At trial, when prosecutor Barry Albert asked her about the thigh swab, Gilchrist testified that she had identified "the ABO blood group antigen H, again indicative of type O blood, PGM (1), no ABO secretor blood group substances detected."

In the same sentence, Gilchrist said that she didn't detect any secretor substances, yet she found antigen H, which is the secretor substance for O positive. If that stain was Pierce's semen, it should not have showed antigen H, because he was a nonsecretor.

Albert led his witness to a conclusion that was equally ambiguous.

"The blood type of the semen donor [would] either be a type O or nonsecretor," Gilchrist testified. "But, in my opinion, I don't have a quantity of semen—the level was insufficient for me to say anything about the blood type of the semen donor because all the information, genetic marker information I'm getting, is consistent with that of the victim. He's either got to be the same blood type and secretor status and PGM marker information as the victim or he's going to be a nonsecretor and I can't say anything about the blood typing because the quantity's just not sufficient."

> Q [ALBERT]: *Okay. So he's either going to be a person with the identical blood type and genetic markers of S. B.—*
> A [GILCHRIST]: *Correct.*
> Q: *—or he's going to be a nonsecretor.*
> A: *That's correct.*
> Q: *And Mr. Pierce is a nonsecretor.*

Blood type, secretor status, and enzyme size are all separate and distinct. A nonsecretor does not release blood-type indicators in other bodily fluids—but all the enzyme markers are evident in the fluids of both secretors and nonsecretors. Gilchrist's and Albert's confusion of blood type and enzyme markers is too clever to be unintentional. Gilchrist states that either the suspect shares the same enzyme markers as the victim (which Pierce does not) or he is a non-secretor (which Pierce is). Albert and Gilchrist use the fact that Pierce is a nonsecretor to explain why the electrophoresis results did not pick up his PGM enzyme marker. Secretor status has nothing to do with enzyme markers.

Brian Wraxall had trained Gilchrist in electrophoresis. He is sure that Gilchrist knew the difference between blood typing and electrophoresis.

Gilchrist said that because Pierce was a nonsecretor, she could not eliminate him as the semen donor. What Gilchrist did not say was that using that level of evidence, she could not eliminate any other male in the population.

"It's well known within the scientific community," Wraxall said, "that if you find no blood type, secretor status, or PGM information but that which matches the victim, you have to assume that all that information came from her fluids."

Gilchrist did this when it suited her, by saying that whenever the PGM (1) marker showed up it must have come from the victim. Yet when she felt she needed to distinguish between Pierce's fluids and the victim's, she did that as well.

And Albert must have been in on it—that's the only way an experienced and intelligent trial lawyer could avoid asking the next logical question: "So, what serological evidence do you have that implicates Jeffrey Todd Pierce in the rape of S. B.?" To which an honest answer would have had to have been, "None."

After leading Gilchrist through the serological evidence, Albert turned to hair. Gilchrist used the term *microscopically consistent* to describe the hair matches she made between Pierce's hair and the hairs recovered from the crime scene. Albert liked this wording and went one step further. He repeatedly said "microscopically consistent in all respects?" and Gilchrist agreed. In the discussion of one hair found on the victim's skirt, Albert asked, "There was not even a scintilla of inconsistency under the microscope?" Gilchrist answered, "No." When the jury heard phrases like "microscopically consistent" and "not even a scintilla of inconsistency" they understood the hair matches to be positive identifications.

In her direct testimony, Gilchrist stated that she noticed a change in pigmentation on each of the hairs she matched to Pierce, indicating that he wore a bandanna. The hair covered by the bandanna, according to Gilchrist, did not become sun-bleached.

In an affidavit filed after the trial, John Wilson stated that Gilchrist's testimony about the "bandanna effect" was "a statistical impossibility and . . . seriously mislead the jury." Wilson points out that "for each of the twenty-eight scalp hairs to have an identical band caused by the headband would require each hair to have come from the same relative position on the scalp, for each of the hairs to be in the same phase of growth and all other hairs not matching this criteria must be excluded."

On cross-examination of Gilchrist, Raymond Burger brought up the fact that Pierce surrendered hair samples on March 1, when his hair would not be sun-bleached. Was this peculiar "bandanna effect" the reason why Gilchrist requested additional hairs from Pierce on July 30? Had Pierce's samples somehow gotten mixed up with the evidentiary hairs from the crime scene? In her lab report, Gilchrist does not count the number of known hairs submitted by Pierce. We don't know how many hairs she took from him, only that she matched twenty-eight scalp hairs and three pubic hairs from the crime scene to him. Raymond Burger questioned why there were so many hairs at the crime scene and wondered whether Pierce's sample hairs had gotten commingled with the known hairs. Two forensic scientists, Edward Burwitz of the FBI and Ann Reed of the Oklahoma State

Bureau of Investigation, later stated in reference to this case that it was rare to have more than five hairs left by the suspect in a rape or murder, unless a handful of hair was pulled out during the assault, which was not the case in the hair evidence used in the Pierce trial.

Raymond Burger later said that he had not educated himself on hair and semen evidence because he didn't realize how important it would be in the trial. Burger told the *Tulsa Tribune* that at the beginning of the Pierce trial he thought hair evidence "was going to be weak." By the end of the trial, he said it was "the most atrocious weapon of the state."

Burger had hired Brian Wraxall's Serological Research Institute (SERI), but Gilchrist only sent Wraxall the bodily fluid evidence. Since he could not distinguish between the blood type, secretor status, or enzyme markers of the victim and the suspect, Wraxall had to assume that everything came from the victim. Gilchrist did not send Wraxall any of the hair evidence. At trial she said that she remembered SERI didn't do hair comparisons. In fact, Wraxall had made arrangements with another lab to examine the hair evidence. Since Gilchrist didn't send the samples, he had no hair evidence to examine. Although Gilchrist had clearly dragged her feet on discovery, it was the defense's responsibility to follow up and make sure that she delivered all the evidence for reexamination, which Burger did not do.

Burger made another critical mistake when he allowed testimony about the detectives' suspicion of Pierce's being responsible for the Weichert murder to be introduced. When Burger cross-examined Bill Cook, he asked the detective about another suspect who had been excluded (Randall Cannon, who was convicted and sentenced to death for the rape and murder of Ada Hawley). Cook stated that the victim had identified another suspect during a photo identification, but that suspect had already been excluded by Gilchrist's hair comparisons, not in the rape case, but in the murder and rape of Judy Weichert.

A [COOK]: *The hairs of Mr. Cannon were compared by Joyce Gilchrist to the pubic and scalp hairs found on the dead body of Judy Weichert.*
Q [BURGER]: *So, good deal. She excludes him, then from the crime of raping S. B.*
A: *She matched those hairs, S. B.'s and Weichert's. To exclude one would exclude the other.*
Q: *She matched the hairs of S. B.'s and Weichert's.*
A: *Yes, sir.*
Q [ALBERT]: *Need to be more descriptive, officer.*
A: *Sir, we found hairs on the body of a homicide victim. Hairs were found on the body of S. B. Those hairs were compared together and found to be the same.*

When Burger elicited this testimony, he opened the door for Albert to ask questions about the Weichert case, which led the jury to believe that Pierce was not only a rapist but also a murderer.

In Pierce's defense, Burger examined twenty-one character witnesses, many of whom also testified that they had never seen Jeffrey wear a belt or bandanna or black leather gloves. Pierce's coworkers testified to his alibi, being on lunch break during the time the attack occurred. Pierce also took the stand in his own defense.

Albert devised a complicated and bizarre scenario to account for all the discrepancies in the state's case. Jeffrey Todd Pierce had no record of violent or sexual crimes, yet Albert painted the picture of a pathological misogynist who hated women because his parents had gotten divorced and he didn't like his stepmother. After returning to the apartment complex grounds following his lunch break, Pierce was working a leaf blower. He worked quickly and got way ahead of his coworkers. Then he slipped into a rest room in the main office, where he put on his "dominance uniform" of a red bandanna, black leather gloves, tan T-shirt, leather belt with a large buckle, and expensive running shoes. This costume, Albert argued, was what Pierce wore whenever he attacked a woman, because it gave him power. Pierce raped S. B., Albert hypothesized, then changed back into his work clothes and reassumed the leaf blower before his coworkers even noticed he was gone.

In his closing arguments, Barry Albert told the jury that the evidence against Pierce was "overwhelming." He said that the odds of Gilchrist being wrong about the hairs matching would be "totally astronomical."

On October 13, 1986, Pierce was convicted of first-degree rape, oral sodomy, anal sodomy, first-degree burglary, and assault with a dangerous weapon. He was sentenced to a total of sixty-five years in prison. The jury had deliberated for almost eight hours over the course of two days. At one point, they sent a note to the judge saying they were unable to reach a unanimous verdict. The first vote was seven to five favoring acquittal. A later vote was eleven to one for conviction.

"We started with a prayer and ended with a prayer," James R. Foshee, the jury foreman, said. "It took some time for all of us to get emotions out of it and really concentrate on the judge's instructions and decide the case on the evidence."

Pierce had twin sons, who were seventeen months old when he went away to prison. While still believing in his innocence, Pierce's wife divorced him and moved to Michigan. She had to pawn the diamond earrings he had bought her in order to pay for the move. The couple had decided that it would be better for the children if they left Oklahoma and started a new life without Jeffrey.

"I didn't do this because I didn't believe Jeff or love Jeff," Kathy Pierce said years later. "I did it because I had to take care of our kids.

I didn't think I could go on for sixty-five years and do monthly prison visits."

For nearly fifteen years, Kathy Pierce struggled to find a way to tell her children that their father was in prison. She never did.

While in prison, Pierce consistently maintained his innocence. He denied himself the possibility of an earlier parole by refusing to enter a sex-offender program, saying he wasn't a sex offender.

David Autry handled Pierce's case on appeal. John Wilson examined the police reports and Gilchrist's testimony (he was unable to examine the evidence itself). In his affidavit, dated April 22, 1987, Wilson called Gilchrist's hair comparisons "factually incorrect." Wilson also found that "her interpretation of those comparisons was wrong and substantially misled the jury."

Wilson concluded that Gilchrist's own electrophoresis tests "positively and without question exonerate Mr. Pierce as the attacker." He pointed out that Gilchrist's testimony regarding secretor status had nothing to do with the absence of Pierce's PGM enzyme marker, because "secretor status is irrelevant to the presence or detectability of this enzyme." In testifying that this serological evidence supported her opinion that Jeffrey Todd Pierce was the suspect, "Gilchrist violated her professional ethics," according to Wilson.

Autry included Wilson's affidavit in his appeal brief. In 1990 the Oklahoma Court of Criminal Appeals decided that the PGM (1) enzyme found in the evidence Gilchrist had identified as semen could have been consistent with the victim's, or else was just a false reading. The court also found that although Gilchrist was under a court order to send all evidence to SERI, "she took it upon herself to determine the portions of the Order with which she wished to comply. . . . The failure to abide by a valid order by a trial court will generally have serious consequences and will always be considered error." The court stated that while it "cannot take Gilchrist's breach of the law lightly," it did not find the error serious enough to reverse, because the defense experts had had ample time to demand the evidence from Gilchrist, which they did not do. No continuance had been requested, and the defense had stated that they were ready to proceed to trial.

During testimony at the trial, Joyce Gilchrist swore that she was a member of the American Academy of Forensic Sciences. She was not a member, having been suspended for nonpayment of dues. When this was pointed out to the Oklahoma Court of Criminal Appeals, the judges found that "Gilchrist's testimony, while potentially misleading, was harmless error in light of her other, ample qualifications as an expert."

The court affirmed Pierce's conviction. In a special concurrence, Judge Ed Parks wrote: "It is utterly incomprehensible that a professional of Joyce Gilchrist's alleged competence wantonly violated the terms of a court order." While Parks agreed that this was not reversible error, "I wish to stress, however, that such a violation will not escape the type of serious consequences herein eluded under a less compelling set of circumstances."

Jeffrey Todd Pierce stayed in prison.

CHAPTER TWELVE

THE FACTORY
BREAKS DOWN

IN JANUARY 2001 THE OKLAHOMA INDIGENT DEFENSE SYSTEM (OIDS) asked the OCPD to reexamine the semen evidence in the Jeffrey Todd Pierce case. By this time, Laura Schile had been hired by the crime lab. She was in the office one day, examining the Pierce file when Joyce Gilchrist walked in.

"What are you doing with that evidence?" Gilchrist demanded.

"I'm going to send it out for DNA testing," Schile replied.

"No you're not," Gilchrist shouted.

After appealing to Captain Byron Boshell, head of the laboratory services division of the OCPD, Schile eventually did send the evidence to Brian Wraxall for DNA tests. And Wraxall's tests proved what Pierce had been saying all along—that he was an innocent man.

When Bob Macy was notified of the DNA results, his face turned red and "he was just sick," according to David Prater, who was there with him at the time.

However sick it might have made him feel, when shown undeniable proof that his office had convicted an innocent man, Macy himself refused at first to believe it. He ordered additional tests to be performed by another lab. When those came back, also proving that Pierce was innocent, Macy said he would wait for the written report before he made a decision concerning the case. In the meantime, Pierce remained in prison.

Here was a clear miscarriage of justice, one that even Bob Macy had to admit. This time, there was no arguing with the evidence. Macy could not claim, as he did with Clifford Henry Bowen or Robert Lee Miller, that he still believed Pierce was guilty.

Although he had not prosecuted the case himself, Macy was responsible for the charges against Jeffrey Todd Pierce being filed. Barry Albert was dead. The OCPD detectives had retired (and Bill Cook was dead). Quickly, the blame focused on Joyce Gilchrist.

Chief M. T. Berry placed Gilchrist on administrative suspension and scheduled a hearing. She continued to receive her annual salary of $59,528, and Berry did not make the suspension public until months after he had ordered it. Gilchrist's suspension was due not just to the Pierce case but also to the Boshell memo and other criticisms of her work.

While the follow-up tests on the Pierce evidence were still being conducted, Berry asked the FBI to investigate Gilchrist's work in that case and seven others. Those eight cases had been "randomly selected" from a list the OCPD had identified as "significant." In fact, these were the cases in which Gilchrist's work had been most severely criticized by defense lawyers, expert witnesses, and appellate judges.

The FBI report, prepared by Supervisory Special Agent Douglas W. Deedrick, was finished on April 4. It was made public three weeks later. Deedrick had reviewed Gilchrist's laboratory notes, trial testimony, and the physical evidence. He conducted his analysis in the OCPD crime lab, using their equipment.

Deedrick found that Gilchrist had been wrong in all of the hair matches he had been able to review from the Pierce case. He also questioned "[t]he extremely high number of 'matching' head hairs," considering the quality of Gilchrist's examinations. And Deedrick criticized Gilchrist's trial testimony, where she offered her hair and blood analysis as linking evidence but did "not offer that these results are independent."

In addition to the Pierce case, Deedrick found that Gilchrist had been wrong in six out of the seven other cases he reexamined. She had misidentified hairs in five cases and misidentified fibers in one other. Hairs that Gilchrist had matched to suspects' "were either too limited for meaningful comparison or associated incorrectly," the agent wrote.

Regarding Gilchrist's testimony on hair evidence, Deedrick concluded that she had "made statements that went beyond the acceptable limits of forensic science." Gilchrist had repeatedly stated or implied that hairs were "unique" or that it was impossible not to be able to distinguish hairs from two different individuals. "These statements," Deedrick wrote, "would improperly place too much significance on the hairs associated in the cases and leave jurors with the impression that hair associations were identity." Deedrick saw no indication that Gilchrist ever qualified her statements about hair with the standard disclaimer that hair is not identity-specific.

When FBI agents testify about hair evidence, Bureau policy requires them to state the following disclaimer: "It is noted that hair does not possess a sufficient number of unique characteristics to be positively associated with a particular person to the exclusion of all others."

This disclaimer, or something like it, should be included in any report on hair comparison and should be stated in testimony. Deedrick noted that Gilchrist did not make a formal disclaimer. While she often qualified her hair comparisons with wording similar to that of the disclaimer quoted above, Gilchrist would then go on to testify as if she was not bound by the limits she had just described. In fact, Gilchrist would leave the jurors with the impression that hair matches were a positive identifier. At trial Bob Macy or one of his prosecutors would ask, "Have you ever in your experience seen two hairs from two different people that matched?" Gilchrist would answer, "No." While Gilchrist herself may not have ever seen two hairs from different sources match microscopically, the literature on microscopic hair comparison is filled with examples of false-positive identifications. Several hair examiners told me that they themselves have seen false matches.

In one study, the Law Enforcement Assistance Administration (where Bob Macy once worked) tested the forensic work in 235 crime labs. They found microscopic hair comparison to be the weakest area of competence, with an error rate as high as 67 percent. The majority of crime labs were incorrect in four out of five hair samples analyzed, according to the LEAA. A majority of the laboratories could not even identify the species of hair in four out of five samples.

Deedrick made a series of recommendations, including a review of all the cases in which Gilchrist's hair and/or fiber comparisons were "significant to the outcome of the trial." Protocols and procedures should be established at the OCPD crime lab, Deedrick wrote, including peer review, qualification requirements, and proficiency testing for hair and fiber analysts. And all examiners should include a "qualifying statement" about the limits of such comparisons in their reports and testimony.

One of the problems with the evidence in the Pierce case is that Gilchrist did not mount and photograph the hair evidence when it came into the lab. Mounting hair evidence is vital to protecting the chain of custody and disproving claims of evidence contamination. Hairs are placed individually on a clean microscopic slide and a coverslip is permanently mounted. The hair cannot be removed, nor another hair added, without breaking the coverslip or using a chemical to eat through the bonding agent, called Permount, which is so strong that forensic chemists are now having trouble unmounting hair evidence for DNA tests.

Gilchrist usually kept evidentiary hairs in envelopes until she had matched them with sample hairs, also kept in envelopes. Having loose hairs all over her work area made cross-contamination not only possible but probable. Several defense attorneys have argued that Gilchrist could easily have switched hairs from one envelope to another, whether intentionally or unintentionally, thereby creating "matches" between the suspect's and the evidentiary hair.

In the Pierce case, Gilchrist has also been accused of benchmarking the hair samples. Benchmarking, or dry-benching, involves taking a large number of unknowns from the crime scene, matching only a couple of known samples, and concluding that they all match. Benchmarking is universally condemned by the scientific community, not just in hair comparisons but also in analyzing bloodstains, semen samples, and other serological evidence.

Hair comparison is slow and tedious work. It is the most time-consuming of all forensic examinations, taking longer even than DNA. A case relying on hair evidence can take months for the lab work to be completed. Gilchrist was always under a great deal of pressure and continually missed deadlines to wrap up her investigations and turn the evidence over to the defense on discovery. She could have resorted to benchmarking in part due to these time pressures. And benchmarking can help make a weak case seem stronger. When Gilchrist matched thirty-one evidentiary hairs to Jeffrey Todd Pierce, the sheer number of hairs was understood by the jury as powerful evidence of guilt. It is possible that Gilchrist was wrong thirty-one times. It is also possible that she didn't examine all of the hairs. When you consider the fact that none of the hairs were Jeffrey Todd Pierce's, benchmarking could have helped Gilchrist get away with her faulty matches. By comparing only a few sample hairs from Pierce to the evidentiary hairs, she would minimize the chances that she might find obvious dissimilarities.

This is all assuming that she conducted her hair examinations in good faith. Whether she benchmarked or allowed cross-contamination of the sample and evidentiary hairs, Gilchrist clearly exaggerated common attributes between the evidentiary and sample hairs by leading the jury to believe that hair matches were identity-specific and testifying to similarities like the "bandanna effect" that were clearly intended to prove the defendant's guilt.

Following the Deedrick investigation, the FBI undertook a thorough review of Gilchrist's casework. The Oklahoma legislature granted OIDS $650,000 to investigate Gilchrist's cases. The Oklahoma County DA's office began conducting its own investigation, with David Prater personally reexamining Gilchrist's cases and acting as spokesman for the office.

Oklahoma Attorney General Drew Edmondson announced that his office would review the thirteen pending death row cases in which Gilchrist had testified. Edmondson promised that if his office's investigation uncovered problems similar to the ones discovered by Deedrick, he would ask for a delay in execution until further testing was performed.

"Every capital case that she touched needs to be thoroughly examined," Governor Frank Keating said. "And every noncapital case she touched needs also to be thoroughly examined."

Even as Keating and other state officials stressed the seriousness of the Gilchrist investigation, they insisted that no innocent person had been executed.

How did they know?

When the OSBI began reviewing 1,694 of Gilchrist's cases, three years of case files could not be found. These were the files from 1980, 1981, and 1990 that Boshell had reported missing. Those files included not only Gilchrist's work but also cases handled by other chemists. Since the logs also could not be located, the OSBI wasn't even sure how many files were missing.

By now Gilchrist had hired an attorney, Melvin Hall, who said that his client "stands behind her work" and predicted that "she will be completely vindicated."

A May 2 *Oklahoman* editorial urged that Gilchrist be presumed innocent until proven guilty: "It has not been established that Gilchrist's alleged sloppy work has resulted in the execution of an innocent person or even the conviction of an innocent person."

When this editorial was published, the results of the second round of the Pierce DNA tests were already known to prosecutors. Bob Macy was only waiting for written confirmation of those tests.

The written reports arrived at the DA's office on May 7, 2001. That day, Bob Macy formally dropped the charges against Pierce. The district court ordered that Pierce's conviction and sentences be vacated. Later that day, Jeffrey Todd Pierce walked out of Joseph Hart Correctional Center a free man. As Pierce left prison, he said that he planned to leave Oklahoma and to try to rebuild a life with his family.

Pierce blamed Joyce Gilchrist for his incarceration.

"She's ruined me and countless lives," Pierce said. "I'm just one who opened the door. There will be a lot more coming out behind me."

Pierce's first full day of freedom was his wife's birthday—and sixteen years to the day since S. B was raped at the Woodlake Apartments complex.

The *Oklahoman* declared that Pierce's release "actually represents a victory" for the criminal justice system. Macy and his prosecutors were now making the same argument. They also claimed that Pierce had been convicted because DNA testing was not available to them at the time. The Oklahoma state legislature issued Pierce a formal apology, although one state legislator refused to coauthor the bill, saying it was premature. "I gather the state of Oklahoma has done nothing wrong," Representative Ray Vaughn (R-Edmond) said. "I don't see why we are apologizing."

Three months later, the semen sample from the S. B crime scene was matched to a DNA profile in Oklahoma's convicted offender database. Owen May was already in the same prison where Pierce had spent nearly fifteen years. May was serving forty-five years for a 1992 rape at the Woodlake Apartments complex. The statute of limitations on the 1985 rape charge had already expired, so he couldn't be tried for the S. B. rape.

Pierce's release set off a media firestorm that quickly went national. The *New York Times, Washington Post, Time* magazine, *Nightline,* and CBS News descended on Oklahoma City, a community unaccustomed to the hot lights of big media.

When Dan Rather was getting ready to interview Joyce Gilchrist, the CBS anchor worried that he might not be able to get her to admit that she had been called "Black Magic." Expecting her to deny it, he prepared several follow-up questions. Instead, he was visibly surprised when she copped to it immediately.

"That was in reference to a defense attorney who said I could find evidence that no one else could," Gilchrist said, apparently proud of the nickname. Throughout the interview, Gilchrist refused to accept any blame for the Jeffrey Todd Pierce case, or any others she had worked on.

"I would accept responsibility if I'm wrong," Gilchrist said. "But I've never done anything wrong in a case I've ever been involved in. Using the technology we had at the time, I did the best job I could and I presented the facts to the court and let the jury decide what they believed."

During the interview, Gilchrist appeared nervous and tired. Gone were the polish and self-confidence that so many courtroom observers had previously noted. Gilchrist had agreed to let Rather interview her on the condition that he also spoke to Dave McBride, her old boss, a former OCPD chief. If Gilchrist was expecting McBride to defend her, she was in for a surprise.

"I think Joyce Gilchrist may have fallen into an internal feeling that she was on the police team, she was on the prosecution team," McBride said. "And what scientists should always feel like is they are on the side of science."

In interviews with local media, Gilchrist defended her work and said that the only reason she was being singled out for criticism was that she had upset the police administration by making a sexual harassment charge against Major Garold Spencer.

Two weeks after Pierce's release, Bob Macy retired with eighteen months left in his term. While he has steadfastly refused to admit that the Pierce case and the media frenzy it provoked forced him to resign, Jeffrey Todd Pierce is the only person his office convicted whom Bob Macy will admit was innocent. And he blames Joyce Gilchrist.

"Pierce is the only one I can think of out of the hundreds of cases that Gilchrist was wrong," Macy told me. "If you look at the cases that were tried and convicted and compare that against the number that were reversed, it's just tiny."

The cops also blamed Gilchrist; however, she would not have determined that the evidence implicated Pierce if the detectives hadn't wanted her to come to that conclusion. And even while they thought Pierce was the suspect, Detectives Cook and Koonce should have recognized the problems in their case and performed due diligence to resolve them.

Even the jurors blamed Gilchrist.

"I feel like I was part of a scam," Roy Orr, a juror in the Pierce trial said. "The evidence wasn't correct and we counted on the police department and forensic specialists to be honest and truthful, and that wasn't the case."

"They matched his hairs. It must have been him," Mast Doolittle, another juror, said. "I think it's the same as fingerprints. No two hairs are alike. That's what they said."

To this day, S. B. still believes it was Jeffrey Todd Pierce who raped her.

Even if they place all the blame on Joyce Gilchrist, at least Oklahoma authorities are willing to admit that Pierce was innocent. Why can't they admit the same about Robert Lee Miller? Bob Macy dropped the charges against Pierce the day he got the official DNA results back. Why did he keep Robert Lee Miller in jail for three years after similar tests proved that he was innocent?

"I think race was certainly an issue," OIDS attorney Jamie Pybas said. "And Pierce wasn't on death row."

In other words, according to Pybas, because Miller was facing execution, Bob Macy was even more reluctant to admit he was innocent.

I asked Macy about the two cases.

"These people that get out, the media makes heroes out of them, and most of them are, from what I know of their backgrounds, pretty unworthy individuals," Macy said. "If they hadn't been convicted of that rape, they'd be convicted of something else."

Neither Jeffrey Todd Pierce nor Robert Lee Miller had a record of violent crimes. Since their release, they have not been in trouble with the law.

Even though Jeffrey Todd Pierce was not sentenced to death, he had come very close to death row. The police believed, and so did the jury, that he was responsible for the murder of Judy Weichert. If the cops had had any other evidence besides Gilchrist's erroneous hair comparison, Pierce could have been charged with that murder and possibly sentenced to death.

This pattern of shoddy investigation is the exact opposite of what I had assumed about death penalty cases. I thought that since the stakes were so high—literally life and death—death penalty cases would be held to higher standards than noncapital felonies. I figured that there would be more intensive investigations, a higher burden of proof, and cops and prosecutors (as well as judges and juries) more willing to err on the side of uncertainty rather than conviction. Instead, the death penalty, at least in Oklahoma County, exerted pressures upon everybody involved. These pressures made it difficult, perhaps even impossible, for those responsible to admit mistakes, express doubt, point out problems, or even ask obvious questions.

As egregious as Gilchrist's lab work and testimony were in the Pierce case, she did not convict him herself. It took a team of detectives, prosecutors, a judge, and a jury to send an innocent man to prison. The direct responsibility lies with Barry Albert. I believe Albert recognized and understood the weakness (perhaps even the exculpatory nature) of the forensic evidence against Pierce and yet went ahead and prosecuted him anyway. As district attorney, responsible for the formal charges, Bob Macy should never have filed the Pierce case. From the first day that Pierce was brought into the police station, Macy was directly involved. The detectives told Macy they had the suspect and he pressured them to get a confession. When they couldn't get a confession, Macy went ahead and filed on Pierce anyway. Then, because it wasn't a death penalty case, he let Barry Albert prosecute.

The OCPD detectives, Bill Cook, Bob Horn, and Larry Koonce, built the case against Pierce in a series of steps by which they convinced themselves that he was the suspect—ignoring or explaining away evidence that did not fit their theory.

It started with Koonce's hunch that the suspect would be a maintenance worker. When they found a Can Do employee who had been working on the premises the day of the rape, roughly fit the suspect's description, and had quit working for the company shortly after the rape occurred, they thought they had their man. When the victim identified Pierce in a photo lineup (this is assuming that the photo lineup was legitimately conducted) they were certain. The detectives took Pierce in for questioning, hoping they could break him down. When he didn't confess, they had Gilchrist take hair and blood samples, telling her that Pierce was the suspect they liked, not just for the S. B. rape but also for the Weichert murder. Gilchrist came back with hair matches and just enough blood work that she would be able to say she could not exclude Pierce as the suspect.

As in the Robert Lee Miller case, a thoroughly innocent man was sent to prison because everyone on the prosecution believed he was guilty. If anyone had any doubts, they didn't speak up. Bob Macy and Barry Albert, Joyce Gilchrist and the OCPD detectives all convinced themselves and one another that this hardworking young husband and father was a sexual psychopath. No one had the honesty or the courage to take a close look at the evidence (or lack of it) and ask the questions that it provoked: How does Pierce's alibi fit into the time line? Why are there so many clear discrepancies between the suspect's description and Pierce's appearance? How exactly did the serological evidence point toward Pierce? Aside from Gilchrist's hair comparisons, was there any physical evidence linking him to the crime?

When Pierce was released, Macy and his defenders said that it was the result of their not having DNA technology available to them at the time of his trial. (DNA technology was available to them in the Robert Lee Miller case, and they declined to use it.) The problems with the Pierce case have nothing to do with DNA—except for the fact that his innocence would probably never have been conclusively proved without it. DNA is a powerful investigative tool and can serve as virtually irrefutable evidence. In many ways it has revolutionized law enforcement. Yet DNA will never and should never replace good old-fashioned detective work. One of the most important tools a detective has is the ability, and the honesty, to listen to the evidence and follow where it leads, no matter where that takes him. If the OCPD detectives had not been so eager to believe that Jeffrey Todd Pierce was guilty, they would have looked more closely at the evidence and been led to realize that he was not the suspect. But during the Macy years, these detectives had become so convinced of their own righteousness that they lost the ability to examine evidence objectively. They were more interested in winning a conviction than solving the case. And no one would tell them they were wrong.

One of the reasons why Jeffrey Todd Pierce was wrongfully incarcerated was that Bob Macy's office and the OCPD were accustomed to investigating and prosecuting and winning cases like his. They had full run of the criminal justice system; there was no governing authority to stop them.

"When someone says that prosecutorial or police misconduct is harmless error," Bob Ravitz said, "remember Jeffrey Todd Pierce."

The *Washington Post* said in an editorial dated May 28, 2001, that "questions about [Gilchrist's] work serve as a reminder of the grave harm that a single person in the criminal justice apparatus can cause—either through malice or incompetence, if the rest of the system offers little more than malign neglect."

I asked several people if they thought Joyce Gilchrist's mistakes were due to malice or incompetence. Laura Schile put it this way: "If you prove competence, you prove malice."

In other words, if Gilchrist knew and understood the science, then she must have intentionally skewed, suppressed, or fabricated some of her forensic results. If she were simply incompetent, her mistakes would have been all over the map. Instead, her mistakes benefited the prosecution. And when she gave misleading testimony, it concerned matters in which she knew and understood herself to be vulnerable. Even if she wasn't a terribly competent scientist, Gilchrist knew enough to understand what she had to cover up. Using Schile's formulation, I believe this proves malice.

Joyce Gilchrist was an important part of this conspiracy of willful ignorance. Because she dealt with science and terminology that many did not understand (or at least said they didn't understand), she was an easy target for blame. And while her work in the Pierce case and others was not merely incompetent but unconscionable, Joyce Gilchrist is not alone responsible for what is wrong with the death penalty in Oklahoma. Still, the controversy continues to swirl around her.

By mid-August 2001, when the Tenth Circuit Court decision overturning Alfred Brian Mitchell's death penalty was issued, Gilchrist was under investigation by at least six different agencies—the FBI, the state attorney general, the OSBI, the OIDS, the Oklahoma County DA, and her own police department. She was called before a city disciplinary panel to determine whether or not she should be fired. The panel conducted a closed hearing, during which it heard two weeks of witness testimony. After that, the panel spent another week compiling a final report. It was the longest hearing in the state's history.

One of the chief concerns during the proceeding was how to document Gilchrist's errors in a thorough and detailed fashion without exposing the city to liability. If too strong a case was made against her, the very evidence the panel had gathered might be used against the city in future lawsuits. Even with this consideration, the panel appears to have found overwhelming evidence of not just supervisory mismanagement but also serious problems with Gilchrist's casework, testimony, and responses to internal investigations. The report was sealed under a state law protecting personnel records. Everybody who has seen it is under a gag order not to discuss its contents. However, I was able to confirm that the report contains allegations which, if proven, could support indictable criminal charges against Joyce Gilchrist.

Following the hearing, Gilchrist's employment with the OCPD was terminated on September 25, 2001. The reasons given for her firing included "laboratory mismanagement, criticism from court challenges and flawed casework analysis."

In April 2002, Jeffrey Todd Pierce filed a civil suit against Joyce Gilchrist, Bob Macy, and several government bodies. Representing Pierce in the suit were Tulsa attorneys Clark Brewster and Guy Fortney. The suit charged:

- Joyce Gilchrist had connected the S. B. rape and Weichert murder "with an intent to deceive and provide fraudulent and predictable results."

- Detectives Koonce and Cook "induced, solicited and encouraged Gilchrist's false findings."

- Gilchrist had conducted her examination of the Pierce and S. B. evidence "with an intent to deceive and provide fraudulent results."

- Gilchrist also "concealed the exculpatory evidence" from the defense.

Brewster and Fortney looked beyond the Jeffrey Todd Pierce case to see a "pattern and practice" of Macy and Gilchrist's conspiring together in several criminal cases to convict defendants even when evidence indicated that they were innocent.

The suit described Gilchrist's career as being "littered with documented instances of misconduct, professional and ethical breaches of her duty, false reporting and suborning of false testimony. These numerous bad acts represent an intentional and deliberate indifference to the rights of all accused individuals." Gilchrist's "malfeasant conduct" was the policy of Bob Macy "and condoned and tolerated" by Gilchrist's supervisors and the DA's office.

"Under Macy's administration," the suit charged, "the Oklahoma County District Attorney's Office became perverted, seeking convictions of any targeted accused even when the investigations by the OCPD and the District Attorney's Office uncovered exculpatory evidence which clearly demonstrated his or her innocence. Gilchrist and others were coached, directed and influenced during the investigation of a case to provide reports that were consistent with the OCPD's and Macy's theories of the cases in order to gain a 'victory' and conviction regardless of guilt."

The lawsuit asked for $25 million in compensatory damages and $50 million in punitive damages. The defendants deny any liability.

One prominent Oklahoma City attorney called it "the best plaintiff's civil rights case I have ever seen."

When I spoke with Jeffrey Todd Pierce, I was impressed by how calm he remained while he described what had happened to him. Even when I asked him about very sensitive issues, his voice didn't rise from his usual soft-spoken, polite manner. He is a man against whom a terrible injustice has been done, but you don't hear any anger.

While he was in prison, Pierce had hope that his case would be reversed on appeal (while all death penalty cases get automatic appeals, other felonies are heard by appellate courts according to the merits of their cases). After the Oklahoma Court of Criminal Appeals refused to reverse his conviction, Pierce lost hope and resigned himself to a lifetime in prison. His wife and children were lost to him. He would have to make the most out of his life in prison. Trying to tune out as much as possible the ugliness and cruelty of prison life, he did what he could to survive, making friends with several other convicts whom he believed had also been wrongly convicted.

Pierce finally got the freedom he had dreamed of, yet it wasn't easy. He returned to his family as a stranger. His wife had been remarried and divorced. His sons—both honor students and athletes popular with their classmates—never knew their father until they were sixteen years old. They had not been told he was in prison and, when he came back, they did not remember him.

"Kathy and I started up like it was yesterday," Pierce said, "but the boys didn't know me. Kathy had to reintroduce me as their father."

After spending nearly fifteen years in prison, Pierce found it difficult to adjust to even the simplest things. He didn't know how to work a newfangled gas pump. Computers and cell phones were foreign to him. When his two sons went to get their driver's licenses, Pierce took the test with them, because his own license had expired. All three passed.

Even if Jeffrey Todd Pierce wins his lawsuit, he will never get fifteen years of his life back. He missed his sons' childhoods.

"We were never given an opportunity to become a family," Kathy Pierce said. "We never got to sit down at mealtime, to go to baseball games, do the family vacations, birthdays, Christmas, or holidays."

No amount of money can replace what was taken from Jeffrey Todd Pierce. Yet the lawsuit may help explain how and why he was put "over a barrel" by Bob Macy and the OCPD.

Shortly after Pierce's suit was announced, Joyce Gilchrist herself filed a lawsuit against Oklahoma City, the city manager, Chief M. T. Berry, and eight past and present employees of the OCPD. Saying she was the victim of retaliation after she had complained about Major Garold Spencer's "unwanted touching and caressing" of a civilian. Gilchrist claimed that Spencer, along with Byron Boshell and Deputy Chief Robert A. Jones conspired to demote and terminate her. Also named in the lawsuit was Laura Schile. "Joyce Gilchrist's termination was arbitrary, capricious and without a rational basis," the lawsuit charged. "The degree of outrageousness and the magnitude of actual harm inflicted upon Joyce Gilchrist by the defendants is truly conscious [sic] shocking." Gilchrist asked for $20 million and to be reinstated in the crime lab.

"I know one thing," one high-ranking police official told me, "she will never work for the OCPD again."

Joyce Gilchrist was the lead forensic chemist in twenty-three death penalty cases. Because several adjoining counties use the OCPD crime lab, one of these cases was outside of Oklahoma County. Twelve convicts whom Gilchrist had helped send to death row had already been executed. All of Gilchrist's eleven pending death penalty cases were reinvestigated by OSBI and the attorney general's office, and state authorities decided to set three cases for further review: John Michael Hooker, who was convicted in 1988 for the stabbing deaths of his girlfriend and her mother; Michael Edward Hooper (the case outside Oklahoma County), who was convicted for the 1993 murder of his ex-girlfriend and her two children; and Curtis Edward McCarty, who was convicted for the 1982 murder and rape of an eighteen-year-old girl. (McCarty's original convictions had already been reversed twice by the Oklahoma Court of Criminal Appeals.) OSBI also decided that Dewey George Moore's 1985 conviction for the rape and murder of Jenipher Gilbert also deserved a closer look, although Gilchrist had been Janice Davis's subordinate in that investigation.

Meanwhile, the feds were still on the case, even if they found themselves in something of a bind. With the media attention and resulting political pressure that the Gilchrist scandal had generated, the feds had to do something about her, particularly since any state or local investigation would be criticized for partiality toward one of their own. Indeed, such criticisms were already being heard, which is certainly one reason why the federal grand jury was impaneled. Unfortunately for the feds, the statutes of limitation on charges of perjury, evidence tampering, or obstruction of justice had already expired. If someone had been wrongfully executed, however, they could prosecute her for a federal civil rights violation.

The feds subpoenaed evidence from ten of Gilchrist's murder cases. (Nine of those had already resulted in executions. The other case had resulted in a sentence of life without parole.) Federal prosecutors are saying nothing about their inquiry, but at the time of this writing, the jury had spent most of its time reviewing case files, Gilchrist's personnel records, and other documentary evidence. One of Bob Macy's former top assistants happened to be serving as a juror.

By the end of 2001, OSBI had nearly concluded its initial reexamination of Gilchrist's cases. The five-member investigative team had looked at 1,191 of Gilchrist's case files and recommended 196 for further review. The OSBI stated that these cases were set aside because of "concerns."

OIDS is actively testing what DNA evidence remains in other cases to see if anyone else has been falsely accused. So far they have found evidence used to free Arvin McGhee of a rape conviction in Tulsa (McGhee was one of Pierce's friends in prison). OIDS is hindered by a lack of physical evidence, the sheer enormity of cases, and statutory restraints, like the fact that a convict who has already served his term and been released does not have recourse to state-funded DNA tests.

What about the people who have already been executed?

"Nobody cares about the dead," Jack Dempsey Pointer said. "Oklahoma is not going to spend money to find out that they have executed someone who might have been innocent."

And even if the state of Oklahoma wanted to determine whether any of the fifty men and women it has executed had been innocent, much of that evidence is lost, missing, or destroyed.

After she had been transferred out of the crime lab, but before her suspension from the OCPD, Joyce Gilchrist was found rummaging around in the DNA lab. After decontaminating the lab, Melissa

Keith found blood samples from the still-unsolved murder of Judy Weichert in the cabinet drawers that Gilchrist had been caught searching. Was Gilchrist looking for the Weichert evidence? (At this point, the Pierce evidence had been sent out for testing, but the results had not yet been reported.) Was she planning to destroy it? Or was she hoping it might prove that Pierce was guilty of the Weichert murder—despite the fact that the only evidence linking him to the crime were her own erroneous hair comparisons?

"Oklahoma authorities," the *Washington Post* wrote in the same editorial quoted earlier, "say they are confident that nobody has been wrongly executed as a result of Ms. Gilchrist's testimony. We hope they are lucky enough to be right."

Have innocent people been executed in Oklahoma? The average Oklahoman would say yes. Jeffrey Todd Pierce's release and the Gilchrist scandal led Oklahomans to believe that innocent people had been convicted and even executed. Nearly 75 percent of Oklahomans believe that wrongful convictions occur either "frequently" or "now and then," according to a poll conducted by the *Oklahoman* and the University of Oklahoma. Asked how often they think similar errors have led to the wrongful execution of innocent people, 14 percent answered "frequently," 28 percent said "now and then," and 45 percent think it happens "rarely." Only 7 percent of those polled believed that an innocent person had not been executed. Sixty-eight percent said that mistakes like these did not shake their support of the death penalty.

Oklahomans believe in the death penalty. And no one believes in it more fervently than Bob Macy.

CHAPTER THIRTEEN

THE IMPACT OF VIOLENCE

BOB MACY RAN A PROSECUTORIAL MACHINE THAT SENT SEVENTY-THREE people to death row. Macy called it the "best capital litigation team in the country." Judging the system merely by the numbers, perhaps Macy's claim has some merit. Examining the quality of the detective work, the scientific analysis and testimony, and the way the prosecutors ran the cases and conducted themselves, I came to a somewhat different conclusion.

Every case begins with the investigating detectives. They build the foundation upon which the prosecution will eventually rest. In many of the cases I examined, the OCPD detectives ignored exculpatory evidence, failed to follow up significant leads, and generally put together shoddy, half-baked cases. Their investigations often effectively ended once they decided that a certain suspect was guilty of the crime. Most of the time, they had the right suspect.

Detectives often work off hunches. When their hunches are wrong, hopefully the detectives realize it before charges are filed. This is where the crime lab should play an important role in the truth-seeking function of the investigation. If the evidence excludes the suspect, the criminalist has to tell the detectives. Not only was Joyce Gilchrist often reluctant to do this, but she appears to have used her lab tests to confirm the detectives' hunches rather than seek independent scientific results. She also tried to control the results of her tests, either by keeping them at a less determinative (and therefore more subjective) level or by ignoring results when they didn't say what she wanted them to. She treated discovery requests with contempt and kept evidence from the defense. She systematically destroyed evidence at the very time when she knew that much of that evidence might be retested.

Bob Macy created a machine for prosecuting death penalty cases whose ambition seems to have been racking up as many convictions as possible rather than seeing that justice is done. He trained a generation of prosecutors who continue this practice. At trial, Macy repeatedly allowed his expert witnesses to give testimony that he should have known was inaccurate, irresponsible, or simply false. His public statements helped precondition the jury pool in favor of death penalty convictions. His political power kept him from being held accountable—for a time.

The Oklahoma City defense attorneys are not blameless. Most of them were intimidated by Bob Macy. Some gave up when they should have been fighting the hardest—while their clients were on trial for their lives. Others fought hard and still lost.

The juries simply responded to what they believed or wanted to believe. Brainwashed by Macy's propaganda, selected for their willingness to send convicts to their death, and succumbing to peer pressure, Oklahoma County juries voted for guilty verdicts and death penalties in cases that never satisfied the burden of proof.

Many district court judges in Oklahoma County consistently ruled in the prosecution's favor, allowing Macy to get away with prosecutorial misconduct and Gilchrist to give misleading testimony.

Sometimes Macy and Gilchrist would be criticized by a Court of Criminal Appeals that reversed several cases on those grounds but consistently found reasons to affirm convictions that should have been overturned. Because the district court judges faced regular election campaigns and the appeals court judges ran on retention ballots, their ability to stand up to Bob Macy was compromised, especially once he established his political power.

Finally, the people of Oklahoma County kept reelecting Bob Macy. They were very proud of "America's Leading Death Penalty Prosecutor." Many of them still are. In 1998, when Macy was clearly in physical and mental decline, he ran for reelection and spent one afternoon in his office raising money. After he had gotten pledges for $50,000 (a significant war chest in Oklahoma County politics) no one would run against him. At a time when he was probably unfit to hold office, Macy ran unopposed.

A couple of years later, when criticism of his record could no longer be ignored, this driven, ambitious man retired with eighteen months left in his term. Macy said he wanted to spend more time with his family. He lives alone.

I visited Bob Macy at his home. We had scheduled a meeting for Easter Saturday. That morning I called him to confirm. Macy told me that his brother was dying and he had not slept that night. I asked whether he wanted to cancel the interview. Macy said no, he had driven back from Plano, Texas, just to see me. He asked that I give him an hour. He needed to take a shower and have some coffee.

Stephen Weeks and I drove to Harrah, a small rural town about twenty minutes outside Oklahoma City, where Macy lives on his cattle ranch. Above the entrance to his driveway is a gate that reads "String Tie Ranch." Macy was at the door to greet us. His eyes were filled with tears.

"My brother just died," he said, shaking my hand. He had just heard the news minutes earlier.

I asked again if he wanted to cancel the interview. He said no.

Before I met Bob Macy, I had read thousands of pages written about him and spoken to dozens of people who knew him, worked for him and against him, loved him and hated him. I wanted to meet Bob Macy face-to-face. I knew the danger of caricature and media cliché. I wanted to give Macy the chance to prove the popular image of him wrong.

The man who stood before me now was over seventy years old. His hair was white. He walked slowly, almost shuffled. His barrel chest had shrunk. His hands had once been large and powerful; now they were trembling and covered with age spots. On his walls and bookshelves were photographs, awards, and other mementos of his career. He was an old and lonely man. His children were gone. His marriages had broken up. Few friends came to see him. Macy showed me the guest bedroom he kept for his friend Wilford Brimley, the actor, when he came to visit. Brimley hadn't been there in a while.

Bob Macy sat and talked with us for three hours. The conversation covered a broad range of subjects. We talked about our favorite Western movies and traded crime stories. Macy showed us his collection of memories from his career as a prosecutor and rodeo roper. At times he was sharp and attentive; sometimes he drifted off. These lapses in attention usually occurred when a troubling question was asked. He had a quiet stubbornness. Sometimes he wouldn't answer my questions, but he never got angry. He was a man who didn't get rattled easily. And he was deeply grieved by the death of his brother—the first of his siblings to die.

We went over several of his famous death penalty cases. In each one of the cases I mentioned to Macy, he had one detail or anecdote which proved, if not the defendant's guilt, then at least that he was a bad person. This was our third conversation, and I was hearing many of the same anecdotes. Macy had a prepared defense for almost every question I asked, as if he had been waiting for this interview for years (perhaps he had, and he just didn't know I would be conducting it).

"I tried a bunch of death penalty cases," Macy said, "and they were the sorriest lot of SOBs."

Bob Macy believes in the death penalty. For him, it is an article of faith. He clearly hasn't thought out many of the philosophical questions about it, yet he has his reasons, and he sticks to them. Most of all, he believes that the death penalty is an effective deterrent.

"I couldn't understand why we were having all these horrible murders in Oklahoma City," Macy said. "Part of my motivation was, if we give them the death penalty and execute a few of them, maybe it will go down."

I asked him what made him seek the death penalty.

Macy said that his decision was always based on whether he believed the defendant would kill again.

"Every time, before I asked for the death penalty," Macy said, "I was satisfied that if I didn't get it for them, they would go out and kill again."

Macy also said he would not seek the death penalty if the suspect was truly remorseful. When Steve Weeks pointed out that remorse can only come with a confession, Macy was silent for a moment. Then he said, "I never thought of that."

I asked Macy what he would change about the death penalty. The only proposal he had was expediting the process.

"I think it would be better," Macy said, "if we could get it over with more quickly."

Had Macy ever witnessed an execution himself?

"There wasn't any reason why I wanted to see an execution," Macy replied. "I don't think it would have changed my ability to do my job if I had. I thought about going a few times, then I said, what the hell for?"

I asked Macy about Joyce Gilchrist.

"I was a trial lawyer for thirty years and I think I can read people pretty good and I think Joyce was doing the best she could," Macy said. "She may have made some mistakes, but hell, who doesn't?"

I reminded him of the judicial decisions in McCarty and Mitchell and LaFevers, and of what John Wilson had been saying for years and the FBI had eventually confirmed.

"She was criticized for giving her opinion," Macy replied. "That's what an expert witness does."

Macy maintained that he had trusted Joyce Gilchrist and believed that she was competent. The only mistake he would admit was giving too much credence to a forensic science (microscopic hair comparison) that was not as determinative as he had thought.

"We gave hair evidence a lot more credit than it really deserved," Macy said. "But we believed in our hearts that what we were doing was right."

Macy's defenders have tried to frame the debate over the death penalty as a dispute over the accuracy and probative weight of microscopic hair comparison.

"Lots of people working both sides of the fence, defense and prosecution, genuinely believed and accepted that hair comparison was fundamentally reliable within certain parameters," Assistant District Attorney Richard Wintory said. "Now nobody can tell us what those parameters are."

The parameters had been established long before Joyce Gilchrist ever entered the OCPD crime lab. They were the same parameters then as they are today. Microscopic hair comparison is similar to other comparative forensic sciences like tire tracks, shoe prints, and bite marks. In these fields, trained experts perform analyses and render opinions based on their education and experience. When their conclusions are testified to, the expert witnesses can visually demonstrate the similarities they found. This is not possible with hair comparisons, because the characteristics of hair are not as easily recognized by nonexperts. Other comparative forensic techniques also share one advantage that hair analysis lacks—they cannot be contradicted by DNA.

The problem isn't with the science but the manner in which it was used. Brian Wraxall remembered one case he worked in Oklahoma during the early 1980s where mistakes had been made during the comparison of a known blood sample from a suspect with an unknown semen sample from the crime scene. Upon reexamining the evidence, Wraxall determined that the suspect could not have been the semen donor. The OCPD lab had not gotten the blood analysis right—the suspect didn't have the same ABO type. He told Bob Macy, who responded, "Wait a minute, we've got a sixteen-point hair match on the suspect." Macy thought that a sixteen-point match on hair was a positive ID. After all, you only needed eight points on a fingerprint. Wraxall told Macy that twelve to fourteen of those matching characteristics were found in everybody's hair. Macy reluctantly dismissed the case.

If Macy didn't understand hair evidence, he should have. Instead, he chose to accept Gilchrist's testimony, because she told him what he wanted to hear. After fielding my repeated questions about how Joyce Gilchrist's incompetence had put him in a bad position, Macy snapped back, "It looks like you're trying to get me to turn on Joyce."

He made it clear that he wouldn't do this. We spoke with Macy before Gilchrist's lawsuit was filed. I wonder if he regrets not telling us more about her.

If he could live in any other time, I asked Macy, which time would he pick?

"Back in the Wild West," Macy said, smiling, "with Wyatt Earp and Doc Holliday."

I asked him what was his favorite movie.

"Lonesome Dove," Macy replied. He went on to describe his favorite scene, when Gus was dying and said to his friend Woodrow, "It's been one hell of a party." When Macy said this, his eyes filled with tears.

Not only was Bob Macy a living legend to the people of Oklahoma County, but he believed the legend himself. He believes in the myth of the Cowboy West. Macy didn't just dress like Wyatt Earp, he tried to be him. During the 1980s and 1990s, when the world changed so much and so quickly, Macy fought to turn back time to a past that never existed. He wanted justice to be simple. He thought revenge could be his. He wanted not just to fight crime but to wipe it out entirely. He believed, most of all, in the death penalty.

I wonder if Macy still believes. Looking in his tired, teary eyes, I wondered if he was looking back at his long career and wondering which other convicts might have been innocent. When he was in power, he never questioned himself, and he was never questioned. Now that he has lost his power, the doubts that he had suppressed for so long threaten to overwhelm him.

After visiting Bob Macy, Steve and I went to the Oklahoma City Bombing Memorial. The bombing of the Alfred P. Murrah Federal Building in Oklahoma City on April 19, 1995, was a horrible crime against not only the people of Oklahoma City but the entire nation. One hundred and sixty-eight people were killed. Nineteen of them were children.

From the street, the memorial is unassuming, almost hidden. It takes a moment to realize that a building once stood there. On the Cyclone fence outside the west entrance are hundreds of flowers, letters, photographs, stuffed animals, police department patches, poems, and gifts placed there by visitors from all over the world.

Entering the west side, you see two tall polished stone walls at either end of a reflecting pool. One wall is engraved with 9:02. The other says 9:04. The minute in between is when the bomb went off, and everything changed forever.

On the south side of the memorial is a lawn with a gentle rise. One hundred and sixty-eight chairs sit on the lawn, facing the reflecting pool. Each chair is engraved with the name of a victim. Children are represented by small chairs. The chairs are simple, even austere, yet deeply moving.

On the north end, rough stone steps lead toward an elm tree that somehow survived the blast. They call this the Survivor Tree. Its branches were charred black, yet small green buds were sprouting.

I had already seen the memorial during the daytime. At night it is even more beautiful, with lights illuminating each chair and shining on the reflecting pool. There were several visitors wandering silently around the memorial grounds. Oklahoma City was quiet for a city on a Saturday night. Beyond the memorial, lights in the city's two biggest office towers were burning in the form of two large crosses.

The official inscription over the entrance to the memorial reads: "We come here to remember those who were killed, those who survived and those changed forever. May all who leave here know the impact of violence. May this memorial offer comfort, strength, peace, hope and serenity."

Graffiti on a nearby wall says: "We search for the truth. We seek justice. The courts require it. The victims cry for it. And God demands it."

Those words were spray-painted on the wall by a team of rescue workers on the day of the bombing. They echo Bob Macy's closing arguments in several death penalty cases. When the building on which the words had been written was renovated, the memorial commission had the words repainted on the wall.

Macy had been at his office, just two blocks away from the federal building, when the bomb went off. The working day had just begun. Macy was meeting with a couple of detectives, talking about a case. All of a sudden the courthouse building shook violently. The two detectives were knocked off their feet.

"Boys, you better get out of here," Macy said, "this building is coming down."

Before the three men could leave, Macy's chief came in and said that someone had just bombed the federal building. Macy ran outside and kept running until he got to the site.

Several women ran up to him, screaming, "Mr. Macy, help us find our babies."

Macy rushed into the wreckage and began helping the firemen and rescue workers recover victims, alive and dead. His son Brett was one of the first policemen at the scene. Father and son worked side by side searching for bodies. Just being near the bomb site was extremely dangerous. The entire face of the building had been torn off by the blast. Parts of the building's structure were collapsing and debris fell constantly. Ignoring any danger to themselves, Macy, Brett, and the others performed heroic feats of rescue. Many of the victims they recovered were already dead. Some of them were their friends.

One of Macy's closest friends, DEA Agent Kenny McCullough, was among the missing. Macy himself found McCullough's body trapped under a beam. He was dead. Macy helped pull the body out from under the beam and put him in a body bag.

"As we turned to carry Kenny out of the rubble," Macy recalled, "I saw two lines of federal agents and police officers. They saluted as we carried out his body."

Telling this story, Macy could no longer hold back his emotions. He broke down crying and could not speak for nearly a minute.

Macy kept working at the bomb site for eight days. He went home only a couple of times to shower and change his clothes. When he tried to sleep, he couldn't. So he went back to the bomb site.

I asked Macy what he felt like doing to the man responsible for all this carnage. Macy said, "I wanted to slit his throat."

Of course, Timothy McVeigh was arrested for the crime. Macy had wanted to prosecute McVeigh himself (at one point he said he'd like to execute McVeigh 168 times).

"For sixteen years I handled everything of a criminal nature in Oklahoma County," Macy said. "We had a good homicide unit. My office were among the best death penalty litigators in the country. All of a sudden we have the worst crime in the nation and I'm cut out of it."

The feds took the case away from Macy.

"All they let us do was park their cars," Macy said with contempt.

When McVeigh was convicted and given the death penalty, Macy promised to prosecute him on state charges, because he claimed that the federal death penalty law had too many loopholes, and the people of Oklahoma would be more certain of an execution if he was tried in the state courts. When McVeigh waived his appeals, Macy turned his attention elsewhere.

Two days before Christmas 1997, Terry Nichols was convicted in federal court of involuntary manslaughter and sentenced to life without the possibility of parole. Macy began preparing to prosecute Nichols on state charges, despite the fact that polling indicated some 87 percent of Oklahomans were opposed to such a trial.

In a letter to the *Oklahoman,* published on December 12, 1999, Macy wrote: "I am required by ethics to say Terry Nichols is presumed innocent of the charges he faces until and unless he is proven guilty beyond a reasonable doubt." After this grudging disclaimer, Macy went on to say: "There is only one appropriate sentence which justice demands for these murders . . . Terry Nichols should pay, not merely with his freedom but with his life."

On October 16, 2000, a judge disqualified Macy from the Nichols case because of that letter and other media comments.

"I have never seen such a blatant open violation of the rules of professional conduct," District Court Judge Ray Dean Linder said.

"There is no doubt in my mind that Mr. Macy is too closely involved."

Linder's disqualification was upheld by the Court of Criminal Appeals, who also decided that Macy's staff could continue with the case.

When the Murrah Building was bombed, none of Macy's death penalty convictions had been executed. That would soon change. Bombing victims and their families lobbied both the Oklahoma state legislature and Congress for legislation speeding up the appellate process of death penalty cases. In 1996, state and federal laws were passed that greatly streamlined the appeals process. These changes helped result in the high number of executions in Oklahoma and throughout the country during the next few years.

As McVeigh's own death date neared, nearly half of the victims and their families were now opposed to his execution. But these weren't the ones to whom authorities listened. McVeigh himself wanted to die. That, according to some, was reason enough not to kill him. My eleven-year-old daughter said: "They shouldn't have killed him. They should have left him in jail for the rest of his life so he could think about what he did."

When Wes Lane was appointed district attorney to serve out the remainder of Macy's term, Lane said he might drop the Nichols case. On July 30, 2001, Lane met with family members of the bombing victims and, in his words, "prayed about it." A little more than a month later, Lane held a press conference near the Survivor Tree to announce that he would go ahead with the prosecution. Sandy Stensaas, the wife of Ray Elliot, who prosecuted Robert Lee Miller, will head up the prosecution team.

Wes Lane can prosecute Nichols and convict him and execute him—and then what? There will be no one else left to punish.

Standing at the Oklahoma City Bombing Memorial, I couldn't help but think of murder and vengeance. There is only so much a homicide detective can do. He can solve a murder, but he can't bring the dead back to life. He can't restore them to their loved ones. And he certainly cannot act as avenger, no matter how justified or righteous he feels.

"You and I kinda come from the same place. We've been to crime scenes. We've seen what those bastards do," Bob Macy said near the end of our first conversation. "I kinda got the feeling that if you and I got to know each other, we'd find out we got a lot in common."

I saw what I had in common with Bob Macy and it scared me. I know the sense of righteousness that comes with crime fighting; I have given in to hatred and revenge. Yet Macy's career showed me the futility of vengeance. Evil cannot be met with evil, no matter how it is justified. The whole point of law enforcement is to serve justice, not your own ego, ambition, or pathology. We take an oath to uphold the law, not dance around it; to serve others, not ourselves.

Bob Macy believed that if he executed enough people, he could wipe out violent crime in his town. One lunatic with a truckload of fertilizer proved him wrong. Macy acted heroically during the rescue. Yet after all that death, Macy's only response was more death.

"HEINOUS, ATROCIOUS AND CRUEL"

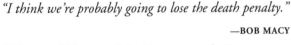

"I think we're probably going to lose the death penalty."

—BOB MACY

"Macy could be one of the big reasons why."

—DAVID AUTRY

I USED TO BELIEVE IN THE DEATH PENALTY. IT WAS AN ARTICLE OF FAITH for a cop. During my twenty years on the force, I saw so much death, pain, and misery that I never questioned whether or not capital punishment was just. There were some people who deserved to die. That's what I thought, and so did my fellow cops.

We often expressed our support for the death penalty with crude terms and lofty rationalizations. We never used the word *revenge*. Instead, we called it justice, but it was cloaked in hate and anger. When we talked about the death penalty it was always with contempt for the suspect. "Fry the fucker," we'd say, "drop the pill on that asshole." That was the way we talked and the way we felt. I was empowered by my peers and that led to a feeling of self-righteousness. I had a closed mind about the issue and refused to accept any facts that might shake my worldview. There was no good reason, that I saw, to be against the death penalty, unless you wanted criminals to get away with murder. It seemed absolutely right and justified.

The death penalty was reestablished in California when I was a second-year officer, but I was never involved in a death penalty case. The standards for death penalty are very high in California, and the only murders that might qualify are usually handled by special divisions like Robbery/Homicide. Early on, the DA's office decided not to seek the death penalty in the O.J. Simpson case and nobody was particularly upset by that decision.

When I retired from the force, I began to broaden my perspective. In each book that I wrote, I found severe problems with police behavior and wound up investigating the investigations, not just the murders that stimulated them. In *Murder in Brentwood,* I uncovered a conspiracy between police and prosecutors to cover up mistakes made by detectives Phil Vanatter and Tom Lange. In *Murder in Greenwich,* I found a small-town police department completely unequipped to investigate a brutal murder. In *Murder in Spokane,* I saw how the incompetence and mismanagement of a serial killer task force led to delays in arresting a suspect and the deaths of at least ten more women.

When I started working on this book, I thought that since death penalty cases carry the highest punishment, they would be investigated more thoroughly and professionally. I quickly realized that the opposite is true. Catastrophic errors occur in many death penalty cases, because of the pressure to make a strong case and get a capital conviction.

Death penalty cases are all high-profile. Maybe you don't see them on the evening news, but within that jurisdiction, even in Oklahoma County, where they were so commonplace, a death penalty case creates the same pressures and scrutiny, the same temptations to cheat or cover up, that I saw in the Simpson trial.

Once a prosecutor announces the death penalty will be sought, anything less than a capital conviction is seen as a failure. If Bob

Macy hadn't asked for the death penalty in these cases, Joyce Gilchrist and the rest of the OCPD wouldn't have felt so much pressure to not only solve the case but also ensure a capital conviction. That pressure was self-reinforcing among those involved in a death penalty case. It gathered a momentum that swept everybody along with it. No one could afford to go against the flow.

The first place where a death penalty case goes wrong is with the detective. His investigation is the foundation on which the prosecution is built. It is up to him whether the crime is investigated thoroughly, professionally, and responsibly. It would be easier if the detectives were simply incompetent, yet certain efforts to hide the mistakes and holes in their cases indicate that they were competent enough to know when they were wrong.

Cops are supposed to follow the rules. That's what makes us different from criminals. What I saw in Oklahoma was that the more law enforcement felt superior to criminals, the more they started to act like them.

The problem isn't just Oklahoma County or Bob Macy or Joyce Gilchrist. It's the death penalty itself. Capital punishment is driven by two emotions—revenge and ambition. The public says it wants revenge for horrible crimes. But they want that revenge secondhand, carried out discreetly by clinical professionals in a small room very far away. The mob cries for blood—they just don't want to actually see it. And so they are never satisfied with, or sickened by, the revenge that is carried out for them. They never learn that revenge has no end; it just completes the circle of violence. The loss that the family of a murder victim feels is not made any less painful by the execution of their loved one's killer. If there ever is any closure for the family of murder victims, it should be based on forgiveness, not revenge.

"The death penalty creates a whole new class of victims whose only crime was to love another human being," defense attorney Steve Pressen said.

Bob Macy said, "When someone commits a crime, it's like a stone being thrown into the water. It creates ripples that spread out far and wide. Everybody's affected."

Macy was talking about the victim and his or her family, friends, neighbors, and the society at large. He could have included the family of the criminal himself. They have done nothing themselves, but they must carry the burden of shame and punishment, and the pain of loss and death, with them for the rest of their lives. This struck me when I saw that young girl in her Easter dress leaving the visiting room at McAlester—it was reinforced in my conversations with Jim Fowler. Of course, a criminal should pay for his crimes. Yet now I realize that punishment is not so clear and unambiguous as I wanted it to be.

Ambition comes into play when prosecutors seek political power by trying death penalty cases. If they win, they can brag about it. If they lose, they can blame liberal judges, corrupt defense attorneys, or the criminal justice system as a whole, forgetting for the moment that they are an important part of it. Either way, they've got their law-and-order position staked out for the next campaign.

As a political issue, the death penalty has become a litmus test on law and order. It is a way for politicians to demonstrate that they are tough on crime. Bill Clinton flew back to Arkansas during the heat of the 1992 campaign to sign the death warrant on a man so retarded he saved a piece of pie from his last meal to eat later. Clinton did this to demonstrate he was not the squishy liberal that some people thought. I would prefer that politicians support law enforcement by simply supporting law enforcement. That would mean giving cops and prosecutors the tools they need to fight crime.

Politically, there is very little to gain, and much to lose, by calling the present death penalty system into question. The death penalty enjoys support from a substantial majority of Americans. Yet that support is not as strong as many think. According to a recent Gallup poll, 66 percent of Americans supported the death penalty; however, 90 percent of them believed innocent people have been executed, and they believe the percentage of innocents executed to be around 10 percent. These findings indicate the fault lines of death penalty support. We want to believe that the death penalty is just, yet we don't think it's fair. We cannot reconcile our faith with the facts. There will soon come a time when we can no longer sustain this contradiction.

Earlier in this nation's history, executions were held in public. The citizens attending the execution had a mix of complex emotions concerning the killing of one of their own. They truly believed that the death penalty was a just punishment. At the same time, they pitied the condemned, praying for them, even turning them into folk heroes—without forgetting the crimes they committed. Back then, people saw the condemned as human beings, in part because they saw the man or woman standing on the gallows. Still, they supported the state's decision to kill them and saw it as a moral necessity. There was a ritual aspect to public executions, in which the public was purged of collective guilt at the same time the person directly responsible was punished. There was also an element of theater; an execution drew bigger crowds than any other public event.

Now we have to hide our executions. They occur in sterile chambers, witnessed by only a few with close ties to the victim or the condemned. If capital punishment is so popular in Oklahoma, and the process of lethal injection is so painless and clean, why doesn't the state broadcast each execution? Why are Department of Corrections officials so afraid that a video of an execution might "get into the wrong hands"?

We're not squeamish about other forms of violence. Yet executions somehow trouble us. We aren't comfortable with them, so we avert our eyes and thereby avoid responsibility.

One question that is posed to prospective jurors prior to a death penalty trial in Oklahoma is: "Would it do violence to your conscience to vote for the death penalty?" Most people say no. If they say yes, they're usually excused.

But it should do violence to your conscience to vote for a death penalty. Even if you believe that a death verdict is just, it should never be an easy decision—unless you are made to feel that somehow you're not responsible.

The investigating detectives, the forensic experts, the prosecutors, the jurors, the trial and appellate judges, the prison officials, the pardon and clemency boards, the governors, and finally the three men in black hoods standing in the execution room mixing the chemicals all say that they are only one small part of the machinery.

Macy himself used those very words. During the penalty phase in his first capital trial to result in an execution, Macy told the jury they were "just a small piece of the machinery that is designed to take people like Scotty Lee Moore and put them on death row."

If we didn't feel guilty about the death penalty, we wouldn't have to erect such a complex mechanism in order to achieve it. Lately, that guilt has expressed itself in concern that innocent people are being convicted and possibly executed. From the reinstatement of the death penalty in 1977 to the time I am writing this, of the one hundred people released from death row, only eight of those cases involved DNA evidence.

Statewide, Oklahoma has one wrongful conviction for approximately every forty death sentences passed since 1973. These are cases of demonstrated innocence, not cases overturned because of reversible error. Of the seven innocents released from McAlester's death row, two of them, Clifford Henry Bowen and Robert Lee Miller, had been prosecuted by Bob Macy.

Lee Ann Peters said, "After Robert Lee Miller, how can you continue to execute people and feel good about what you've done?"

"What if an innocent person is executed?" I asked Bob Macy. "Is that sacrifice worth keeping the death penalty?"

"I'd have to say yes," Macy replied.

I don't agree with Macy. I think that one innocent man's life is worth losing the death penalty. I'll go one step further. I think the nearly eleven years that Robert Lee Miller spent in prison are reason enough to lose the death penalty.

When you work in law enforcement, it's us versus them. Good guys and bad guys. You erect a wall between yourself and the criminals. Sometimes during my police career I let down that wall and developed a rapport, even an understanding, with a suspect. This often happened during interrogations. For a moment, I would see the suspect as a man. I would have empathy for him. That made it difficult to do my job, so the wall went back up again.

In order to execute people, we have to demonize them, deny their humanity, and mark them with the stigma of evil so great that there is no choice but to kill them. The system is built to minimize any feelings of empathy or responsibility. There is a sense of inevitability in death penalty cases that gradually achieves momentum until nothing, not even the United States Supreme Court, can stop an execution.

Justice is supposed to be blind, but we all know it's not and never will be. We want it to be perfect and flawless, unlike any other human endeavor.

"As long as the criminal justice system is administered by human beings," Jim Fowler said, "we should not have a punishment that is one hundred percent irrevocable."

Throughout my research and writing of this book, I wanted to have it both ways. I wanted to support the death penalty. When I found problems with it, I wanted them to be identified and fixed. I soon came to realize that the problem was the death penalty itself. We have tried tinkering with the system, when the Supreme Court overturned the death penalty nationwide in *Furman* v. *Georgia* and then established guidelines for state legislatures in *Gregg* v. *Georgia*. It took only a few years before prosecutors like Bob Macy were arguing that almost every murder was "heinous, atrocious and cruel" and therefore satisfied the aggravators that the Oklahoma legislature had established in accordance with the Supreme Court's decisions. Bob Macy used the vagueness of the Oklahoma statutes and court precedent concerning the death penalty to create a system in which almost any murder, from domestic violence to armed robbery to a drive-by shooting, was deserving of the death penalty.

Every murder is "heinous, atrocious and cruel." By executing the innocent we have committed an act just as "heinous, atrocious and cruel" ourselves.

In my career as a detective, both as a police officer and an author, I have always followed the evidence, wherever it led. My investigation of the death penalty in Oklahoma County has brought me to this conclusion: death penalty cases are not investigated or prosecuted at a level that can guarantee justice, or even that the accused is actually guilty.

I no longer believe in the death penalty. I no longer have faith that it is administered fairly or justly. I fear that innocent people have been executed.

That's why I am calling for the abolition of the death penalty, not only in Oklahoma but in every state. The federal government should reserve the right to execute only those guilty of treason, terrorism, and political assassination. In these circumstances, we as a nation would be executing the criminal, and it would no longer be up to individuals like Bob Macy and Joyce Gilchrist. These federal executions should be televised and broadcast on the Internet. If we don't have the stomach to watch executions, we shouldn't be performing them.

I could make all sorts of arguments about deterrence, cost-effectiveness, wrongful convictions, politics, philosophy, and so on. But it boils down to this—the death penalty brings out the worst in all of us: hatred, anger, vengeance, ambition, cruelty, and deceit.

This book has been a journey. I had to reach deep down within myself to come to this conclusion and the words to express it. I was wrong about the death penalty. I chose revenge instead of justice. And I was not alone. Instead of being an individual, I was just another ugly face in the crowd, chanting for death. Now I recognize the need to change not just our laws but ourselves.

Murder creates a pain that can't be forgotten or ignored. Our efforts to bring justice to those responsible should not make that pain any worse. In seeking the death penalty, horrible mistakes were made that cannot be undone. However, once we admit these mistakes, we have taken the first step toward reconciling and working together to ensure those mistakes don't happen again. Then we can begin to right the terrible wrongs that have been committed, not just against death row inmates but against our system of justice and therefore all of us.

In my investigation into the death penalty in Oklahoma, I began to rethink much of what I had believed for twenty-five years in law enforcement. I learned that justice is not as simple as I would have liked it to be; that anger and revenge only cause more pain and take more lives.

This book has challenged me as a journalist and as a man. I realized that I had not been brave enough to stand alone in my opinion about the death penalty. Instead of seeking the truth independently, I let my environment and my peers think and feel for me. The lessons of this book are not over for me. In fact, they have just begun.

Jim Fowler showed me the peace that forgiveness and compassion can offer. If he, who has suffered so much, can forgive, then why can't the rest of us? The story of the death penalty in Oklahoma, and throughout America, is sad, even depressing. But it is not without hope. The solution rests with each one of us to see the truth and then act on it. To choose justice over revenge.

MACY'S DEATH PENALTY CASES

While Bob Macy did not personally prosecute every one of these cases, they were convicted while he was district attorney.

CONVICTS EXECUTED

1. SEAN SELLERS

Sellers was sentenced to death in 1986 for killing his mother, Vonda Bellofatto; stepfather, Paul Bellofatto; and Robert Paul Power, a convenience-store clerk. Sellars was seventeen years old when he was convicted. Sellers was executed February 4, 1999.

2. SCOTTY LEE MOORE

Moore was sentenced to death for the 1983 murder of Alex Fernandez, a motel desk clerk. Moore was executed June 3, 1999.

3. MALCOLM RENT JOHNSON

Johnson was sentenced to death for the 1981 rape and murder of seventy-six-year-old Ura Alma Thompson. Johnson was executed January 6, 2000.

4. RONALD KEITH BOYD

Boyd was sentenced to death for the 1986 murder of Oklahoma City Police Officer Richard O. Riggs, after Boyd and his female accomplice robbed a convenience store. Boyd was executed April 27, 2000.

5. JAMES ROBEDEAUX

Robedeaux was sentenced to death for the 1985 murder of Nancy Rose Lee McKinney. Robedeaux was executed June 1, 2000.

6. EDDIE LEROY TRICE

Trice was sentenced to death for the 1987 murder of eighty-four-year-old Earnestine Jones. He was also given three 999-year sentences for the rape and robbery of Earnestine Jones and the beating of her mentally disabled son, Emanuel Jones. Trice was executed January 9, 2001.

7. WANDA JEAN ALLEN

Allen was convicted for the 1988 shooting death of her lover Gloria J. Leathers outside the Village police station. Allen was executed January 11, 2001, the first woman to be executed in Oklahoma history.

8. FLOYD ALLEN MEDLOCK

Medlock pleaded guilty to the 1990 rape and murder of seven-year-old Katherine Ann Busch and was sentenced to death. Medlock was executed January 16, 2001.

9. MICHAEL DONALD ROBERTS

Roberts was sentenced to death for the 1988 murder of eighty-year-old Lula Mae Brooks. Roberts was executed February 10, 2001.

10. MARILYN KAY PLANTZ

Plantz was sentenced to death for the 1988 murder of her husband, Jim Plantz. Her lover, William Cliff Bryson, also received a death sentence. Their accomplice, Clint McKimble, received a life sentence in return for testifying against them. Plantz was executed May 1, 2001.

11. ROGER BERGET

Berget was sentenced to death for the 1985 murder of Rick Patterson, a high school math teacher. His accomplice, Mikell Patrick Smith, got a life sentence. Berget was executed June 8, 2000.

12. WILLIAM BRYSON

Bryson was sentenced to death for the 1988 killing of Jim Plantz, his lover's husband. Marilyn Plantz was also sentenced to death. Bryson was executed June 15, 2000.

13. LOIS NADEAN SMITH

Smith was sentenced to death for the 1982 murder of Cindy Baillee, her son's ex-girlfriend. Her son Greg Smith was given a life sentence for his role in the murder. Lois Smith was executed December 4, 2001.

14. SAHIB AL-MOSAWI

Al-Mosawi was sentenced to death for the 1992 stabbing death of his wife, Inaam Al-Nashi, and son-in-law Mohammed Al-Nashi. A third stabbing victim, Fatima Al-Nashi, survived the attack. Al-Mosawi was executed December 6, 2001.

15. DION ATHANASIUS SMALLWOOD

Smallwood was sentenced to death for the 1992 murder of Lois Frederick, his girlfriend's adoptive mother. He beat Frederick to death with a croquet mallet, then put her body in a car and set it on fire. Smallwood was executed January 18, 2001.

16. MARK FOWLER

Fowler was sentenced to death, along with Billy Ray Fox, for the 1985 murders of three supermarket employees. Fowler was executed January 23, 2001.

17. BILLY RAY FOX

Fox was sentenced to death, along with Mark Fowler, for the 1985 murders of three supermarket employees. Fox was executed January 25, 2001.

18. LOYD WINFORD LAFEVERS

LaFevers was sentenced to death, along with Randall Cannon, in the 1985 beating death of Addie Mae Hawley. The eighty-four-year-old victim was abducted from her home, beaten, raped, and set on fire. LaFevers was executed January 30, 2001.

19. JOHN JOSEPH ROMANO

Romano was sentenced to death for the 1985 stabbing murder of Lloyd Thompson and the 1986 stabbing murder of jeweler Roger Sarfaty. His accomplice, David Wayne Woodruff, was also given a death sentence for the Sarfaty killing and a no-parole life term for the Thompson killing. Romano was executed January 29, 2001.

20. DAVID WAYNE WOODRUFF

Woodruff was sentenced to death, along with his accomplice, John Joseph Romano, for the 1985 stabbing murder of jeweler Roger Sarfaty. He was given a no-parole life term for his part in the 1986 stabbing death of Lloyd Thompson. Woodruff was executed January 31, 2001.

CONVICTS ON DEATH ROW

21. CURTIS EDWARD MCCARTY

McCarty was sentenced to death for the 1982 stabbing murder of eighteen-year-old Pam Willis. Twice the Oklahoma Court of Criminal Appeals overturned McCarty's death sentence. Each time he was sentenced to death again.

22. DEWEY GEORGE MOORE

Moore was sentenced to death for the 1984 abduction and killing of twelve-year-old Jenipher Gilbert. The Tenth U.S. Circuit Court of Appeals returned the case to federal district court to conduct an evidentiary hearing concerning charges of evidence planting. Oklahoma Attorney General Drew Edmondson has also ordered a reinvestigation of the forensic evidence in the case.

23. DON WILSON HAWKINS JR.

Hawkins was sentenced to death for the 1985 kidnapping and murder of Linda Thompson. He was also convicted of kidnapping Thompson's two daughters, two-year-old Katie and four-year-old Lorie. The girls were returned unharmed the next day, but their mother was raped and killed. Hawkins's accomplice, Dale Austin Shelton, received five life sentences for his role in the crime.

24. JOHN PAUL WASHINGTON

Washington was sentenced to death for the 1984 murder of Air Force Security Officer Arlie Virgil Newsome. He was given a five-hundred-year-sentence for the rape of Newsome's wife, Bobette.

25. RANDALL EUGENE CANNON

Cannon was sentenced to death, along with Loyd LaFevers, for the 1985 beating death of Addie Mae Hawley. The eighty-four-year-old victim was abducted from her home, beaten, raped, and set on fire. LaFevers was executed on January 30, 2001.

26. CYRIL WAYNE ELLIS

Ellis was sentenced to death for the 1986 murders of his fiancée's sister, Teresa Thomas, and employment supervisors Carl D. Lake and James L. Rider. He also received sentences of 2,000 years, 3,000 years, and two 1,000-year terms for the shooting of four other victims, including Thomas's boyfriend Robert Dumas, and her six-year-old daughter, Tameca, and two other work supervisors, Gordon Allin Moore and Ansel Davis.

27. GARRY THOMAS ALLEN

Allen pleaded guilty in the 1986 shooting murder of his ex-girlfriend Gail Titsworth and received a death sentence.

28. WINDEL RAY WORKMAN

Workman was sentenced to death for the 1987 beating murder of two-year-old Amanda Holman, the daughter of his live-in girlfriend.

29. KENNETH D. TATE

Tate was sentenced to death for the 1987 murder of his ex-wife Rosalee Tate outside a grocery store. He also received a life sentence for the murder of her neighbor Jeff White and ten years for pointing a gun at a store employee. The state Court of Criminal Appeals ordered a new sentencing hearing because the jury should have been allowed to consider the option of life in prison without parole. He was resentenced to death.

30. MICHAEL WAYNE HOWELL

Howell was sentenced to death for the 1987 murder of Sgt. Charlene Cal-houn during an attempt to steal her car. Howell was also sentenced to death in Tennessee for killing a Memphis convenience-store clerk less than twenty-four hours before Calhoun's slaying. His accomplice, Mona Lisa Watson, received life sentences for each killing.

31. JOHN MICHAEL HOOKER

Hooker was sentenced to death for the 1988 fatal stabbings of his girl-friend, Sylvia Stokes, and her mother, Drusilla Morgan.

32. ROBERT DON DUCKETT

Duckett was sentenced to death for the 1988 murder of his lover, John E. Howard. Duckett had escaped from prison in 1987, where he was serving time for a 1983 robbery and beating of a fifty-six-year-old man.

33. EARL ALEXANDER FREDERICK SR.

Frederick was sentenced to death for the 1989 beating death of fellow Vietnam veteran Bradford Beck. He also is accused of shooting seventy-seven-year-old Shirley Fox to death in Texas five days after the Beck murder. Following his Oklahoma conviction, Texas prosecutors decided not to try Frederick for the Fox murder. Frederick gave up his appeals and is awaiting execution.

34. WALANZO DEAN ROBINSON

Robinson, a gang member from Los Angeles, was sentenced to death for the 1989 murder of Dennis Eugene Hill following a dispute over drugs.

35. VICTOR WAYNE HOOKS

Hooks was sentenced to death for the 1988 fatal beating of his common-law wife, Shalimein Blaine, who was six months' pregnant. He also received a five-hundred-year sentence for manslaughter in death of Blaine's unborn child.

36. BARNEY MARSHALL JR.

Marshall pleaded guilty to the 1990 murder of twelve-year-old Helen LeFlore. He confessed to raping the girl, then throwing her from a bridge, holding her head underwater until she lost consciousness, slitting her throat and stabbing her twice in the chest. Marshall was sentenced to death.

37. ERNEST MARVIN CARTER JR.

Carter was sentenced to death for the 1990 murder of security guard Eugene Manowski, while Carter was attempting to steal a wrecker from the Oklahoma Auto Auction. Codefendant Charles Summers was found guilty of first-degree murder and received a sentence of life without parole.

38. JIMMIE RAY SLAUGHTER

Slaughter was sentenced to death for the 1991 murder of his former lover Melody Wuertz and their eleven-month-old daughter, Jessica. Slaughter's wife, Nicki Slaughter, was named as an accomplice but charges against her were dismissed.

39. DANNY KEITH HOOKS

Hooks was sentenced to death for the 1992 murders of five women in an Oklahoma City drug house. According to prosecutors, Hooks had tried to force Sandra Thompson, Phyllis Adams, Carolyn Watson, Fransill Roberts, and LaShawn Evans into an orgy. When they resisted, he stabbed all five of them to death and left their naked bodies at the house. The murders remained unsolved until 1997, when Hooks's DNA from a California case was matched to bloodstains found at the crime scene.

40. HUNG THANH LE

Le was sentenced to death for the 1992 murder of his friend, Hai Hong Nguyen, whom he had met in a refugee camp in Vietnam. Le stabbed Nguyen several times during the course of a robbery attempt.

41. GEORGE OCHOA

Ochoa was sentenced to death for the 1993 murders of Maria Yanez and her common-law husband, Francisco Morales. Each victim was shot nine times. Osbaldo Torres was also sentenced to death for his role in the killings, which had no apparent motive.

42. OSBALDO TORRES

Torres was sentenced to death for the 1993 murders of Maria Yanez and her common-law husband, Francisco Morales. Each victim was shot nine times. George Ochoa was also sentenced to death for his role in the killings, which had no apparent motive.

43. RICHARD FAIRCHILD

Fairchild was sentenced to death for the 1993 murder of his girlfriend's three-year-old son, Adam Broomhall. The victim was beaten and had severe burns on his back from being held against a heater. Stacy Broomhall received a five-year deferred sentence for permitting the abuse of her son.

44. YANCY LYNDELL DOUGLAS

Douglas was sentenced to death for the 1993 murder of fourteen-year-old Shauna Farrow, who was killed during a gang-related drive-by shooting. Farrow was not the intended target of the shooting.

45. PARIS LAPRIEST POWELL

Powell was sentenced to death for his involvement in the 1993 murder of fourteen-year-old Shauna Farrow, who was killed during a gang-related drive-by shooting. Farrow was not the intended target of the shooting.

46. MARCUS CARGLE

Cargle was sentenced to death for the 1993 murders of Richard Paisley and his wife, Sharon Paisley. Codefendant Christopher Todd Williams was given two life terms for the crime; codefendant Christopher Jackson testified against Cargle and Williams in exchange for immunity from prosecution.

47. BOBBY JOE FIELDS

Fields pleaded guilty to the 1983 shooting murder of seventy-seven-year-old Louise Schem during a burglary. The judge sentenced Fields to death.

48. ROCKY DODD

Dodd was sentenced to death for the 1994 murders of his neighbors Kari Sloniker and Shane McInturff. The state Court of Criminal Appeals overturned Dodd's conviction and death sentence in 1999. The court questioned the reliability of the prosecutors' jailhouse informant, Kenneth Bryant, who had helped Oklahoma County prosecutors in six death-penalty cases. In his second trial, Dodd was convicted and given the death penalty.

49. RODERICK LYNN SMITH

Smith was sentenced to death for the 1993 murders of his wife, Jennifer Smith, and her four children. Smith and her sons were stabbed; her daughters were strangled.

50. GEORGE JAMES MILLER JR.

Miller was sentenced to death for the 1994 murder of motel clerk Gary Kent Dodd. The victim was stabbed, beaten, and burned with acid. Miller had done maintenance work at the motel just prior to the killing. He also goes under the name Jay Elkins.

51. LARRY KENNETH JACKSON

Jackson was sentenced to death for the 1994 fatal stabbing of his former girlfriend Wendy Cade after he had escaped from a prison work detail. Jackson had been serving a thirty-year sentence for the 1985 shooting death of his then-girlfriend Freda Laverne Washington.

52. TERRY SHORT

Short was sentenced to death for the 1995 murder of Ken Yamamoto. Short threw homemade explosives through the patio door of the apartment of Brenda Gardner, a woman he had been dating. The fire caused neighbor Yamamoto's apartment to collapse. Yamamoto died later from burns to 95 percent of his body.

53. NAPOLEON LEWIS JR.

Lewis was sentenced to death for the 1995 murder of his ex-girlfriend Anita Bebout. Bebout and her daughter, Tressa, were set on fire. Bebout died shortly after the assault. Six-year-old Tressa was permanently disfigured. Lewis received a life sentence for child abuse. Lewis died of a heart attack in prison on Thanksgiving Day, 2000.

54. JOHN CAMP BERNAY

Bernay was sentenced to death for the 1995 shooting death of Pamela Wolf Chief. In 1951, Bernay was sentenced to life in prison for first-degree murder. After serving sixteen years of that sentence, he was paroled.

55. STEVEN LYNN ABSHIER

Abshier was sentenced to death for the 1995 murder of his twenty-two-month-old daughter, Ashley, who was beaten to death. Stephanie Abshier pleaded guilty to second-degree murder and testified against her husband in exchange for a twenty-five-year sentence.

56. KEVIN YOUNG

Young was sentenced to death for the 1996 murder of Joseph Sutton. The killing occurred at an alleged gambling house during the course of an attempted robbery. Young received a death sentence for the Sutton murder and a combined sentence of fifty years for convictions related to the wounding of a second patron and attempted robbery with a firearm.

DEATH SENTENCES STRICKEN

57. CLIFFORD HENRY BOWEN

Bowen was sentenced to death for the 1980 murders of Ray Peters, Marvin Nowlin, and Lawrence Evans. Bowen's conviction was overturned by the U.S. Court of Appeals in 1986. Bowen was released and the DA's office dropped charges against him the next year.

58. BENITO BOWIE

Bowie was sentenced to death for hiring Dexter Tyrone McDade to commit the murder of Eric Douglas Dunn. The sentence was reversed because the jury was not instructed on the option of life without parole. Bowie is now serving a life sentence.

59. JAMES TERRANCE FISHER JR.

Fisher was sentenced to death for the 1982 murder of Terry Gene Neal. The victim was stabbed in the throat with the broken neck of a wine bottle. Fisher was granted a resentencing hearing in 1999 by U.S. District Judge Tim Leonard, who characterized Fisher's defense as "nonexistent." In March 2002 the Tenth District Court overturned Fisher's murder conviction, saying that his lawyer had been "grossly inept." Former state senator Melvin Porter "sabotaged his client's defense," according to the court, by speaking only nine words during the sentencing phase of Fisher's trial. ("Waive. Rest. Judge I object to that. We waive.") Porter later said that his "personal feelings" toward his client affected his representation. "At the time," Porter said, "I thought homosexuals were among the worst people in the world."

60. RICHARD GLOSSIP

Glossip was sentenced to death for the 1997 murder of motel owner Barry Alan Van Treese. Twenty-year-old Justin Sneed, pleaded guilty in exchange for a sentence of life without parole. In 2001, Glossip's conviction and death sentence were overturned due to ineffectiveness of counsel. The court said that no forensic evidence was presented to link Glossip to the crime and the evidence supporting Sneed's testimony was "extremely weak." The court did not overturn on the evidence, however, because it found that trial counsel's conduct was so ineffective "we have no confidence that a reliable adversarial proceeding took place." Glossip is awaiting a new trial.

61. KENNETH EUGENE HOGAN

Hogan was sentenced to death for the 1988 fatal stabbing of Lisa Stanley, during an argument at her home. Hogan claimed that he was acting in self-defense. He was convicted in 1988, but a three-member panel of the Tenth U.S. Circuit Court of Appeals ordered a new trial, stating that the jury should have been given the option of first-degree manslaughter. The attorney general's office is appealing that ruling.

62. EMMANUEL LITTLEJOHN

Littlejohn was sentenced to death for the 1992 murder of convenience-store owner Kenneth Meers in a robbery attempt. Prosecutors said that Littlejohn and Glenn Roy Bethany went to the Root 'n' Scoot convenience store with the motive of robbery. Prosecutors said Littlejohn was the triggerman. Bethany was convicted of first-degree murder and robbery and sentenced to life in prison without parole. The Oklahoma Court of Criminal Appeals affirmed Littlejohn's conviction but vacated his death sentence, finding that the state had only satisfied one "aggravating circumstance." Littlejohn is awaiting a new sentencing hearing.

63. ROBERT LEE MILLER

Miller was sentenced to death for the 1986 murder of Anna Fowler and the 1987 murder of Velma Cutler. Both victims were also robbed and raped. DNA evidence eventually proved that Ronnie Lott was the suspect. Oklahoma County Special Judge Larry Jones dismissed the charges against Miller in February 1997, saying there was not enough evidence to justify his continued imprisonment. Miller's original conviction was overturned in 1995, and he was granted a new trial. The prosecution decided to drop charges and Miller was released. In 2001, Ronnie Lott was convicted of the crimes and is now on death row.

64. ALFRED BRIAN MITCHELL

Mitchell was sentenced to death for the 1991 rape and murder of Elaine Scott at a local recreation center. In 1999 the Federal District Court vacated the rape and sodomy convictions. Two years later, the Tenth Circuit Court overturned Mitchell's death sentence and ordered a new sentencing hearing.

65. ALVIN "KING" PARKER

Parker was sentenced to death for the 1985 murder of police detective Gary Ward, who was shot with his own gun when he attempted to arrest Parker for stealing a television set from a Holiday Inn. In 1989 the Oklahoma Court of Criminal Appeals overturned King's conviction and ordered a new trial because the first trial was "replete with prosecutorial misconduct." Bob Macy was criticized by the court for making comments that "served no purpose but to inflame the jury's passions and prejudices." The next year Parker was convicted and given a 199-year sentence.

66. KENNETH WAYNE PAXTON

Paxton was sentenced to death for the 1989 murder of Donna Kay Neal. In 1999 the Tenth Circuit Court vacated Paxton's death sentence, saying that Bob Macy "clearly and deliberately made two critical misrepresentations to the jury," by implying that Paxton had killed his wife, Gloria Jean Paxton, in 1979. Paxton had been charged with the murder, but those charges were dropped when he passed a polygraph test. Macy, whom the court said knew about the polygraph results, said he didn't know why the charges had been dropped. "Mr. Macy's conduct crossed the line between a hard blow and a foul one," the judges wrote. The court also found that the trial judge improperly allowed hearsay evidence and denied the defendant a chance to present mitigating evidence. Paxton was eventually resentenced to life without parole.

67. HENRY WESLEY SMITH

Smith was sentenced to death for the 1984 murder of Garry Wayne Palone, a convenience-store clerk. His accomplice, Ricky Lynn Tyree, offered a surprise guilty plea during arraignment and was given a life sentence. At trial, Smith said he was acting on God's instructions when he shot Palone. Smith's death sentence was reversed by the Oklahoma Court of Criminal Appeals, which ruled that the judge erred in telling the jury "It is up to the defendant to prove that he was insane." Macy agreed with the reversal. Facing a second trial, Smith pleaded guilty and received a sentence of life without parole.

68. BIGLER JOBE "BUD" STOUFFER II

Stouffer was sentenced to death for the 1985 murder of elementary school teacher Linda Reaves and the wounding of her boyfriend, Doug Ivens. Stouffer had been dating Ivens's estranged wife, Velva Ivens. The Tenth U.S. Circuit Court of Appeals ruled that Stouffer receive a new trial because of the "unexplained and unsupportable ineptness of trial counsel." Stouffer is awaiting a new trial.

69. CHARLES FREDERICK WARNER

Warner was sentenced to death for the 1997 rape and murder of eleven-month-old Adrianna Waller, the daughter of Warner's live-in girlfriend. The victim had a six-inch skull fracture, a broken jaw, three broken ribs, bruised lungs, and a lacerated liver and spleen. In 2001, Warner's conviction and death sentence were overturned by the Oklahoma Court of Criminal Appeals, which found that the trial judge had erred in denying defense motions to dismiss some of the potential jurors (one of the jurors knew the case detectives, another expressed a bias toward the death penalty). Warner is awaiting a new trial.

70. CURTIS LEE WASHINGTON

Washington was sentenced to death for the 1996 murder of his ex-wife, Celia Ann Washington. When Macy filed charges against Washington, he mistakenly listed prior convictions in Illinois for attempted murder and armed robbery. But those convictions belonged to a different man who had the same name and birth date. In 1999 the Oklahoma Court of Criminal Appeals overturned Washington's death sentence and modified it to life without parole. The court found that Macy made improper statements, that the aggravating factor was not sufficiently proved, and that letters from the victim and her father that were improperly used during the sentencing phase. Washington is now serving a sentence of life without parole.

71, 72, 73. PATRICIA BETH JONES, RONNIE LEE FLOYD, AND ALFREDO OMALZA

Separate juries found Jones, Floyd, and Omalza guilty of the murder of Kim Gayleen Grant and Harrel Lloyd Robinson, whose bodies were found near Lake Stanley Draper. Grant was a key witness in a drug smuggling case involving Jones that was about to go to trial. Accomplice David Lee Flippo was sentenced to life without parole. In 1995 the convictions of Jones, Floyd, and Omalzo, as well as Flippo, were overturned by the Oklahoma Court of Criminal Appeals, citing "prosecutorial misconduct" and errors by judges. In retrials, all four were convicted and given sentences of life without parole.

INDEX